Lewis Sergeant

The Franks

From their Orgin as a Confederacy to the Establishment of the Kingdom of France

and the German Empire

Lewis Sergeant

The Franks
From their Origin as a Confederacy to the Establishment of the Kingdom of France and the German Empire

ISBN/EAN: 9783337171360

Printed in Europe, USA, Canada, Australia, Japan

Cover: Foto ©ninafisch / pixelio.de

More available books at **www.hansebooks.com**

THE FRANKS

*FROM THEIR ORIGIN AS A CONFEDERACY
TO THE ESTABLISHMENT OF THE
KINGDOM OF FRANCE AND
THE GERMAN EMPIRE*

BY

LEWIS SERGEANT

AUTHOR OF "JOHN WYCLIF: LAST OF THE SCHOOLMEN AND
FIRST OF THE ENGLISH REFORMERS," ETC.

SECOND EDITION

London
T. FISHER UNWIN
PATERNOSTER SQUARE

Copyright by T. FISHER UNWIN, 1898.

PREFACE.

THE story of the Franks, especially of the earlier Franks, is rich in fable but poor in history. In the legend of Clovis, and even in the legend of Charles the Great, it is a work of considerable difficulty to separate what is historically accurate from that which has at best a dubious origin. My aim in writing this volume has been to present a general outline of the history of the Franks, and, in doing so, to confine myself almost exclusively to facts which have a sure foundation. That aim implied that the greater part of the volume should be devoted to periods in which the historical foundation was least secure—to the long struggle between Romans and Teutons, during which the tribes on the east of the Rhine were perpetually combining against their enemies until the Frank confederacy clearly emerged, and to the subsequent Merovingian period, during which the Franks were gradually subjecting the whole of Gaul. It is in this domain, overgrown as it is with fable, and meagrely as its central facts have been dealt with by historians, that the student of history should find his greatest attraction.

I have ventured in the following pages to support an interpretation of a particular passage in Gregory of Tours which has been either ignored or repudiated for more than a thousand years. The reader must decide for himself as to the probable origin of the Franks, and the position of Gregory's "Dispargum"; but in any case it is impossible that we should continue to attach the slightest credence to the imaginary Belgic Thuringia.

CONTENTS.

I.

THE CONFLICT OF RACES 1–10

Introduction—Romans, Gallo-Romans, and Germans—The Kelts in Gaul and in Britain—The Roman Church—Limits of the subject—The Franks ultimately retire from, or are rejected by, France.

II.

WHO WERE THE FRANKS? . . . 11–20

Obscure Origin of the People—The Gallo-German Frontier—Cæsar and the Sicambrian League—Earliest occurrence of the name—Vopiscus, Sulpitius, Gregory of Tours—The Trojan Legend—A Historical Puzzle and a Word-Study.

III.

CÆSAR'S FRONTIER POLICY 21–34

Hereditary Foes—The Roman Conquest of Gaul—The Westward Migrations—Compression and Expansion—Cæsar's Policy—Continued by Augustus—Hermann—The Disaster of Varus—The Revenge of Germanicus—Marbod—The Julian Emperors—The Story of Civilis.

Note on the German Tribes (according to Tacitus)   34–36

IV.

THE GERMAN RACE . . . 37–47

The Home of the Teutons—Roman Inconsistencies—German Raids—Romanised Germans—The Flavian Emperors—The Rhine Frontier—The Roman Rampart—The Cradle-Land of the Franks—The *Decumates Agri*.

V.

THE DECLINE OF ROME 48–57

Franks, Allemans, and Goths—"Deum Ira in Rem Romanam"—Growth of the Christian Church—Romanised Gaul—Pagan and Christian Letters—Gallic Poets.

VI.

THE COMING OF THE FRANKS 58–79

The Frontier broken—Incursions of Allemans, Vandals, and Franks—Postumus the Traitor—Gallic Insurrections—Aurelian—More Frank Raids—Probus—Diocletian—Augusti and Cæsars—Legati, Duces and Comites—Constantius—Constantine—Julian—Salian Franks settled in Belgic Gaul—A Frank Consul—A Frank Emperor-Maker—Stilicho—The Poet Claudian.

VII.

THE MEROVINGIAN FRANKS . . . 80–98

Establishment of the Merovingians in Gaul—Their Origin—Clodion and Merowig—Gregory of Tours—Dispargum (Divisio-Burgum ?)—The Thuringian Scheidungen-Burg—Salian Franks—Riparian Franks—Læti and Leti—Cambrai and Tournai occupied by the Franks—Aëtius—An Impossible Task—Attila the "Scourge of God"—The Yellow Terror—Childeric—The Mother of Clovis—Childeric's Tomb.

Note on the Origin of the Merovingians . . . 98–100

VIII.

KING CLOVIS   101–119

The Political State of Gaul at the end of the Fifth Century—The four Frank Kingdoms in Gaul—Allemans, Goths, and Burgundians—The Armorican Land—The Conquests of Clovis—Defeat of Syagrius—The Cup of Soissons—War with Thuringia—Queen Clotilda—Expulsion of the Allemans—The Conversion of Clovis—Saint Remy.

IX.

CONQUESTS OF CHRISTIANITY   .   .   120–131

The Western Church—A new Imperium—The Penance of Theodosius—Policy and Victories of Christian Rome—The Church in Gaul—Rome appeals to the Teutons—Invokes the aid of the Franks—Orthodoxy and Arianism—The Council of Nice—Victory of the Trinitarians—Effects of the Frank Conversion.

X.

THE SUBJECTION OF GAUL   .   .   132–152

Wars of Clovis with the Burgundians—Gundobald and Godegisil—Aredius—The Burgundian Codes—Councils of the Gallic Church—Theodoric the Goth opposes Clovis—The Meeting of Clovis and Alaric—The Council of Agde—The Conquest of Aquitaine—Clovis as Roman Consul—Removes from Soissons to Paris—Subjection of the minor Frank Monarchies—Death of Clovis.

XI.

CHARACTERISTICS OF THE FRANKS   .   .   153–164

The Growth of a Nation—Character and Institutions of the Teutons—Their Codes—Origins of Teutonic Law—Salic Law—Wehrgeld—Ordeals—Slavery and Enfranchisement.

XII.

THE SONS OF CLOVIS . . . 165–179

Subdivision of the Realm of Clovis—Conquest of Burgundy—Old Age and Death of Clotilda—Conquest of Thuringia and Bavaria—Clotilda the Younger—Conquest of Provence—Belisarius—The Romance of Totila and the daughter of Theodebert—The Plagues—Clotair, second Sole King of the Franks—Genealogy of the Merovingian Kings.

XIII.

THE SONS OF CLOTAIR 180–193

Subdivision of the Realm of Clotair—Siegbert and Chilperic—Brunhilda and Fredegonda—Fredegonda's Crimes—Death of Chilperic—Gontran of Burgundy and Childebert—Brunhilda's Machinations—Clotair II., third sole King of the Franks—The Kingdoms of Neustria and Austria—The Frank Reich and the Oster Ric.

XIV.

THE MAYORS OF THE PALACE . . . 194–206

Origin of the Office—Increase of authority during the minority of the Kings—Warnaher and Rade—Pepin "of Landen"—Grimoald and his Son—Rois Fainéants—Genealogy of the hereditary Mayors—Charles Martel—Pepin the Short, Mayor and King.

XV.

ROME APPEALS TO THE FRANKS . . . 207–220

The Roman See—The Lombards in Italy—Pope Stephen appeals to Pepin—Pepin crowned at S. Denis—The Hercynian Wolf—Development of Frank Authority—Approach of the Franks to full Civilisation—Land Tenure under the Frank Kings—Serfdom under Teutonic Rule—The Sons of Pepin—Accession of Charles.

XVI.

CHARLES THE GREAT . . . 221-232

Franks and Saxons—Destruction of Irminsul—A Thirty Years' War—Pope Adrian's appeal to Charles—Charles defeats the Lombards in Italy—Visits Rome—Becomes Dux of Rome and King of Italy—His Benefactions to the Pope—Fresh Campaigns in Saxony and Italy—The Assembly of Paderborn—Mission of Ibn-el-Arabi—Charles invades Spain—Battle of Roncesvalles—The " Song of Roland."

XVII.

THE WESTERN EMPIRE REVIVED . . . 233-247

Witikind the Saxon—Conversion of the Saxons—Final subjection of Saxony—Other Wars of Charles—Tassilon of Bavaria—Charles on the Danube—Death of Pope Adrian—Renewal of the Understanding with Charles—Leo expelled from Rome—Restored by Charles—Charles crowned Emperor at Rome—The Policy of the Pope—Rome and Byzantium.

XVIII.

THE GOVERNMENT OF CHARLES . . . 248-266

Imperial Rule—The Palace at Aachen—The Basilica—Spoils from Italy—Instruments of Music—Haroun-al-Raschid—Missi Dominici—Incompatibility of Franks and Gauls—A Barrier of Speech—Charles's Preference for the East—General Assemblies under the Carolingians—The Capitularies—Archbishop Hincmar—The Personal Government of Charles.

XIX.

The Court of Charles . . 267–285

The Emperor's Mother—His Wives and Family—Ealhwine of York—Alcuin and the School of the Palace—Alcuin's Method of Instruction—A Revival of Learning—Caligraphy—The Scriptorium at Tours—Eginhard—Charles as a Writer—The "Caroline Books"—Correspondence of Charles—Dawn of Teutonic Literature.

XX.

The Life and Work of Charles . 286–297

Last Years of Charles the Great—Inroads of the Northmen—The Emperor's Sons—The Death of the Emperor—His Life and Work—Obstacles to Mental Evolution—The Legend of Charlemagne—Influences of the Franks—Charles and Offa, King of the Mercians.

XXI.

The Partition of the Empire . . 298–319

Louis the Pious and His Sons—Genealogy of the Carolingians—Constituent Parts of the Empire—Weakness of Louis—Revolt of his Sons—Battle of Fontenai—Louis the German and Charles the Bald—The Oaths of Argentaria—Lingua Romana and Lingua Teudisca—Nationalities at Fontenai and Argentaria—Treaty of Verdun and Partition of the Empire—The Imperial Succession—Encroachments of the Northmen—Rollo, Duke of Normandy.

XXII.

FRANCE AND GERMANY . . 320–334

The Last Carolingians—The Dukes of France—Hugues Capet—The Kingdom of France—Hereditary Fiefs—Origins of the Feudal System—The Word " Frank "—The Imperial Title—The Holy Roman Empire—Conclusion.

INDEX 335

ROMAN NAMES AND MODERN EQUIVALENTS . . 342

LIST OF ILLUSTRATIONS.

	PAGE
GALLIC BRACELET	8
MAP OF WESTERN GERMANY	*To face* 28
PORTA NIGRA (ROMAN)	51
PNEUMATIC ORGAN, FOURTH CENTURY	56
MONUMENTAL TOMB (ROMAN)	63
STATUE OF JULIAN	71
FROM AN ALTAR TO CERNUNNOS IN PARIS	76
SKETCH-MAP	85
CEREMONIAL SWORD IN SHEATH (FROM THE TOMB OF CHILDERIC)	95
BUCKLE (FROM THE TOMB OF CHILDERIC)	96
MOUNTED TOOTH (DITTO)	97
AXE-HEAD (DITTO)	98
SPEAR-HEAD (DITTO)	99
FRANK WARRIOR (TYPICAL)	106
STATUE OF CLOVIS (XII. CENTURY)	112
STATUE OF CLOTILDA (XII. CENTURY)	115
THE BAPTISM OF CLOVIS	118

LIST OF ILLUSTRATIONS.

	PAGE
ALTAR TRAY AND CHALICE	123
TOMB OF S. REMY	127
A GALLIC COUNCIL	137
AMBOISE IN THE SIXTEENTH CENTURY	140
RUINS OF MARMOUTIERS	142
DIPTYCH OF SIVIDIUS OF TOURS	146
EARLIER FRANK SETTLEMENTS IN BELGIAN GAUL	156
IRON SAUFANG	161
GAUL AFTER THE DEATH OF CLOVIS	168
VOTIVE CROWN OF KING SUINTILA	174
REALM OF THE FRANKS UNDER CLOTAIR II. (613)	190
REPUTED THRONE OF DAGOBERT	198
SAXON REALM OF CHARLES THE GREAT	229
THE SWORD OF CHARLES THE GREAT	237
DIADEM OF CHARLES THE GREAT	244
ORGANISTRUM (IX. CENTURY)	250
THREE-STRINGED CROUT (IX. CENTURY)	250
LYRE (IX. CENTURY)	251
TINTINNABULUM (IX. CENTURY)	264
CHIMES (FROM A IX. CENTURY MS.)	273
BYZANTINE ENAMEL RELIQUARY (X. CENTURY)	279
CHRIST AND HIS MOTHER (IX. CENTURY FRESCO)	295
TURRET BELL NOW AT SIENA (1159)	331

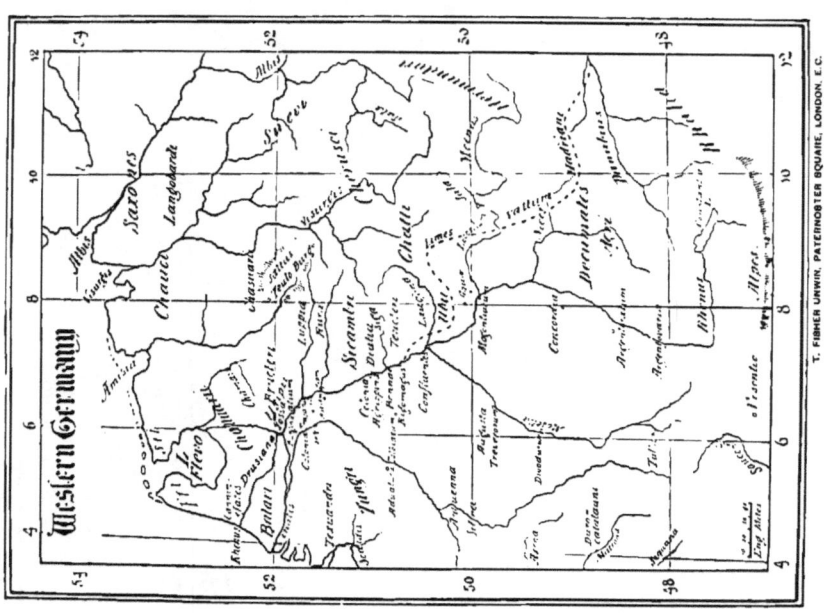

I.

THE CONFLICT OF RACES.

It is sometimes said that historians who dwell on the operation of historic laws, in accordance with which they believe that history is continuously evolved, seek to build too great an edifice upon a series of simple observations, and magnify mere coincidences into the necessary results of co-operating causes. But if there is any exaggeration of this kind sufficiently serious to produce a misapprehension of historical facts, it is not so unfortunate in its consequences as the opposite exaggeration of those who represent the facts of history as little else than a chronological succession of casual events.

To say that history is developed in accordance with law is only to admit that such permanent causes of human action as the race and its tendencies, the country and its climate, the nation and its institutions, must in successive ages bring about similar results from similar combinations of circumstances. Nations, like individuals, act in the long run according to a fairly constant law of their being, so that from the recorded events of the past we can often account for and explain the present, whilst the present condition and character of a nation will sometimes enable us to interpret and understand its past.

In dealing with a people like the Franks, and especially with the Franks who entered Gaul and helped to create France, there is one consideration which must be always borne in mind. The mixture of races in any country, and even the mixture of various branches of the same race, constantly modifies the type of each. For a time the grafted tree will bear two different kinds of fruit, both of which may persist as long as the tree survives. But rarely will several grafts·continue to flourish on the same stock ; either one of them will prevail over all the rest, or the stock will prove itself more vigorous than the introduced branches, and will produce its original fruit in greater abundance, whilst the grafts dwindle away, or give but slight evidence of their distinct character. Law is still at work ; the type persists and displays itself; but with sundry types in one composite nation there is a struggle for predominance, and the historian cannot always follow this struggle as closely as he would desire amidst the intricacies of national development.

Nowhere can we study the laws of national development, or follow up the human struggle for existence, with greater satisfaction and profit than in the early history of England and France. The reason is the same in both cases, and the elements of the inquiry, though differing in some important respects, are in a large measure identical. In Britain and in Gaul the race that was original—so far as our present knowledge permits us to speak of the original —was the race of Kelts. The Greeks called them Kelts; though indeed Herodotus, writing in the fifth century before Christ, said that the Danube rose in their territory, and that a people whom he called Kynesioi were the westernmost race in Europe. In any case the Kelts were in Britain and Gaul; and in the latter country, nineteen hundred years ago, they had already been pressed hard by the Germans when the Roman armies overwhelmed them. In both countries a Roman occupation gave them several centuries of comparative peace and civilisation.

The Cæsars rolled back from Gaul successive tides of invasion. The valleys of the Rhine furnished a thousand battlefields for the age-long conflict between a dying empire and a young invincible race. To such a conflict, amongst the most momentous and important which humanity has known, there was but one possible end. Before the destined masters of the world, who were to carve out four mighty empires in Europe, and to rise to heights of knowledge, culture, and disciplined strength such as even Greece and Rome had never attained, the imperial organisation gradually weakened and gave way. For five centuries, and for part of a sixth, the Roman stood between the Kelt and the German, striving against fate, stemming what to him was a tide of barbarism, yet working out as he did so the beneficent laws of civil evolution, by tempering to finer consistency the hard metal of the northern races—metal which Rome could grind and set, but could never break.

In the end Rome abandoned the hopeless struggle, and withdrew from the circumference of her empire because her very existence was threatened at the centre. Whilst the last of the Western emperors and the later Roman *duces* were fighting in vain against successive inroads of Goths, Alans, Huns, and Lombards—whilst the Christian Church in Rome, by virtue of its compact organisation, began to assume civil rule in the ravaged and dilapidated city, and thence to extend its influence to the countries which Rome had conquered and colonised, the Kelts and Germans renewed their interrupted warfare. The Rhine-Germans, no longer opposed by highly-trained Italian or mercenary legions, established themselves in Gaul; the coast-Germans broke through the defences of the Saxon shore, and carved an England out of Britain; whilst the forest-Germans, ever pressing from behind upon the fluid tribes of the western and northern Teutons,[1] at once impelled them into the struggle and reinforced their ranks.

Thus were the new States of Europe founded; yet not by the harmony and co-operation of the tribes which made up this later Aryan development, but by their competition, and in the teeth of their mutual internecine ravages. The first Sicambrian and Chattan Franks in Gaul had to hold their own against Batavians and Chamavians, who preceded or followed them, just as the Gallo-Roman-Franks succumbed

---

[1] The words "German" and "Teuton," as used in this volume, must be regarded as generally equivalent. "Teuton" originally had a more restricted meaning, but it was soon employed by Latin writers in the same sense as "German."

to the Northman sea-kings in the ninth century, and as the Anglo-Saxons of England succumbed to the Norman-French in the eleventh century.

The actors are virtually the same, though the arena changes ; the pressure and the conquest are always from the last-formed waves of the advancing tide, from the newer and ruder Northmen, such as are still least affected by civil status and civilisation.

Our intention is to consider the period of Frank development and predominance in Western Europe, and to estimate the Franks in relation to and comparison with the tribes and races which surrounded them. Side by side with these tribes and races we shall behold another growing and aggressive dominion, Semitic in origin, Greek in expression, Roman in organisation, a marvellous counterpart of the *imperium* whose deserted capital it appropriated, whose methods it adopted, whose eagles it followed into every land, and whose fate it experienced with the most significant exactitude. It is by no mere coincidence that the empire of the Roman Church, in the clash of conflict with Greeks, Italians, Iberians, Kelts, and the various Teutonic nations, gained substantially the same victories and received substantially the same checks as the empire of Roman arms.

The separation of the Eastern and Western Empires was followed in due time by the separation of the Eastern and Western Churches. The grafting of an imperial Church on the old Italian stock led successively to the limitless assumptions, the incredible corruptions, and the eventual humiliation of Christian Rome, so that the Eternal City, as

Hadrian called it, has been twice head of the world and twice the prison of its Pontifex Maximus. Amongst the Kelts, the Roman Church has found, as the Roman State before it had found in its oldest Province, its most docile, exalted, superstitious, and faithful subjects. State and Church alike encountered in the Teutons a staunch, unconquerable foe, who spurned their control, shattered their power, and finally built up an edifice of their own on durable foundations. All this has been but the working out of the same historic laws through the instrumentality of the same peoples. With certain characters, amidst given circumstances and conditions, we have arrived in each case at very much what might have been expected and predicted beforehand.

To trace the effects of such historic laws as these is naturally more difficult, as has already been said, when we have to do, not with the marked characteristics of single tribes or races, but with the composite characters of national amalgamations. Thus it is a task of greater complexity to disentangle the motives which tend to shape the acts of the nation of Kelts, Gallo-Romans, Basques, Franks, and Scandinavians, whom we call Frenchmen, or of the nation of Kelts, Teutons, and Norman-French, whom we call Englishmen, than it is to understand the comparatively simple development of the almost unmixed people of Germany.

At any rate we have the same Teutonic elements more or less distinctly present in France, England, and Germany. Even the Franks are among our common ancestry, from whom we derive both blood and ideas. They fill a page in our island history, a volume in the histories of France and Germany. They are especially important as having been, more than the Goths, or the Angles, or the Saxons, a hinge of ancient and modern civilisation ; for in the rise of the new nationalities they were ever nearest, in arms, in settlement, and in law, to the vanguard and the outposts of Rome. Yet in spite of this fact, and although the first Frank emperor, a century before the time of Alfred in England, attained to a civilisation which was not a mere afterglow of Roman culture, but was in some measure Teutonic, the Franks themselves, in presence of the Gauls, the Romans, and the Northmen, were not destined to be the persistent race in the land which they had conquered. In Britain there was a conquering German race which did persist, under very similar conditions, against Kelts and Romans and Northmen ; but the Franks, who were the flower of the Teutonic family, and whose victories were greater and more striking than those of the Anglo-Saxons, left comparatively slight traces behind them in the country to which they gave their name. It is only in a limited sense that the Franks can be called the makers of France. A few characteristics of the Salic law, two or three of the customs which went to build up the feudal system, a certain inevitable blending of the population in the centre and north of Gaul, with a larger admixture of the Germanic element in the north-east, especially in the provinces which came to be known as Alsace and Lorraine, added, of course, to the national consolidation which might never have been attained, or would not have been so thoroughly attained, without the Merovingian and Carolingian conquests—these are the principal items of the legacy which was bequeathed by the victors in arms to their victors in religion, in language, and in such art and letters as the times admitted.

It was, indeed, the very strength of their own national characteristics that led to the failure of

GALLIC BRACELET.

the Franks—if failure it must be called—to acclimatise themselves thoroughly in Gaul. They were always the most German of the Germans, in their final conquest of the Thuringians, Saxons, and Allemans, as in their early struggle with the Romans, and in their victories over the Goths, Burgundians, and Lombards. Their domination in the west was largely due to the assistance of the Church, without which they would scarcely have been able to extend their borders to the Mediterranean and the Atlantic, and would certainly not have succeeded in converting their kingdom into an empire. The Church, after all, was the real victor, and the Church in Gaul was essentially Gallo-Roman. The Franks, it is true, became very good Christians ; but they ended, as they began, by being essentially warriors, and they never ceased to cherish their German institutions, language, and national traditions. They were in Gaul for centuries, but of Gaul they never were, in any thorough and durable sense. The nostalgia which perpetually haunted them became with large numbers an irresistible force. When they realised that the Gallo-Romans and the northern and western Kelts could never be Germanised, and that on the Seine and Loire and Rhone they must either become Gauls themselves or be content to live amongst a race alien in language, thought, and daily habit, then, by natural and inevitable gravitation, they practically reverted as a nation to their ancestral seats.

Charles the Great showed by many evident signs that his ideas and preferences were German rather than Gallic, Austrian rather than Neustrian. He built the broad foundations of a German empire between the North Sea and the Alps, dwelling constantly in the Rhinelands, and leaving Aquitaine, Provence and Italy to the charge of his sons. A generation after his death his grandchildren divided his possessions ; the empire passed permanently into Germany, and all that was most essentially German amongst the Franks tended to fall back upon the Rhine. If there was no wholesale and manifest re-migration of Franks from Neustria and Western Gaul, there was at any rate a continuing current from west to east of the elements which were more distinctly Teutonic, and which had shown themselves least fitted or disposed to coalesce with the Gallo-Roman. From the year 843 we may reckon that the part of the Franks in the making of France was practically complete, the kingship falling (partly, perhaps, by marriage with a Frank princess) to the Angevin family of Robert the Strong, whose great-grandson was Hugues Capet. From the same year the male descendants of Charles the Great reigned in Germany alone, and at the end of the ninth century the splendid mission of the Franks in Gaul had been accomplished.

The object of this volume is to trace the rise and development of the Franks, from their obscure origin as a confederacy, rather than as a nation, to their attainment of full and distinct national life; to follow them through the successive phases of their growth, to the time when the Carolingian empire towered in strength and renown above all other contemporary dominations; and, beyond that, to .the time when the mighty stream of human energy, receding from Western Europe, recovered force and impulse at its fountain-head, and reflooded the plains of Germany with imperishable and imperial strength.

II.

WHO WERE THE FRANKS?

THE origin of the Franks, like the origin of their name, is lost in obscurity. The first thing to note about them is that we have no facts on which to found a definite statement. They appear suddenly and casually in the pages of history, and the Gauls or Romans who heard them mentioned for the first time by their new title must have wondered who they were, and whence they came. There are maps still in circulation which include Franks amongst the Teutonic tribes who occupied Germany at the beginning of the Christian era; but, there were no Franks for two or three centuries after Christ, and the Franks were not a tribe of the Teutons, though they were indisputably Teutonic.

The earlier Roman historians knew nothing of this people. Tacitus, who lived into the second century, and who mentions some seven and forty branches of the Teutonic race, gives us no particulars of a tribe or combination of tribes possessing the distinctness and prominence which subsequently marked the Franks. Teutonic leagues there naturally would be—alliances for a single campaign, whether aggressive or defensive; associations for a special purpose, enduring until the purpose was fulfilled; treaty-obligations between two or more tribes, entered into after a fight, or in order to avoid fighting. Cæsar and Tacitus describe several of these leagues, the most important being that which was formed by the Sicambrians, amongst the tribes on the right bank of the Rhine, extending northwards between the lands of the Ubii and the Usipii—that is, approximately, between the confluences of the Mosella and the Luppia (Lippe) with the Rhine.

This was the most vulnerable section of the Rhine frontier. Lower down, the waters, higher up the mountains, created natural defences, aided in the latter case by a *limes* and a *vallum*, a stockade and a rampart. On the eastern bank of the Rhine, nearly corresponding with the eastern part of what is now called Rhenish Prussia, north and south of the river Sieg, which enters the Rhine opposite to Bonn, the Sicambrians and their allies repeatedly braved the power of Rome.[1] It was the very place where we should expect to find an anti-Roman league, at any time during the Roman occupation of Gaul. The Rhine-Germans were always fighting, or preparing to cross the river, or recovering their energies after a defeat. Those who would not fight migrated eastwards in their shame, amongst the marshes and forests, and became hewers of wood and drawers of water. Those who remained were constantly reinforced by Chasuarians, Cheruscans, Chattans, and volunteers from every quarter, wherever the greatness of the Roman name and the

[1] Tacitus, "Annals," ii. 26, iv. 34.

memories of their own ancestry attracted the bravest warriors to the front. Of those who fought, some few made good their footing in Gaul, either in spite of Gauls and Romans or in agreement with them, defending their new settlements against invaders who came after them. Others were put to flight by the Roman generals, who every now and then pursued them across the Rhine. In the long series of wars which were waged between the Gallo-Romans and the Rhine-Germans, millions must have perished on both sides of this historic frontier, by the sword of their enemies or by the ravage and starvation which followed in the wake of victory.

Cæsar tells us, in his account of the Gallic War, of a combination of the Tencteri and Usipii, to the number of 330,000, who crossed the Lower Rhine into the Belgian settlements of the Menapii, after they had been driven from their own territories by the warlike Suevi—for whom, they declared, not even the immortal gods could be a match. The intruders would not retire at Cæsar's bidding, even when he offered to transfer them to the country of the Ubii, whom the Suevi had placed under tribute, though they could not drive them from their fields. Cæsar fought and defeated them ; and, not content with that, he ordered his cavalry to fall upon their women and children. It was a shameful deed, for which, as Cato said at Rome, the conqueror ought to have been handed over to the vengeance of the survivors.

In this way, amongst others, the Romans welded together their indomitable foes. That forced migration of the two tribes, expelled from their homes by a fierce enemy of their own race, wandering for three years with their families and the remnants of their property, seizing the fields of the Menapii, expelled again by the Romans, cut to pieces by Cæsar's army, witnessing the butchery of their wives and little ones, whom even the irresistible Suevi had spared, was in fact the origin of the first riparian league of Germans —or, at any rate, of the first strong league of the Rhine-Germans which history records. For the survivors of the massacre, including a large number of horsemen, recrossed the river near its junction with the Meuse, and, with another body of horsemen who had not been engaged in the battle, betook themselves to the Sicambrians, with whom they entered into alliance.

Cæsar determined to follow up his victory by striking a blow at his enemies on their own ground. He built his famous bridge of wood, probably, as Mommsen says, between Cologne and Andernach, and led his army into the territory of the Sicambrians. The allies did not venture to face him. They took refuge in the woods—" finibus suis excesserant, suaque omnia exportaverant, seque in solitudinem ac sylvas abdiderant." Some of the neighbouring tribes sent embassies to the invader; but the Suevi raised their standard, and began to assemble an enormous host of fighting men, which would doubtless have tested the valour of the Romans to the utmost. Cæsar therefore withdrew, cutting the bridge behind him. And, whilst he was absent on his first expedition to Britain, the fugitives returned to their homes, cemented their alliance, and made a joint attack on Aduatuca Tungrorum (the modern Tongres).

Now this Sicambrian League has generally been regarded as the original, or at all events as the direct forerunner, of the confederacy which at a later date acquired the name of Franks. Some of the earliest commentators on Cæsar's text assert that the descendants of the Sicambrians and their allies who fought against Rome in the century before the birth of Christ were subsequently called by this name. There is nothing to prove an actual descent. All that we can affirm is that a people who were known as Franks, and who were undoubtedly Teutons, constantly invaded Gaul in the third and following centuries. The historian Vopiscus, who wrote a life of his contemporary Aurelian, says that the latter, when he was tribune of the sixth Gallic legion, fought a battle near Mogontiacum (Mayence or Mainz), and defeated a force of the "Franks," "who had invaded the empire, and were ravaging the whole of Gaul." Aurelian died in the year 275, and Vopiscus appears to be the first writer who made use of the name of Franks, though Sulpitius, writing two centuries later, names three "Frank" leaders who broke the Roman rampart in 238. The passage proves nothing as to the origin of the particular Germans who fought Aurelian. They might have been in Gaul for many years, or they might have crossed with other Germans at any point between Rigomagus and the sea.

Gregory of Tours (544–595), who wrote a "History of the Franks," records the baptism of King Clovis, whose cruel deeds and Christian fervour he sets down with much impartiality. According to his account Remigius (whom we also know as S. Remy, archbishop of Reims) prepared a little speech for the royal catechumen, beginning with "Mitis depone colla Sigamber"—"Bow thy neck meekly, Sicambrian!" Thus in the year 496 we have the representative and flower of the Frank race addressed as a Sicambrian. But that, again, proves nothing as to a special Sicambrian origin for the people and the name of Franks. It was a natural turn of rhetoric for Remigius to use; but Clovis, as we shall hereafter see, was a Salian rather than a Sicambrian Frank. And the Salians had their origin on the borders of the Hercynian Forest, where the river Sala (Saale) flows into the Main.

It would be idle to attempt to define the territorial limits of the Franks during the earlier centuries of their history, even if we could rely upon the accuracy and precision of every one who used the term up to the establishment of Clovis in Gaul. We read of the Riparian Franks, of the Sicambrian Franks, of the Salian Franks, of the Chamavian Franks, and so forth. Of the Salian Franks, again, there are two denominations, which we will attempt to distinguish in a future chapter; and it is doubtful how far to the eastward we ought to look for the original home of the Franks before Clovis, towards the central watershed of Germany, amongst the Chattans and Hermundurians, or even amongst the Suevians. Clovis himself, the real founder of the Merovingian dynasty, had to fight the Thuringians and the Allemans, and to oust the king of the Riparian Franks, before he could establish his authority over the Burgundians and Aquitanians. In other words, he, an undisputed Frank by origin, found himself opposed to other undisputed Franks, and to Germans who were not demonstrably Franks, as well as to Gauls and Gallo-Romans.

It is unnecessary to say that a Trojan origin was claimed for the Franks—as for the Danes and the Britons, and as a Macedonian origin was claimed for the Saxons. The work which goes by the name of Fredegarius, and which is partly based on Gregory of Tours, is especially responsible for the Trojan legend ; and it must be confessed that Fredegarius is not without warrant for claiming Virgil as an authority for his statement. What Virgil says[1] is this :—

> "Antenor potuit, mediis elapsus Achivis,
> Illyricos penetrare sinus, atque intima tutus
> Regna Liburnorum et fontem superare Timavi,
> Unde per ora novem, vasto cum murmure montis,
> It mare proruptum, et pelago premit arva sonanti.
> Hic tamen ille urbem Patavi sedesque locavit
> Teucrorum."

That is to say, Antenor the Trojan migrated to the furthest gulfs of the Illyrian coast, to the northern shore of the Adriatic, to Pannonia and Venetia, where he founded the city of Patavium, or Padua—whence, say some, the origin of the Batavians. Now, Gregory himself mentions Pannonia as a reputed home of the Franks ; and in an age which accepted Virgil as an authority in history it would not seem at all unreasonable to conclude that the Pannonians and Venetians

[1] Æneid, i. 246.

were of Trojan origin. But, whatever this may argue as to the parentage of these two peoples, it throws little or no light upon the parentage of the Franks.[1]

The derivation and meaning of the word *francus*, which is clearly not Latin in origin, will provide us not only with a very interesting historical puzzle, but also with a word-study of exceptional value and variety. Many words now in constant use, geographical and other, have been derived from this common appellation (for as such it came to be employed) of the Germanic settlers in Gaul; but whence did they originally derive it?

There is in the Breton division of the Keltic tongue a word "franc," which means "ample," "open," "at large," and, by natural inference, "free." The meaning suits, and some fairly good authorities, like the German Diefenbach, have been satisfied with this explanation. If it were accepted, one might go so far as to attach a new signification to the derivative word *franchir*, and find a harmony in the ideas suggested by this verb and by the epithet applied to the irrepressible Teutons, who so constantly leaped the barriers of Gaul.

Grimm and others have looked for a solution to the Gothic *freis*, and the German *frei*, one adding the word *ancke*, "youth," and then contracting *frei ancke* into *frank*. Others again refer us to an English or Saxon word *franca*, signifying "a dart," or even to a Teutonic word *framea*, with the same signification. These are not happy guesses, and we should still be

[1] The Trojan legend is discussed at some length by Dr. Rydberg, in his "Teutonic Mythology."

without any better suggestion than that of the Breton word *franc*, if it were not for a distinct statement, in historical form, which, though not of conclusive authority, commends itself to our careful consideration. Sigebert of Gembloux, a Belgian chronicler who died in the year 1112, writing of the Franks, says, " Valentinianus Francos Attica lingua appellavit, quod Latina lingua interpretatur feroces." And another writer says, with greater detail, " Sicambri haec audientes caesos Alanos (Allemannos) deleverunt. Romani Attica lingua tunc eos Francos, id est feroces, appellaverunt ; diuque a tributo liberi vixerunt." If we read " Hattica," or " Chattica," for ' Attica," and if we accept the substance of the two statements as fairly likely to be based on an older and stronger authority, we may conclude that the German warriors of the central cantons were called " Franci," that is to say ferocious or formidable, by Romans with whom they were at the time virtually in alliance. Probably enough they accepted the term as complimentary rather than in the opposite sense. According to the writer last quoted, the name was given by Romans to Sicambrians, though borrowed from the Chattan dialect ; but we need not suppose that he drew any sharp distinction between the two tribes, or, on the other hand, that the vocabulary of a Chattan differed much from that of a Sicambrian.

There is, however, a discrepancy in the statement of Sigebert as compared with the passage already quoted from Vopiscus. The first Valentinian was born in the year 321, but Vopiscus, who wrote part of the " Historia Augusta," must at the latest have died before Valentinian I. came to man's estate. Either the derivation of the word "Franci" was introduced into the Life of Aurelian by a younger hand than that of Vopiscus, or else the Valentinian that Sigebert refers to was not the first to make use of it.

We have another and considerably earlier explanation of the term from the Byzantine Lydus, who wrote a book on Roman magistracies in the first half of the sixth century. According to Lydus, the Gauls or Romans called these invaders Franks after the name of one of their leaders.[1] There is clearly a choice of difficulties, and the matter must be left without definite conclusion. The most we can do is to find reason for preferring the explanation that the German word "frank," whoever first applied it to this seed of a nation, was adopted by the Romans, ever ready to apply a nickname to their enemies or auxiliaries, and that in this way it passed into general acceptation.

And to the present day there is no word in the French language which, as we shall hereafter see, is more monumental in its record of historical origins and successive developments.

[1] Φράγγους αὐτοὺς ἐξ ἡγεμόνος καλοῦσιν ἐπὶ τοῦ παρόντος οἱ περὶ 'Ρῆνον καὶ 'Ροδανόν (iii. 56).

III.

CÆSAR'S FRONTIER POLICY.

IT follows from what has already been said that there can be no such thing as a precise and comprehensive story of the Franks, at any rate before the time of Clovis. The name which has become so famous in the history of the world was always undefined, and never more than conventional. What we know is that it was applied to certain German warriors —probably in the first instance to Sicambrians, Chattans, and Hermundurians, nearly corresponding with the Hermiones of Pliny—and that from them it was gradually extended to other bold and aggressive Teutons, dwelling on or near the banks of the river Sala, of the Main, and of the Middle and Lower Rhine. But we could not at any period take a map of Europe and say with confidence, " Here were the Franks, and here they ceased to be." We could not be sure that in dividing the German cantons between Franks and not-Franks we were including all that ought to be included, and excluding all that ought to be excluded. We could not take the descriptions of Germany and of its national characteristics, as furnished by Cæsar, Strabo, Pomponius Mela, Pliny, and Tacitus, and say, "This applies in particular to Germans who took the name of Franks, and this to Germans who remained in their ancestral seats, and never called themselves Franks." As we are shut out from any exact definition by the nature of our subject, it is necessary to begin by laying down limits for ourselves.

It will be interesting if we follow the general progress of the struggle between Romans and Germans, on both sides of the imperial frontier, from the time of Julius Cæsar onward. Proceeding on these lines, and watching the general retrocession of the Roman dominion, up to the time when the Rhine became German on both banks, throughout the whole of its course, we may take note of the earlier occurrences of the name and personality of the Franks, without drawing any more positive conclusions in regard to them than our last chapter may appear to warrant. Not until we approach the middle of the fifth century shall we be entitled to speak, as the introduction to the Salic code of law will be found to speak, of the Franks as a nation.

From the time of Clovis to the time of Charles the Great we shall have to do with a comparatively distinct kingdom, or with distinct kingdoms, of the Franks; and thereafter we shall see a new empire, with Franks in place of Romans, recoiling before a new invasion of irrepressible Northmen.

When Julius Cæsar went to the transalpine Province of Gaul as proconsul, in the year 58 B.C., more than forty years after the memorable defeat by Marius of the Cimbrians at Aquae Sextiae (Aix), and of the Teutons at Vercelli, his command extended as far north as the Cebenna mountains and Lake Lemanus. Of further Gaul, which he describes as held by Aquitanians, Celts, and Belgians, and which up to that time was independent of Rome, the Germans had already occupied considerable districts on the left bank of the Rhine. The river was practically in German hands, from its source to its mouth. Between the mouth and the Vosagus mountains (Vosges), the Belgians, so far as they were Kelts, had been driven back or overrun by Teutons; and, higher still, great hordes of Central Germans had ousted the Helvetians from their native valleys, and driven them to seek a new home in Gaul. The leaders of this vast migration gave Cæsar a pretext for attacking them, which he was not slow to seize. He had come from Rome with an aggressive policy already shaped in his mind, and he took the first step towards the conquest of Gaul by crushing the Helvetian host, and compelling the wanderers, or such of them as had not been slain, or taken refuge amongst the Aeduans, to return to their former territories.

A new and more formidable enemy was now to be encountered. Ariovistus, with an army of a hundred thousand Suevians (an indefinite term which must be regarded as including Germans of more than one tribe) had penetrated into the land of the Sequanians, within a few days' march of Vesontio (Besançon). There Cæsar defeated him, and thence drove him, with the remains of his shattered forces, back across the Rhine.

There were still plenty of Germans left in Gaul, as

Cæsar found to his cost. We have mentioned already the presence of the Menapians amongst the earlier settlers in Belgic territory, the migration of the Tencteri and Usipii, Cæsar's demonstration against the Sicambrian League, and his withdrawal before the general levy of the Suevians. He was both wise and prudent in declining to fight on that occasion. He had come to conquer Gaul, not Germany or Britain. His policy was to subdue the divided Gauls in detail, whether by fighting or by negotiating —and it must be remembered that the wealthiest men in nearer Gaul were already largely Italian in feeling, and well disposed to Rome. He was too great a general to miss his main object by committing himself deeply in the side issues.

Moreover, Cæsar must have seen, with the clear sight of true military genius, that the conquest of Germany, if not actually impossible, was a very different thing from the subjugation of Gaul. He saw that the number of fighting men in Germany was almost unlimited, and that each of them was as brave and intrepid as the best Roman legionary. Physically, indeed, they were bigger and stronger than the Romans and their southern levies; their only inferiority was in discipline and strategy. But what Cæsar would regard as more important—what was overlooked by rasher and younger generals, like Drusus half a century later—was that the Germans, in addition to being a multitude of swarming nations, were also in a condition of constant flux, and this not so much by their own choice as by a combination of natural necessities. His course in Gaul was comparatively smooth sailing, but if he had invaded Germany he would have been caught in a vortex of overwhelming currents. In Gaul he had a fixed mark, whereas in Germany the target would have been incessantly in motion. His first experience as proconsul, when he came from Rome with a single legion, was to encounter a planned and bravely escorted migration of 368,000 Helvetians, moving from east to west, who, if not themselves actually Teutons, were in motion as the direct result of a westward Teutonic pressure. The expedition of Ariovistus was not ostensibly a migration, but it doubtless originated in the same causes, which must have led to the same shifting of wives and families and property. Ariovistus was said to have been called in to the assistance of the Sequanians and Arvernians (corresponding to the present Auvergnats); but he was in Gaul before that, with other objects and other aims. The case of the Tencteri and their allies was more distinctly one of migration initiated by pressure behind, and exerting pressure in front.

If Cæsar recognised these two great growing forces of compression and expansion amongst the German tribes, he probably foresaw something of the course of events during the next few centuries. It would be useless for Rome to conquer Germany: she could not hold it. Her policy must be to stem this human tide, to keep it in check, and by a few well-directed blows at the proper moments to prevent the enemies of the empire from massing themselves in irresistible force upon the frontiers. In this way the compressed populations of the mountain and forest lands, of the valleys and grazing-grounds of Germany, might be held back by strong forts and ramparts, and by unceasing vigilance of frontier-garrisons; but the restrained force would still gather and grow, and the first relaxation of the defence would be followed by an immediate expansion. As Montesquieu has said, "Les violences des Romains avaient fait retirer les peuples du Midi au Nord: tandis que la force qui les contenait subsista, ils y restèrent; quand elle fut affaiblie, ils se répandirent de toutes parts." The truth of this statement was frequently attested, from the time of Marius onward; but it was conspicuously illustrated in the fifth and the ninth century.[1]

The best work of Cæsar in relation to Gaul and the Germans endures to this day, because it was in close harmony with the laws of historic development—not, like the work of many generals and statesmen, in apparent resistance to those laws. "Inasmuch as the great general and statesman of Rome," says Mommsen, "with sure glance perceived in the German tribes the rivals and antagonists of the Roman-Greek world; inasmuch as with firm hand he established the new system of aggressive defence down even to its details, and taught men to protect the frontier of the empire by rivers or artificial ramparts, to colonise the nearest barbarian tribes along the frontier with the view of warding off the more remote, and to recruit the Roman army by enlistment from the

[1] "La même chose arriva quelques siècles après. Les conquêtes de Charlemagne et ses tyrannies avaient une seconde fois fait reculer les peuples du Midi au Nord; sitôt que cet empire fut affaibli ils se portèrent une seconde fois du Nord au Midi" ("Causes de la Grandeur des Romains et de leur Décadence").

enemy's country, he gained for the Hellenic-Italian culture the interval necessary to civilise the West, as it had already civilised the East."

To say that Cæsar did this, and that he had the genius to do it, is another way of saying that the historical development of the world had produced the imperial race of Italy, and that the Italian race had produced the characteristic genius of Cæsar. The character and the culture of Italy had alike matured to bring about this result on the very eve of the Christian era. The genius of Rome, the conquests of Cæsar, the power of the Roman army which was presently to set up and put down the Emperors as its puppets, created an engine of human development whereby not only was Roman culture assimilated in Gaul, Germany, and Britain, but also Christianity was grafted upon that culture, before the Roman Empire came to an end.

This is a root-fact of history which need not here be further dwelt upon; but it is indispensable to any right conception of the story of the Northern races.

The policy of Cæsar was observed by his successors. Augustus spent some three years in the transalpine Provinces (17–14 B.C.), and devoted himself, amongst other purposes, to the consolidation of the frontier defences. During the next two or three centuries, the forts on the Rhine and the Danube, which were often the centres of colonies, and the artificial barrier connecting the two rivers at points where they became wide enough to be easily defended, were constantly restored and strengthened; and many a blow was struck at the riparian tribes when their gathering strength threatened to be formidable again. Augustus did, indeed, advance the frontier-line to the mouth of the Amisia (Ems), so as to include the conquered Frisians, and part of the territory, as far as the Visurgis (Weser), which his stepson Drusus had three times promenaded. After the death of Drusus, his brother Tiberius chastised the Sicambrians, whom we once more find united with their neighbours in a strong anti-Roman league. This time the Chattans are spoken of as their most prominent allies.

The campaigns of the two sons of Livia seemed for the moment to have produced a salutary effect upon the Sicambrians, Chattans, and Cheruscans. A chain of fifty forts was completed, now or not long afterwards, between Mogontiacum and Vetera Castra. Vast numbers of German settlers on the left bank of the Rhine were expelled again, and for a few years the Romans flattered themselves that the warlike Teutons were bowing their necks to the yoke. Augustus made Varus governor of the newly included country, and commissioned him to bring it under the

---

The map attempts to illustrate the history of several centuries. The allocation of tribe names is only approximate. [*Albis*, Elbe; *Amisia*, Ems; *Aquæ Mattiacorum*, Wiesbaden; *Argentoratum*, Strassburg; *Argentovaria*, Artzenheim (?); *Asciburgum*, Asburg; *Augusta Treverorum*, Trèves; *Axona*, Aisne; *Bonna*, Bonn; *Burginatium*, Schenkenschanz; *Colonia Agrippina*, Cologne; *Confluentes*, Coblenz; *Diutia*, Deutz; *Divodurum*, Metz; *Durocatalauni*, Châlons; *Issala*, Yssel; *Laugona*, Lahn; *Locoritum*, Lohr (?); *Luppia*, Lippe; *Matrona*, Marne; *Moenus*, Main; *Mogontiacum*, Mainz; *Nicer*, Neckar; *Rigomagus*, Remagen; *Rura*, Ruhr; *Sala*, Saale; *Sauconna*, Saône; *Scaldis*, Scheldt; *Sequana*, Seine; Siga, Sieg; *Tolbiacum*, Zülpich; *Tullum*, Toul; *Vahalis*, Waal; *Vetera Castra*, Birten; *Visontio*, Besançon; *Visurgis*, Weser.]

jurisdiction of Rome. Hermann, a chief of the Cheruscans, who had served in the Roman army, and had been created a Roman knight under the designation of Arminius, lived on terms of amity with the unsuspecting Varus, meanwhile preparing for him a deadly ambush. One day, as Varus was marching with his three legions through the Saltus Teutoburgius, the Cheruscans and their allies, led by Hermann, fell upon him suddenly from all sides, and in countless numbers. The brave legions sustained the attack for three days, until barely a man was left alive; and then the unfortunate Varus fell by his own hand. In vain Augustus cried to him, at Rome, to give him back his lost legions. The disaster was worse than this, for Hermann's treachery produced its calculated effect, and the conquests of Drusus were abandoned. Germanicus, indeed, avenged the slaughtered legions on their enemies. He took an army of veterans, reinforced by eight troops of Batavian horsemen, to the Teutoburg forest, paid funeral honours to the bones of Varus and his men, defeated Hermann after a year or two of varying fortunes, led a fleet of one thousand vessels through the canal (Drusiana Fossa) which his father Drusus had dug between the Rhine and the Issala (Yssel), and crossed the Lower Ems and Weser. He might have reconquered the country, at any rate for a time, if he had not been recalled to Rome by Tiberius. Thus tamely ended the only serious attempt which was made to depart from Cæsar's wiser policy.

A few years later (A.D. 19), the broken prestige of Hermann left him a prey to the jealousy of the surrounding tribes, and at the age of thirty-six his authority came to an end with his life. It was in the same year that his countryman Marbod, who, like him, had been trained and befriended at Rome, having formed a confederacy of the Southern Suevians, and defied his former hosts, was driven from power by his neighbours, at the instigation of Drusus, the son of Tiberius. It is a curious parallel. Hermann and Marbod were of the same age; probably enough they had consorted together in Rome, and there nursed in common the twofold ambition of defeating Roman armies and creating dominions for themselves in their native land. But the Germans were not yet matured for wide dominion. There was cohesion enough amongst the Teuton warriors to form powerful confederacies, and to face the Roman legions year after year, never accepting defeat as a ground for submission. There was not cohesion enough to obey a common leader for any length of time, or for any other purpose than the defeat of their enemies, the preservation of their liberties, and the acquisition of booty.

The defensive policy against Germany prevailed more or less during the first two centuries of the Christian era. The desultory wars which occurred from time to time under the Julian emperors were, so far as the Romans were concerned, for the most part defensive. Caligula (37–41) sought martial glory in the Roman frontier camps, but, if the stories of Suetonius may be believed, he only succeeded in covering himself with ridicule. Claudius (41–54), whom the Gauls hailed as "father of the Provinces," and by whom large numbers of them were admitted as Roman citizens, was invited by the Cheruscans to arbitrate between opposing factions of the tribe. During the reign of Nero (54-68) a rebellion in Gaul, fostered by Galba, was opposed by Virginius Rufus with an army from Lower (Belgian) Germany; and it was virtually the coalition of the Gallic and Batavian forces which brought about the downfall of Nero, and the elevation of the traitor Galba to the dignity of Imperator. Galba, Otho, and Vitellius, the last of whom marched to Rome with an army largely composed of German levies, were little more than nominal emperors, whose three reigns extended over less than one year. Vitellius, after using the Batavians to crush Otho, dismissed them to their homes, thus reconverting them into enemies of Rome.

It fell to the lot of Vespasian, or of his generals, to crush the rebellions which had come to a head under his weaker predecessor. The Batavians and Frisians, with allies from both sides of the Middle Rhine, had conquered several Roman armies, and occupied some of the larger fortified towns, including Augusta Treverorum and Castra Vetera; but they were eventually beaten.

The story of Civilis, as told by Tacitus—though his narrative has reached us in an incomplete form—is full of romance. He was a Frank before the Franks,[1] who had spent his youth as a mercenary

---

[1] It must be borne in mind that the Batavians were an offshoot from the Chattans. Tacitus ("Germania," xxix.) says:—"Of all these nations the Batavians were especially distinguished for their valour. They dwelt not far from the sea-shore, on an island formed by the

in the Roman army, and had learned to despise and hate his masters. His brother had been put to death on a charge of conspiracy, and Civilis himself, narrowly escaping the same fate, now became what he had been falsely accused of being. He collected a large army of Germans and Kelts, which included the Canninefates and the Frisians, dwelling between the Rhine-mouths and the northern sea. During the years 69 and 71, Civilis gave the Romans a great deal of trouble, defeating the armies of Vitellius and Vespasian, capturing or besieging the fortified places on the Rhine, overshadowing for a time the powerful Sicambrians and Chattans of the south, and making the name of Batavian a terror to Rome.

Much of the influence of Civilis amongst the German tribes was derived from his association with a Bructerian prophetess, Veleda by name, who had foretold a return of prosperity for the Germans, and the destruction of the Roman legions. She dwelt apart, in a tower, and one of her attendants, "as though he were the interpreter of a goddess," carried to and fro the questions submitted to her and the answers she vouchsafed. Her authority gained for the Batavian leader many friends on the east of the Rhine who might not otherwise have espoused his cause. Amongst these were the Tencteri; and when the inhabitants of Colonia Agrippina, who had been constrained to an alliance

<small>Rhine, and were once a part of the Chattan people, who, after an internal quarrel, migrated to their new home." The list given by Tacitus of the various German nations will be found in the Note at the end of this chapter.</small>

with the enemy of Rome, were called upon by this German tribe to level their walls, they made a conciliatory reply, and referred the question to Civilis and Veleda.

In the end, however, Civilis lost his hold upon the anti-Roman confederacy. His fortune waned, and his allies, especially amongst the Gauls, fell away. It may have been that his very intimacy with the wise woman on the banks of the Luppia had led to a relaxation of his own efforts, or to jealousies on the part of his comrades—for human nature has been the same in all ages. At any rate, Veleda herself was alienated, and began to prophesy evil; and the evil followed. A Roman general, Cerealis, who subsequently conquered the Brigantes in Britain, was sent against him with a large army; and Civilis, who had to choose between making terms for himself and being virtually delivered into the hands of his enemy, after some further fighting accepted the invitation of Cerealis to negotiate for peace. The two leaders conferred with each other from opposite banks of the Drusiana Fossa, which connected the Rhine and the Issala.

At this point the narrative of Tacitus comes to an end, and the story of Civilis is left unfinished.

Domitian (81–96) and Trajan (98–117) were both compelled to renew the struggle, for the Chattans, Sicambrians, and their neighbours, the Franks of the future, were ever prompt to wage war against their ancestral enemy. In the reign of Marcus Aurelius (161–180), the descendants of the Southern and South-western Germans whom Marbod had attempted to consolidate a century and a half ago, once more began to cross the higher Rhine—this time conspicuously in obedience to the natural law of westward pressure which was always operative amongst the Germans, though not always with equal force. The invaders, who were called Suevians in the time of Julius Cæsar and Tiberius, were now described by the geographical name of Marcomanni, the men of the marches. So far as it is possible to speak of Teutonic tribes inhabiting the same district at an interval of more than a century by the same name, and as standing to each other in the relation of ancestors and posterity, the "Suevi" of Marbod were ancestors to the "Marcomanni" who, in alliance with the Quadi and other neighbours, were driven upon the legions of Aurelius by the fierce Alans and Slavons in their rear. The peace-loving emperor—who might have exclaimed, and probably did exclaim to himself, like Julian a couple of centuries later, "What a task for a philosopher!" —reaped more than one victory over the German hosts, but died with his task unfinished, apparently as far advanced in the territories of his foes as Vindobona, the modern Vienna. On his death, his son Commodus was content to purchase peace of the unconquered border tribes.

NOTE.

The German tribes are thus enumerated by Tacitus in the "Germania"—(2) Quidam, ut in licentia vetustatis, pluris deo ortos plurisque gentis appellationes, *Marsos, Gambrivios, Suevos,*

Vandalos, affirmant. . . . (28) Validiores olim Gallorum res fuisse. . . . Iulius tradit : eoque credibile est etiam *Gallos in Germaniam* transgressos. . . . Inter Hercyniam silvam Rhenumque et Mocnum amnes, *Helvetii*, ulteriora *Boii*, Gallica utraque gens, tenuere. Manet adhuc *Boihemi* nomen, significatque loci veterem memoriam, quamvis mutatis cultoribus. . . . (29) Omnium harum gentium virtute præcipui *Batavi* non multum ex ripa sed insulam Rheni amnis colunt, *Cattorum* quondam populus . . . nec tributis contemnuntur nec publicanus adterit. . . . Est in eodem obsequio *Mattiacorum* gens. . . . Non numeraverim inter Germaniæ populos, quamquam trans Rhenum Danubiumque consederint, eos qui *decumates agros* exercent. Levissimus quisque Gallorum, et inopia audax, dubiæ possessionis solum occupavere. Mox limite acto, promotisque præsidiis, sinus imperii et pars provinciæ habentur. (30) Ultra hos *Catti* initium sedis ab Hercynio saltu inchoant. . . . Duriora genti corpora, stricti artus, minax vultus, et maior animi vigor. . . . (32) Proximi Cattis certum iam alveo Rhenum, quique terminus esse sufficiat, *Usipii* ac *Tencteri* colunt. . . . (33) Iuxta Tencteros *Bructeri* olim occurrebant : nunc *Chamavos* et *Angrivarios*. . . . Angrivarios et Chamavos a tergo *Dulgibini* et *Chasuarii* cludunt, aliæque gentes, haud perinde memoratæ. A fronte *Frisii* excipiunt. . . . (35) *Chaucorum* gens, quamquam incipiat a Frisiis, ac partem litoris occupet, omnium quas exposui gentium lateribus obtenditur, donec in Cattos usque sinuetur . . . populus inter Germanos nobilissimus. . . . (36) In latere Chaucorum Cattorumque *Cherusci*. . . . *Fosi* contermina gens. . . . (37) Eundem Germaniæ sinum proximi Oceano *Cimbri* tenent, parva nunc civitas, sed gloria ingens ; veterisque famæ lata vestigia manent, utraque ripa castra ac spatia, quorum ambitu nunc quoque metiaris molem manusque gentis, et tam magni exitus fidem. Sexcentesimum et quadragesimum annum urbs nostra agebat cum primum Cimbrorum audita sunt arma. Ex quo si ad alterum imperatoris Traiani consulatum computemus, ducenti ferme et decem anni conliguntur (B.C. 114 to A.D. 96). . . . (38) Nunc de *Suevis* dicendum est, quorum non una, ut Cattorum Tencterorumve gens : maiorem enim Germaniæ partem obtinent, propriis adhuc nationibus nominibusque discreti. . . . (39) Vetustissimos se nobilissimosque Suevorum *Semnones* memorant. . . . (40) Contra *Langobardos* paucitas nobilitat. Plurimis ac valentissimis nationibus cincti, non per obsequium sed proeliis et periclitando tuti sunt. *Reudigni* deinde et *Aviones* et *Anglii* et *Varini* et *Eudoses* et *Suardones* et *Nuithones* fluminibus aut silvis muniuntur. . . . (41) Propior (ut nunc Danubium sequar) *Hermundurorum* civitas. . . . (42) iuxta *Narisci*, ac deinde *Marcomanni* et *Quadi*. . . . (43) Nec minus valent retro *Marsigni*, *Gothini*, *Osi*, *Burii*. . . . Latissime patet

Lygiorum nomen, in plures civitates diffusum. Valentissimas nominasse sufficiet *Arios, Helveconas, Manimos, Elysios, Naharvalos.* . . . Trans Lygios *Gotones* regnantur. . . . Protinus deinde ab Oceano *Rugii* et *Lemovii*. . . . (44) *Suionum* hinc civitates, ipso in Oceano, praeter viros armaque classibus valent. . . . (45) Ergo iam dextro Suevici maris litore *Aestyorum* gentes adluuntur: quibus ritus habitusque Suevorum, lingua Britannicæ propior. . . . Suionibus *Sitonum* gentes continuantur.

IV.

THE GERMAN RACE.

OUR materials for the history of Rome in the time of her later Cæsars, whilst she was engaged, amongst the other tasks of her decadence, on the critical duty of maintaining her frontier against the ultimately irresistible inroads of Eastern and Northern barbarism, are somewhat meagre. Contemporary historians are few, and in such records as remain to us the details of what would now be particularly interesting are neither full nor well connected.

For several generations after the death of Marcus Aurelius we hear comparatively little of the Teutonic tribes, who, nevertheless, gave a constant account of themselves along the whole of the extended frontier of the Roman Empire in Europe.

Before we take up the story of the Franks in its more definite form, at the time when they had come to be known as Franks, and when the defenders of the frontier were found unequal to the work of rolling back the tide of invasion, it will be interesting to make some better acquaintance with them on their own soil, as Germans in Germany, strong in their characteristics, proud of the long-maintained independence of their race, yet already modified by the example and influence of their more civilised neighbours in Gaul and Italy.

Centuries of constant strife against the armies of Rome must in any case have made excellent soldiers out of the unsurpassed raw material of the Teutonic tribes; but their inborn fighting qualities had received direct and effective training in the ranks of the Roman legions. The armies of the Cæsars were very largely recruited from the nations whom they overcame; and from no nation were recruits more willingly drawn than from the Germans, whose personal valour had been proved on so many battlefields. It was a dangerous lesson which Rome taught her ancient foes when she thus proved her inability to rely on Italians for the defence of Italy; and simultaneously she was teaching them other lessons equally fatal to her security.

The attitude of Rome towards her enemies on the European frontier was inconsistent from first to last. The policy of attack, ending in doubtful victories or virtual defeats, was alternated with the policy, or indeed the stern necessity, of defence. In one generation the Romans would regard with supreme indifference the inter-tribal quarrels of the Teutons, whilst in another they would find a pretext for intervention in precisely similar quarrels. Resolute, for the most part, in riding down and cutting to pieces the fugitives who escaped across the river from their Teutonic, Scandinavian, or Slavonian enemies, they would occasionally invite and enrol them in large numbers, Romans leading them to war against Romans, or instructing them in all the arts of treachery and intrigue. One general or emperor would fight them ruthlessly and haughtily, selling their prisoners into slavery, or deporting them to distant lands; another would buy off their hostility with gold. These were lessons, not of firm strength, but of weakness and vacillation and in the long run they taught the Riparians not to respect but to despise.

If the maritime Frisians and Batavians, the enterprising Chaucian merchants, the Sicambrians and Chattans who bore the brunt of the border warfare, learned to see and take advantage of the growing weakness of the empire—especially from the time of Commodus onwards—they had always been attracted by the comforts and luxuries which the Roman legions and colonists brought in their train. They hated the life of cities—a wall had little meaning for them except as the boundary of a prison—but their fighting men loved nothing better than to raid a Roman town, and bring back everything that was portable to their wattled homes on the borders of the forest and the fen. They would barter when they were not fighting, but the raided treasures were the sweetest, and many a German home was full of spoils from Gaul and Rhætia. Their vast herds of cattle were their own natural wealth and material for barter; but the taste for Roman treasure came with the opportunity of securing it. "Argentum et aurum propitii an irati dii negaverint, dubito," says Tacitus: it is an open question whether the gods were kind or unkind in stinting the Germans of gold and silver. But the god of battles gave what other gods had denied, and no people have been keener than the Teutons in their quest of booty.

Apart from war, the Roman civilisation found its way amongst the Germans by trade, by casual intercourse in time of peace between the two banks of the Rhine, by the sojourn of individual Germans in Rome, as we have seen in the case of Marbod and Hermann, and by the return of German legionaries after their service had expired. For such reasons as we have mentioned above, the line of frontier defence, which was pre-eminently a line of war between Rome and her neighbours, became also, for the latter, a line of progressive civilisation. All the Roman frontiers, like the frontiers of every empire which extends its borders amongst savage tribes, or nations less civilised than itself, included of necessity, within the extreme limit of dominion, a more or less considerable element of the nationalities outside that limit. Rome regarded the Rhine as a frontier between Gaul and Germany, but it is doubtful whether, before this definite political arrangement, it was looked upon as much more than a natural obstacle for those who dwelt on either side of it. Cæsar mentions frequent crossings of the river from east to west and from west to east—the stronger movement being that which was caused by the pressure in the east, by the overflow of Asia into Europe, of the arid plains and morasses into the fertile valleys.

When Rome converted the natural obstacle of the Rhine into a more distinctly political boundary, for her own strategic purposes, there were already many settlements on the west of this line, made by tribes which had come from the east. It would be impossible to say how long the westward stream of humanity had been steadily flowing across the northward currents of the Rhine; but the first orientalisation of Europe was at least as old as the settlement of Medians and Egyptians on the Mediterranean coasts, and it is reasonable to suppose that the inflow had continued without long cessation, wherever the geographical barriers were most practicable, and the human barriers least effectual. At any rate Rome drew her frontier on the Rhine and the Danube, and drew it in both cases athwart a running stream of human migration. For Roman statesmen and geographers the Rhine at once created a definite Gaul and a partially definite Germany; but it is well to remember that Gaul, as thus defined, already included a strong Teutonic element, and that the Eastern Belgic tribes were, as Cæsar tells us, actually Germans. Indeed the greater part of the Belgians were merely the first Germans who settled on the west bank of the Rhine, and the first who became imbued with Roman civilisation. They would thus be closely allied with the Frisians, Chaucians, Cheruscans, Sicambrians, and Chattans, who formed the vanguard of the Germans coming next in order, whilst they were also kindred in other respects with the Aryan Kelts who had preceded them. According to Tacitus, the first Germans to cross the Rhine were the Tungri, whose name is preserved in the modern Tongres, and who had settled between the Meuse and the Scheldt.

There is another sense in which the frontier-zone of Gaul exerted a constant civilising influence upon the Germans. It was at all times a refuge for such as wanted peace with Rome, and were willing to accept her terms. The Cæsars were not averse to small migrations of this character, which were easily combined with their general system of recruiting and frontier plantations. The imperial armies were composed more and more of foreigners, who received the citizenship as soon as they were enrolled in a legion. Italians were too political, too dangerous to the peace of Rome, to be made the mainstay of the Roman army. Their number in the ranks was continually decreased, until Vespasian, the first Flavian emperor, entirely excluded them. Most of the officers, and most of the City and Prætorian guards, would continue to be Italian for a long time to come. But the legionary soldiers, who were enrolled for twenty years' service, and the auxiliaries in the Provinces, who served for twenty-five years, were Gauls, Germans, Spaniards, and so forth, who became Romanised during their service, and were frequently settled at the end of it on the fields of their countrymen, which they had enabled a Roman leader to add to the confines of the empire. In this way also a zone of half-civilised Teutonism was created on the eastern boundaries of Gaul.

Having regard to the composite character of the population of Eastern Gaul during the Roman occupation—of the broad belt which, in the third century, was partly a Romanised Germany, partly a Romanised Gaul strongly imbued with German qualities—it will serve our purpose to give some closer attention to the frontier-line of Rome and Germany, the central and cardinal line of Gallo-German and Franco-German history in all ages.

After Trajan, early in the second century, had added Dacia to the list of Roman provinces, the European frontier extended from the Euxine Sea, at a point near the mouth of the Tyras (Dniester), by a vallum, as far as the junction of the Drave and the Danube. From thence it followed the bank of the Danube upwards, to a point a few miles above Regina Castra (Regensburg), at which point the Alcimona (Altmühl) enters the Danube on the northern bank. Instead of keeping to the Danube as far as its source, and passing over to the source of the Rhine, the Roman frontier was artificially constructed between the two rivers, thus uniting points where the streams were broad and difficult to cross. After skirting the Altmühl, and running for some distance westwards, the vallum known as Hadrian's turned sharply northwards, crossed the Neckar somewhere near the town of Wimpffen, and so reached the westernmost of the two great southward bends of the river Moenus (Main). There was here at one time a double rampart, the exact courses of which it is impossible to trace. It is, as Mommsen says, extraordinary that Germans should never have had the enterprise thoroughly to explore the foundations of their oldest historical monument. But at the present moment German archæologists are engaged in repairing this neglect.

It may be that Hadrian was the first to construct,

or at any rate to complete, the vallum which came to bear his name. He built strongly when he did build, as remnants of his wall in Britain will show. At all events the line of garrisoned forts, at strategic points along a difficult tract of country, connected by ramparts which would naturally vary in character from stone or brickwork to earthwork or stockade, doubtless answered its purpose, so long as Rome was strong and vigorous, as a substantial frontier between the restless marauders outside and the comparatively settled colonists within.

Trajan, it would appear, completed or strengthened the Limes Germanicus, which had been at least partially drawn in the time of Augustus. Starting on the Main, and nearly bisecting the great curve of that river already mentioned, it ran northwards, about half-way between the modern Frankfort and Karlstadt; then, taking a wide sweep over hill and valley and morass, amongst the sources of many northward and southward streams, climbing the crests of the Taunus, and the northern limits of the Rheingau, it approached the Rhine opposite to Vosolvia (Ober-Wesel). Hence it ran parallel to the stream, across the Lahn, over against Confluentes (Coblenz), at the embouchure of the Mosella, and past the modern Ehrenbreitstein, ending in what is now called the Westerwald, a little above the town of Bonn and the tributary Sieg.

Not many miles eastward of the Limes Germanicus, a little beyond Locoritum, which probably corresponds with the modern Lohr, a tributary of the Main called the Sala (Saale) flows down from the north-east, across what is known to this day as the land of the Unter Franken. There is another Sala, rising at some little distance to the east again, in the same Thuringian section of the great Hercynian watershed, which flows northward into the Elbe. Here, we have every reason to conclude, near the springs of the two Salas, in and around the Thüringerwald, was the very cradle-land of the people called Franks.

The Limes ended at Rigomagus, now Remagen, on the Rhine, and thence, along the left bank, ran a line of Roman forts, the chief of which were Bonna (Bonn), Colonia Agrippina (Cologne), Durnomagus (Dormagen), Novæsium (Neuss), Gelduba (Gellep), Asciburgum (Asburg), Vetera Castra (Birten), Colonia Trajana, Burginatium (Schenkenschanz), and Noviomagus Batavorum (Nimeguen). From Remagen to Nimeguen is a distance of about 105 miles in a straight line. Near some of these towns there would be permanent Roman camps, whilst some of them were Roman colonies. Colonia Agrippina (with Duitia—Deutz—on the right bank of the river) was founded by the Emperor Claudius, A.D. 51, on a site previously occupied by the Ubii, who, as was probably the case with most of the riparian tribes, had held both sides of the river before the advent of the Romans. It must have happened, whenever the legions expelled the fighting men from a conquered territory, that many remained behind on their native soil, and placed themselves at the mercy of the victors. This would be the natural condition of things along the whole European frontier, and a remnant of the Teutons would continue to live side by side with the Roman settlers. Thenceforth the mixed populations would be safe under the shelter of the Roman power, and there would be few places on the Rhine, on the Limes Germanicus, and on the Vallum Hadriani, where an admixture of Romans and Germans, with the Germans in great preponderance, did not exist.

The springs of Wiesbaden, on the southern slopes of the Taunus range, overlooking the confluence of the Main and the Rhine, where the latter river turns abruptly to the west, were known to the Romans as Aquæ Mattiacæ. This was one of the first spots to receive the protection of the Limes, and at a later period Trajan bridged the Rhine at Mogontiacum (Mainz), so as to give the inhabitants of the town a more easy access to the springs. The rough triangle included by the Upper Rhine, the Upper Danube, and the artificial frontier, of which one apex was near Aquæ Mattiacæ, was especially allotted by Rome to military and other settlers, who paid as rent for their holdings one-tenth of the annual produce. But this was not the first systematic re-peopling of the territory which went by the name of the Decumates Agri. Cæsar speaks of the uppermost reaches of the Rhine as separating the Helvetians from the Germans. When the former nation had been restored to their homes, and the whole of Gaul had been practically subjugated, the territory which now includes Baden, Würtemberg, the western part of Bavaria, and the southern parts of Darmstadt and Nassau, was to some extent denuded of its former

German inhabitants, and many Gallic settlers were introduced. For several centuries to come the mixed population of the Decumates Agri enjoyed a peace and a culture which were considerably in advance of those of their German neighbours on the east.

V.

THE DECLINE OF ROME.

THE century in which the Franks make their first appearance, under that name, in the history of Europe, though in some respects it may seem less attractive for the reader than those which preceded and followed it, nevertheless presents many points of exceptional interest and importance. The third century of the Christian era was an age of many significant developments, in which the disappearance of the old and the substitution of the new continually challenge our attention.

The rapidly decreasing power of the Roman Empire is thrown into stronger relief by the almost simultaneous emergence of the Franks, Allemans (whose Teutonic name of Alle-männer clearly indicates another confederacy), and Goths. These, at three different spots, broke through the frontier which for more than two centuries had resisted the fiercest attacks. It was not the *vallum*, or the *limes*, but the human wall which crumbled to pieces at their approach; and it was not so much the number as the spirit of the defenders which proved itself unequal to the task of defence. Rome fell, as an empire, because its protection had been made to depend upon the nations which it had subjugated, and because the Italians who composed the Prætorian Guard, and who had usurped the right of nominating the emperors, chose at one time a rich man who was willing to bribe them, at another a weak man whom they could overawe, at another an imbecile, or a sot, or a popinjay. When by way of exception—and after the Flavian emperors the exceptions were rare—a soldier of real strength contrived to force himself to the front, the ancient glories of the Roman arms were for a time revived, and the strongest enemies of Rome recoiled before him. But such victories were shortlived, and they only serve to emphasise the defeats which came after them. Rome had had her day; she was now to experience the " deum ira in rem Romanam " which Tacitus had seen approaching.

The fall of Rome concerns us here mainly because it was contemporary with the origin of the new nationalities. The development of the Germanic nations corresponded, step by step, with the shrinkage of the imperial dominion. In the third century, side by side with the repeated purchase of peace by Rome, the successful inroads of the Goths, the revolt of legions and the treachery of generals, we find emperor after emperor drawn from the subjugated tribes. In A.D. 193 the empire had been sold by the Prætorian Guards to the highest bidder; an outrage which was, indeed, speedily avenged by the death of the purchaser and the disbanding of the Guards. The latter were replaced by an army of fifty thousand barbarians, so that the State of Rome passed at this time entirely under the control of foreigners. In 218 the Syrian priest Heliogabalus became emperor. Four years later he was succeeded by the Greek Alexander. After him came the Thracian or Gothic Maximinus, followed after a brief interval by the Arabian Philip, who wore the purple when Rome celebrated her millennium; by the Illyrian Decius and his son Hostilianus. It was during the generation when these six aliens held sway in Rome that the Goths, the Allemans, and the Franks broke the Roman frontier in Dacia, in Rhætia, and in Gaul. It is not to be supposed that the alien emperors—especially such emperors as the Illyrians Claudius, Aurelian, and Probus, and the Dalmatian Diocletian, who ruled in the last thirty years of this century—were worse men or worse emperors than the Italians who had ruled before them. But it is impossible to deny the significance of the fact that soldiers who had their origin elsewhere than in Italy swayed the destinies of Rome during the greater part of the third century. The Illyrian and Dalmatian emperors undoubtedly paved the way for the transference of the seat of empire from Rome to Byzantium.

Another dominion, spiritual at any rate in its foundation and elements, was in the meantime being steadily developed. The Christian Church gained continually in repute and organisation, notwithstanding the frequent persecution of its members. The striking contrast presented by its tenets and its sober rule of life with the outworn pagan creed and the demoralisation of Rome secured for it many

PORTA NIGRA (ROMAN).
(Trèves.)

adherents in every generation. In the wake of the Roman armies followed the missionary zeal of the converts, until there was not a single province of the empire in which there had not been sown the seeds of a future national Church. Before the end of the third century we read of important Christian communities in the province of Gaul—at Augusta Treverorum (Trèves), now the chief seat of Roman government, at Arelate (Arles), at Tolosa (Toulouse), at Augustonemetum (Clermont), and at Lutetia (Paris).

Meanwhile the Romanisation of Gaul had rapidly progressed. The Province of Cisalpine Gaul was already in the time of Cæsar and Augustus one of the most civilised and cultivated portions of the Roman dominions. Thence the regular concomitants of Roman conquest rapidly spread to the transalpine Province, and so northward, eastward, and westward, until Roman cults and customs, institutions, coinage, dress, and language were adopted first by the representatives of Rome and the Roman "party," and then by their clients and dependents. The right of association and the right of citizenship had been followed by all the other rights and privileges of the Roman citizen. Municipal life had grown up on the Roman model. Many amongst the more prosperous and cultivated of the inhabitants of Gaul—of course first and foremost in the Roman colonies, Arelate, Bæterræ (Béziers), Arausio (Orange), Forum Julii (Fréjus), Colonia Allobrogum (Geneva), Decumanorum (Narbonne), Equestris (Nyon), Julia Apta (Apt), Vienna (Vienne), Maritima (Martigues), Nemausensis (Nimes), and the Rhine colonies, Cologne, Trèves, Aquensis (Aix), and Julia Bonna (Bonn)— became students and patrons of Latin letters, and with so much zeal that these cities afforded asylums for Roman learning and culture after many an Italian town had ceased to shelter them. Several of the emperors, from Augustus onwards, established or patronised schools of law, grammar, and rhetoric. Orators and men of literary activity abounded in the Gallic provinces. Varro the historian was a Gaul; Cornelius Gallus and Ausonius were Gauls. Three hundred years after the time of Julius Cæsar there were scores of cities, north of the Mediterranean and west of the Rhine, which in general freedom, in learning and culture, in architecture, wealth, and population, would bear comparison with some of the leading cities of Italy.

The anarchy of the third century, which often submerged the liberties and the lives of men, which undermined and overwhelmed the classical literature of Rome, which menaced civilisation, and in some instances buried its traces under a new flood of barbarism, visited Gaul, like every other portion of the empire ; but it is to be remembered that if there was any permanent upholding of the standard of civilised life, any effective continuity of Roman genius and culture through the darkest ages of the first Christian millennium, we owe it in large measure to the great cities which stood out above the devastating floods, which preserved their institutions, their dwellings, their traditions, their wealth, and something of their "humanity" and literature.

No country did more for the preservation of the best legacy of Rome than was done by Gaul, taking that term in its widest signification—the Gaul, that is to say, which stretched from the Apennines to the delta of the Rhine, and from the Western Pyrenees to the Adriatic Gulf. Let us remember that, so far as the legacy of Rome was the heritage of the Franks, it was the Gallic cities north and west of the Alps which acted as trustees of the inheritance, and preserved it during the minority of the heir. Let us remember again that the Gallic Church, from the fourth century onward, began to preside over the destinies of these cities, and to dispense the learning and the humanities which survived the general wreck. And if we think that the Christian priests and teachers, and at a later period the scholastics, were somewhat narrow in the interpretation of their trust, and suffered much to sink in obscurity which might well have been cherished for its beauty, we must remember how much they preserved which would have been lost without them. The earliest Christians were Greeks and Jews, together with the least cultivated populations, slaves and others, of the Roman towns. It was not to them that the world could look for the salvation of Latin literature. But when men of learning and culture accepted the religion of the cross, they clothed its doctrines in language which at any rate guaranteed the continuous study and comprehension of those doctrines for all time. The patristic Latin is not Ciceronian, but at least it is to Quintilian what Quintilian is to Cicero. Minucius Felix, Lactantius, and in a less degree Augustine were Latin writers with a literary style, and with much of the classical form. If they had not written in a Latin based on classical models—if they had insisted on dressing the homely truths of the gospel in the homely words of their humblest converts— our Christianity of to-day might be something very different from what it is. It might have been better or worse; but certainly, without the thorough Latinisation of the worship and administration of the Church, the later world would have found it a far more difficult thing to get back from its mediæval sterility to the fecund humanity of pagan letters.

"It is in the reign of Commodus," as Mr. Mackail [1] reminds us, "amid the wreck of all other literature, that we come on the first Christian authors." In the fourth century Lactantius is still quoting Cicero, Virgil, Horace, Ovid, and Lucretius. Later in the same century "Christian poetry reached its full development in the hymns of Ambrose and Prudentius, and the hexameter poem of Paulinus of Nola." One if not more of the six writers of the "Historia Augusta" was a Gallic Christian. The Panegyrists were especially in favour amongst the Gauls. Two of the extant panegyrics were delivered at Trèves before the Emperor Maximianus, the colleague of Diocletian. "A florid Ciceronianism was the style most in vogue, and the phraseology, at least, of the old State religion was, until the formal adoption of Christianity by the government, not only retained but put prominently forward. Eumenius of Autun, the author of five or more pieces in the collection,

[1] "Latin Literature," by J. W. Mackail (Murray).

delivered at dates between the years 297 and 311, is the most distinguished figure of the group. His fluent and ornate Latin may be read with some pleasure ... Under the influence of these nurseries of rhetoric a new Gallic school of Christian writers

PNEUMATIC ORGAN, FOURTH CENTURY.
(*At Arles; Gallo-Roman.*)

rose and flourished during the fourth century." Bishop Hilarius, the earliest known author of Latin hymns, presided over the see of Poitiers. Ambrose, another hymn-writer, was born at Trèves. Ausonius, who was of Gallic origin on both sides, was educated at his native town of Burdigala (Bordeaux), and taught grammar and rhetoric at Trèves, which in his time had begun to rival Rome as a centre of civilised life in the Western Empire. He wrote Christian hymns, translations from the Greek, elegiac letters to his friends, epigrams, idyls and eclogues. The longest and finest of the idyls is in praise of the river Mosella. After following its course to its junction with the Rhine, he apostrophises the latter stream :—

> "Caeruleo nunc, Rhene, sinus, hyaloque virentem
> Pande peplum, spatiumque novi metare fluenti
> Fraternis cumulandus aquis . . .
> Dives aquis, dives nymphis, largitor utrique
> Alveus extendet geminis divortia ripis,
> Communesque vias diversa per ostia fundet.
> Accedent vires quas Francia, quasque Chamaves,
> Germanique tremant : tunc verus habebere limes."

"In virtue of this poem," says Mr. Mackail, 'Ausonius ranks not merely as the last, or all but the last, of Latin, but as the first of French poets . . alike by the classic beauty of his language and the modernism of his feeling."

VI.

THE COMING OF THE FRANKS.

WE take up the interrupted story of the Teuto-Roman struggle in the reign of Caracalla, the son of Septimius Severus. Severus died at York in 211, and his eldest son, Bassianus, who had taken the name of Marcus Aurelius Antonius, was nicknamed Caracalla by his soldiers because he affected a Gallic dress—the *caracalla* being a long tunic with a hood. He combined in his character a barbarous cruelty with some elements of statesman-like foresight. He conferred the rights of Roman citizenship on all adult freemen amongst the allies of Rome; and, though he may have been prompted to take this step in order to fill his coffers with the proceeds of the taxes incidental to citizenship, one effect of the decree was undoubtedly to promote the civilisation of the included races.

Early in the third century we begin to hear of the Allemanni, a people dwelling to the south of the Frank confederacy. They are spoken of as auxiliaries of the Chattans in the war of 213, when

Caracalla advanced through Rhætia, and triumphed over the allies on the Main. Alexander Severus, a score of years later, found the Germans so active and audacious that he proposed to repeat the policy of Commodus, and purchase a peace which he could not enforce. He paid for the suggestion with his life in 235; and his successor Maximinus, eager to wipe out the new stain, crossed the Rhine at Mainz, and pushed far into the interior of Germany, whilst the tribes, as usual, fell back before him.

In 253 the internal weakness of the empire, showing itself at this time especially by open rivalries for the imperial throne, drew away several Roman legions from the frontier; and there was a sudden rush of Germans across the Lower Rhine, which Gallienus, son of the ill-fated Valerian, was barely able to withstand.

This, then, brings us to the first occasion on which the Franks are mentioned by Roman writers. As we have already seen, Vopiscus in the fourth century gives the name of Franks to the Germans who crossed in 253 and the following years; whilst in the fifth century Sulpitius, who is quoted by Gregory of Tours, mentions three Frank leaders, Genobald, Marcomer, and Sunno, who broke the Roman Limes whilst Maximinus was at Aquileia, in or shortly before the year 238.

In both cases, be it observed, the invasion was made on the Upper, not on the Lower Rhine. We shall return once again to this question of the origin of the Franks when we come to consider the foundation of the Merovingian dynasty.

When Gallienus was called away from the Rhine, or from his palace at Augusta Treverorum, to another part of the frontier, he left his young son Salonius at Colonia Agrippina, with Postumus in command of the Roman troops. The general at once betrayed his trust, slew the boy and his guardian, and induced the soldiers to proclaim him emperor (260). It was whilst he was thus engaged in his own nefarious designs, and defending himself against Aureolus, a general dispatched from the camp of Gallienus, that the Franks slipped past him in vast numbers, followed by a large force of Vandals. Whilst the latter turned towards the south, sacked Langres in Campania and Clermont in the Arvernian country, to be crushed eventually in the neighbourhood of Arles, the Franks overran a large part of Gaul, plundered many of the cities of Spain, seized a fleet of Spanish ships, and made their way across the sea into Africa. Meanwhile the Allemans broke through the passes of the Rhætian Alps, and penetrated Italy as far as Ravenna, whilst the Goths were pushing their victories in Pontus, Thrace, and Greece.

Postumus, who had distinguished himself by permitting a greater inroad of Franks than had ever previously entered Gaul, won the reputation of a strong and successful governor before he was slain by his soldiers in 269. He was one of the so-called Thirty Tyrants who, in the reign of the worthless Gallienus, assumed authority in various provinces of the empire—some of them, no doubt, less from personal ambition than from the necessity of ruling with a strong hand, and preserving the public peace.

It is during this period of anarchy that we find distinct traces of those popular risings and insurrections in Gaul which, then or later, came to be known under the name of Bagaudæ or Bagats. They remind us, a long time in advance, of our English peasant insurrections, and they sprang from very similar causes—constant famine and frequent pestilence, the cruel exaction of excessive taxes, military and judicial oppressions, and the general discontents which naturally gathered round any champion who strove to effect a redress of grievances. The Church was sympathetic towards these periodical risings, and in course of time she secured the appointment of *defensores*, whose business it was to plead the cause of those who considered themselves to be wronged. But several centuries passed away before we hear the last of the Bagats; and the thing itself remained long after the name went out of use.[1] In 271 the Gallic insurgents

[1] No doubt the true character of the Bagats, as sporadic popular insurrections caused by misery or oppression, and easily degenerating into aggressive plunder, is furnished by Salvian :—" De Bagaudis nunc mihi sermo est, qui per malos judices et cruentos spoliati, afflicti, necati, postquam jus Romanæ libertatis amiserant, etiam honorem Romani nominis perdiderunt : et imputatur his infelicitas sua, imputamus his nomen calamitatis suæ, imputamus nomen quod ipsi fecimus. Quibus enim rebus aliis Bagaudæ facti sunt nisi iniquitatibus nostris, nisi improbitatibus judicum, nisi eorum proscriptionibus et rapinis qui exactionis publicæ nomen in quæstus proprii emolumenta verterant, et indictiones tributarias prædas suas esse fecerant ?" (" De Vero Judicio," bk. v.). Salvian wrote in the reign of Honorius, early in the fifth century. The origin of the word is uncertain, though it is possibly allied to *baguer*, and means simply bands of men combined for a common purpose.

took Augustodunum (Autun) after a long siege, when the city was sacked for the third time in less than half a century. There was a similar insurrection fourteen years later, when the Bagats aped the military pretenders, and set up "emperors" of their own.

Aurelian, a native of Sirmium in Pannonia, was the next Roman general and emperor who had an important influence upon the history of the Germans in Gaul. He was a brave, brilliant, and loyal soldier, who had held the highest commands under Valerian, Gallienus, and Claudius II.; and on the death of the latter he was proclaimed emperor by the legions of Sirmium. During the reigns of Gallienus and Claudius, Gaul was practically divorced from the empire; but the operations of Aurelian, who successively defeated the Goths, Vandals, Allemans, Franks, and allied forces under Tetricus, another of the Thirty Tyrants, restored at once the ancient glories of the Roman arms and the ancient frontier of the empire, from the mouths of the Rhine to the mouths of the Danube.

Scarcely had Aurelian quitted Gaul when the Franks again renewed their raids, and this time with so much success that they are said to have sacked no fewer than seventy cities on the left bank of the Rhine, including Trèves. The Emperor Probus, who, like Aurelian, was a native of Sirmium, and whose career was in many respects a parallel to that of his former master, expelled the invaders in 277, and taught them, by a demonstration on their own side of the frontier, that even yet they were no match for a

MONUMENTAL TOMB (ROMAN).
(*Moselle Valley, near Trèves.*)

Roman army when skilfully trained and led. Probus was equally successful as a soldier and as an administrator. He renewed what had formerly existed on the German bank of the Rhine, though for some generations, apparently, it had been effaced—the riparian *limes*, a depopulated zone of territory on which Rome in her strongest days would not suffer her enemies to reside. He also strengthened the ramparts between the Rhine and the Danube, and to him was probably due the outer and stronger wall at the southern extremity of this rampart, pushed forward into the land of the conquered Allemans—which, however, did not stand long after his death.

A distinct feature in the policy of Probus was his mode of dealing with the peoples whom he subdued, and especially with the Germans, whose personal prowess was a household word with all Roman leaders. He was not content with crushing his foes and restoring the frontiers, but he sought to disperse the more formidable of the warriors, or to find occupation for them at a distance from their former camping grounds. It has been said that Probus re-peopled or re-colonised the old lands of Upper and Lower Germany on the Gallic side of the Rhine—which were now included amongst the increasing number of Roman "provinces" in Gaul [1]—with his Frank captives; and that "these German colonists permanently thrust back the Gallic frontier." That would have been a curious effect of the restoration of the ramparts, and of the riparian *limes*, which were rather

[1] The Gallic "provinces" numbered seventeen in the reign of Constantine.

a pushing forward of the Gallic frontier into Germany. But the precautions of Probus—which were nothing less than a return to the Cæsarian frontier-policy—are quite consistent with the planting of Frank colonies, or the confirmation of settlements already made, within the secured frontier, and under the eye of the Roman garrisons, in Germania Inferior, mainly beyond the Meuse, in the lands of the Tungrians and Texuandrians, and on the lower reaches of the Scheldt. Here their descendants were found by Julian, three generations later, and by him the more peaceable amongst them were again confirmed in their possessions.

Though the records of these earliest settlements of Franks in Gaul are very indefinite, no doubt exists as to the general policy pursued by the Emperor Probus. To his prisoners, and to such as his offers were likely to tempt, he gave the option of entering his legions or of settling peaceably in some of the Gallo-Roman provinces. Many thousands took service under him; but he was careful to distribute them amongst his armies in different parts of the empire, nowhere leaving them collected in formidable numbers. But a band of turbulent Franks who would not be very formidable in the ranks of a well-disciplined legion might become decidedly formidable when no longer kept in awe by armed comrades and stern officers.

An interesting story is told of such a band, which had apparently been planted on the eastern shore of the Euxine, in pursuit of the well-meaning policy of Probus. According to the meagre accounts of

Zosimus and Eumenius,[1] a settlement of Franks had been made in Pontus, probably near the town of Phasis, at the request or with the consent of their leaders; but a certain number of them, unable to change their restless habits, seized some ships and sailed away. No doubt they plundered as they went —and if they were to escape alive, and reach their home again, it would be necessary for them to obtain food, at any rate, at somebody else's expense. They disturbed the whole of Greece; there was bloodshed when they came to Sicily; and they were worsted in an attempt on Carthage. But they managed to escape from their enemies, and sailed "homewards." If they did not put ashore amongst their countrymen already settled in Spain, which is not very likely, they would have to extend their adventurous voyage all round the coast of Gaul, reaching after many months the land of their race-fellows on the northern shore.

Is it enough to say of these wandering Franks of the third century that they were marauders, and nothing more? Those who have told us their story would naturally not be too well affected towards them, and it was inevitable in any case that they

[1] Φράγκων τῷ βασιλεῖ προσελθόντων καὶ τυχόντων οἰκήσεως, μοιρά τις ἀποστᾶσα, πλοίων εὐπορήσασα, τὴν Ἑλλάδα συνετάραξεν ἅπασαν, καὶ Σικελίᾳ προσεχοῦσα καὶ τῇ Συρακουσίων προσμίξασα πολὺν κατὰ ταύτην εἰργάσατο φόνον· ἤδη δὲ καὶ Λιβύῃ προσορμισθεῖσα, καὶ ἀποκρουσθεῖσα, δυνάμεως ἐκ Καρχηδόνος ἐπενεχθείσης, οἷα τε γέγονεν ἀπαθὴς ἐπανελθεῖν οἴκαδε. (Zosimus, Ἱστορία Νέα, bk. i. c. 71). The same incidents are referred to in a Panegyric of Eumenius on Constantius, where we read that the ships were seized in the Euxine, and that after their depredations the freebooters sailed further west from Sicily and Carthage.

should be regarded as robbers at large, desperate pirates who plundered and slaughtered wherever they came. It is useless to look for the virtues of peace and self-restraint amongst these hereditary enemies of Roman civilisation. The Franks were sworn to enmity against the Romans, and these particular Franks had tasted the bitterness of defeat and transportation. But clearly their ultimate object was to get back to their homes again, and for this they ran the gauntlet of a hundred dangers, living, after the manner of their day and their race, by the sword, and well knowing that there was but one shore in all the world which would receive them as friends.

In the reign of Probus, all made for peace except peace. By his colonisation, by his public works at Rome and in the provinces, by such encouragements of industry as the permission of vine-culture in Gaul, which had hitherto been dependent for its wine on Italy and the merchants of the cisalpine and transalpine provinces, he did his best to heal the wounds of war, and to divert the thoughts of men into peaceful channels. But the standing armies of Rome had neither the tastes nor the capacities for peace; and Probus fell by the hands of those on whom he had tried to enforce it. The tide of war flowed on more vehemently for its momentary check, and Gaul, throughout its eastern and northern provinces, was once more the theatre of sanguinary strife. To the incursions of the Germans were added a new Bagat, the formidable insurrection of Carausius, who established himself in Britain and seized the Gallic port of

Bononia (Boulogne), and the inroads of Saxon pirates. The Allemans broke down the wall of Probus, and invaded the Sequanian territories, where they met with a great reverse at the hands of Constantius Chlorus, who slew some sixty thousand of them at Langres. Constantius emphasised his victories over the Allemans and other German tribes by rebuilding the ruined town of Autun, and re-opening the schools for which it had already become famous.

Then followed the important reigns of Diocletian and Constantine. The division of the empire by Diocletian into prefectures, dioceses, and provinces— whereof the dioceses were subsequently adopted as a scheme of ecclesiastical government—marked a grand distinction between military and civil administration. The prefects, their deputies (*vicarii*) in the dioceses, and the *præsides* of the provinces—of whom the last were required to be of a different nationality from that of the provinces over which they presided—were theoretically more effective for purposes of administration than any provincial authorities set up by Rome since the first century, when the proconsuls and proprætors answered most of the needs of newly conquered and only partially civilised lands. The spread of civilisation, and the consequent increase of taxation, especially from the reign of Caracalla, had created fresh needs and difficulties, which had doubtless prompted the organisation introduced by Diocletian; and, though history does not for some time afford much evidence of the success of this organisation, we may reasonably conclude that it was not ineffectual under conditions which are essential to the success of any administration, even in our own days—the uprightness and skill of the administrators. The military authorities which existed side by side with the prefects and their subordinates were the Cæsars (in the absence of the Augusti or emperors), the prætorian *legati* (with restricted powers), the *duces* and the *comites;* and it was only natural that the military authority was often found in conflict with the civil.

The following table shows the family of Constantius, which swayed the fortunes of the Roman Empire for a period of nearly sixty years:—

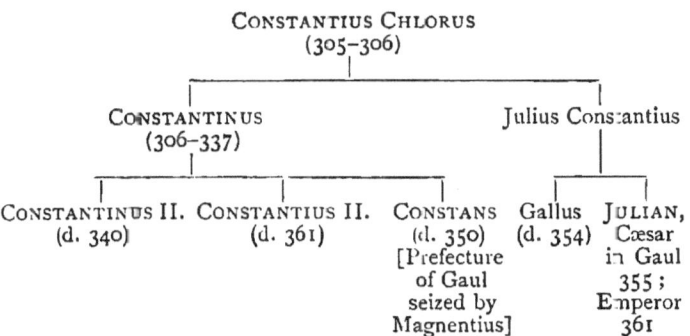

In 325 Constantine summoned the Council of Nice, which was attended by three hundred and eighteen bishops, including Arius, Athanasius, Eusebius, (the confessor of Constantine, who, like the emperor, somewhat inclined to the doctrine of Arius), the Papa of Alexandria, and two representatives of Sylvester, Bishop of Rome. Constantine himself presided over

the Council, which condemned Arius, and declared the orthodox belief of the Christian Church—that the second person of the Trinity is of one substance with the Father, not of "like" substance, as Arius held. But the battle of Arianism had yet to be fought out, as will be seen in succeeding chapters.

The short-sighted policy of Constantius, who employed Allemans to assist him against his enemy, Magnentius, had a disastrous sequel. Magnentius was himself a Frank by origin, in the Roman service; but he rebelled, declared himself emperor, and, with his brother Decentius, gave the Romans a great deal of trouble. The Allemans performed their part of the contract with Constantius, for they defeated the rebels at Agedincum (Sens, the principal town of the old Senones). For their reward they received settlements on the left bank of the Rhine; and, in the result, we find a new story of destruction and plunder laid to their charge. The meaning of the recorded facts may be that their leaders and Constantius were not sufficiently definite in their bargain, that they did not interpret it in the same sense, or did not adhere to it, or could not control their followers. In any case the experiment was a costly one, and Julian had to pay a considerable part of the cost.

In the meantime a second Frank, who had taken the Roman name of Silvanus, assumed the purple at Cologne in 355; and the poor man enjoyed his self-conferred dignity for twenty-eight days, when he was assassinated. Between the hiring of the Allemans and the arrival of Julian, a period of five years, the Germans sacked Cologne, Trèves, Mainz, Strassburg—

STATUE OF JULIAN.
(*In the Cluny Museum.*)

in all no fewer than forty-five cities of the Upper and Lower Provinces of the Gallic Germania.

Julian, the nephew of Constantine and cousin of Constantius, was nominated by the latter as his Cæsar in Gaul, and took up his duties in 356. He cut his way through the Allemans, who had overrun the country as far as Augustodunum and the sources of the Seine, joined forces at Reims with Marcellus, the *magister equitum*, who bore him no good will, and defeated the Franks at Cologne. The German tribes had once again crossed the Rhine, and occupied or destroyed most of the Roman stations on the left bank. The results of Julian's first campaign were limited to the placing of a few garrisons in such of the cities as were capable of being held over the winter, and he himself fell back with a weakened army into winter-quarters at Agedincum, fifty or sixty miles to the south-east of Lutetia. It speaks eloquently of the disorganisation of the Roman power, and the consequent boldness of the Franks and Allemans, that he was pursued as far as this town, and besieged for thirty days by a formidable host.

In the next year Julian defeated a greatly superior army of Allemans under Huodomar and other chiefs, near the town of Argentoratum (Strassburg), fortified and held the town of Tabernæ (Zabern in the Vosges), drove the Germans from various islands in the Rhine, crossed the Decumates Agri as far as the Main, and, returning, expelled a body of Franks who had occupied strong positions on the Meuse. It was earlier in the same year that he recovered some booty from a roving force of Franks, who had come from their cis-Rhenan settlements to the city of Lugdunum (Lyon). They are described by Ammianus as Læti —a name of doubtful signification, which we will consider later on.

Julian spent the following winter (357-8) in the town of Lutetia Parisiorum, which, originally built on an island, was now connected by bridges with the houses on either bank of the Seine. There was already a bishop here when Julian came, with churches and temples side by side, and monuments raised by the Gallo-Romans. At Lutetia Julian, and after him Valentinian and Gratian, resided. Here, in the intervals of war, he wrote and studied. It was here that the pagan philosopher put into writing many of his literary and critical ideas on life and morals, on Christianity and the faith of his forefathers. He exclaims in one place, thinking of the contrast between the pursuits of his youth and his military labours and studies, "Oh, Plato, Plato, what a task for a philosopher!" It was some years later, in his satirical "Misopogon,"[1] that he recalled with affection the days of his sojourn in Paris. "I wintered," he says, "in dear Lutetia—for so the Gauls name the little town of the Parisii, a small island lying in the river, surrounded by walls. The water is very good, clear to look at and pleasant to drink; the inhabitants enjoy a mild winter, and good wine is produced. Some of them grow figs, which they shelter from the cold with straw." Paris was already a noteworthy centre of Latin civilisation.

[1] Μισοπώγων—*i.e.*, The Hater of Bearded Philosophers.

Ammianus, the historian, who was a contemporary of Julian, lays to his charge an act of treachery towards a body of Salian Franks, which reminds one of Julius Cæsar's conduct towards the Tencteri, four hundred years earlier. The story may not be true as it has reached us; Ammianus was not present at the time, and he can have had no better authority when he wrote than the information of men who may have been themselves misled, either by hearsay or by the jealousy of some of those by whom Julian was surrounded.

Julian was setting out on his third campaign, in 358, and, drawing near to a Frank army, was met by a number of emissaries who sued for peace. It is said that he gave them a favourable reply, and sent them away with the presents which would be usual under such circumstances; after which he suddenly fell upon the army, taking it by surprise, and imposing terms more onerous than before. It is probable that whatever happened on this occasion was the creation of circumstances, and that Julian only did what he felt himself compelled to do. The Romans were advancing amongst a hostile race, greatly exceeding them in number; and behind the Salians there was a large force of Chamavians. They had no reason to regard the Germans as trustworthy; a Roman general opposed to the countrymen of Hermann could never hold himself safe under the terms of a truce. Gibbon says that "an inconstant spirit, the thirst of rapine, and a disregard to the most solemn treaties, disgraced the character of the Franks." Still, it is only fair to remember that the first recorded act of treachery between Romans and Germans was committed by the former, on the evidence of the general who was responsible for it.

In this year and in the next, Julian made a strong impression upon the invaders, defeated them in their own country, and restored several of the Rhine fortresses; but it was the campaign of 358, and the arrangements by which it was concluded, that produced the most lasting effect upon the relations between the Gauls and the Franks. Whilst the Chamavians were expelled from the left banks of the Rhine, the Salians were permitted to remain in the fields which they had virtually conquered and held from the time of Postumus, if not considerably earlier.[1] But this concession was made to them on conditions similar to those of Probus—that they should annually furnish recruits for the army, and a stipulated number of cattle by way of tribute. Hence the Præfectus Lætorum was added to the præfects of other foreign elements in the Roman army. It would certainly appear that the immigrants who were content to settle on the pastures which they occupied in the third century, whilst their race-fellows pushed on across the Seine and Loire and Pyrenees, stayed on and were succeeded by their children, though Postumus, Probus, and Julian

---

[1] Julian wrote in his report of this campaign :—$\dot{v}\pi\epsilon\delta\epsilon\xi\acute{a}\mu\eta\nu$ $\mu\grave{\epsilon}\nu$ $\mu o\~i\rho a\nu$ $\tau o\~v$ $\Sigma a\lambda\acute{\iota}\omega\nu$ $\ddot{\epsilon}\theta\nu o\nu\varsigma$, $X a\mu\acute{a}\beta o\nu\varsigma$ $\delta\grave{\epsilon}$ $\dot{\epsilon}\xi\acute{\eta}\lambda a\sigma a$ (Zosimus, iii. 8). Ammianus Marcellinus also, it may be noted, uses the term Salii as one in common acceptation. Julian, he says, "petit primos omnium Francos, eos videlicet quos consuetudo Salios appellavit, ausos olim in Romano solo apud Toxiandriam locum habitacula sibi figere prælicenter" (xvii. 8).

had been able to clear the land of any large body of aggressors, and to check new incursions.

In 359 Julian is said to have delivered from the Allemans, in their own country, no fewer than twenty thousand Gallo-Roman captives—a fact which is eloquent not only of the extent to which the German invasions of Gaul had been pushed in the past generation, but also of the thoroughness of Julian's triumph. In the following year his career in Gaul

FROM AN ALTAR TO CERNUNNOS IN PARIS.

came to an end. Constantius, who had more than once created difficulties for Julian, commanded the latter to send his best troops, Batavians, Herulians, Kelts, and "Petulantes," to reinforce the army in Persia; and these troops, who had engaged only for service north of the Alps, revolted, and proclaimed Julian emperor at Paris.[1] He remained long enough

---

[1] The Roman army included also, about this time, an "ala Francorum," an "ala Vandilorum"; and "cohortes Allemannorum," "Chamavorum," and "Gothorum."

in the West to inflict defeats upon the Chattuarians and a new force of Allemans, and then he marched eastward to meet Constantius.

The quiet of Gaul after the five or six campaigns of Julian was only comparative, and it was not of long duration. The Emperor Valentinian took sundry measures for the maintenance of public order; but his measures were scarcely consistent. It was he who established the *defensores*, or advocates of the citizens—not to use the term "advocates of the poor," which has a special and modern application, though the *defensores* were really in a somewhat similar sense official champions of those on whom the burden of civilisation fell with the greatest severity. He issued this decree on the recommendation of the Christian bishops; and it may have been at their instigation that he prohibited marriages between Roman citizens and barbarians. He was succeeded by his son Gratian, who had married the daughter of Constantius; and Gratian it was who dignified a Frank chieftain, Mellobaudes, by making him a Roman consul. Mellobaudes assisted Gratian, in the year 378, at Argentovaria on the Rhine, to defeat a German invasion of forty thousand men, described as Lentienses—descendants of the Boii, who had come to avenge their ancestors on the Gallo-Romans. The emperor and his Frank consul were both slain a few years later, during the revolt of Maximus.

Arbogast, another Frank, of whom we hear as a *comes* under the Emperor Theodosius, had assassinated Valentinian II. in 392, and proclaimed Eugenius, the *magister officiorum*, as emperor in rivalry to his former master. But this Frank emperor-maker died in the following year, shortly after the defeat and execution of his puppet by Theodosius.

In the last year but one of the fourth century, Trèves was once more in the hands of the Germans, who never ceased to take advantage of any relaxation of watchfulness on the part of the Roman emperors and their *duces*. Stilicho, a Vandal by birth—he may have been a Goth, or a Burgundian, or a member of one of the tribes allied to these, who had gravitated southward and westward from the Baltic shores through the old lands of the Suevians, for to these the common name of Vandals had been given—was *dux* in Gaul under Honorius, the son of Theodosius. He belongs to the line of capable Roman generals who from generation to generation were able with difficulty to stem the barbarian tide, and prolong the existence of the empire; but the Germans on the Rhine frontier were not his only enemies, nor was Gaul his only care. He defeated Alaric in 403, and Radagasius in 405; and, leaving a Gothic lieutenant to represent him in Gaul, pursued in Italy the course of personal ambition which led to his death in 408.[1] Meanwhile, on the first day of the year 407, a huge host of Stilicho's countrymen—Germans of various tribes seeking a refuge in the West from the fury of the advancing Huns — crossed the frozen Rhine on foot, and penetrated far into North-eastern Gaul, sacking the cities as they progressed, and carrying destruction to the walls of Reims, Amiens, and Tournai. There must have been ten or a dozen

[1] Stilicho found a panegyrist in the poet Claudian, who accompanied

fighting tribes in the country during the first decade of the fifth century; and the Franks were prominent amongst them. We read of them at this time as far south as the city of Arles, in the neighbourhood of which place they were beaten by Ulfila the Goth, who had taken service under Honorius. And it was probably during this period that the land of Hainault was definitely held by Frank leaders, who were not only warlike enough to seize and to retain their new home, but also sufficiently zealous for orderly government to implant their native Salic law in Belgic soil.

him in some of his campaigns. Here is one of his apostrophes ("De Laudibus Stilichonis," i. 220):—

> "Rhenumque minacem
> Cornibus infractis adeo mitescere cogis
> Ut Salius jam rura colat, flexosque Sicambri
> In falcem curvent gladios, geminasque viator
> Cum videat ripas, quæ sit Romana requirat:
> Ut jam trans fluvium non indignante Caüco
> Pascat Belga pecus, mediumque ingressa per Albin
> Gallica Francorum montes armenta pererrent:
> Ut procul Hercyniæ per vasta silentia sylvæ
> Venari tuto liceat, lucusque vetusta
> Religione truces, et robora numinis instar
> Barbarici nostræ feriant impune bipennes."

VII.

THE MEROVINGIAN FRANKS.

WE have traced with some detail—perhaps with a wearisome detail, because it has too often lacked the quality of continuity, or the satisfaction of manifest cause and effect — not only the general relations between Rome and Germany during the greater part of five centuries, but also the persistent efforts of the Franks and other Teutons, over the whole of that period, to establish themselves in the Romanised land of Gaul. We have now entered upon the fifth century of the Christian era — the century which brings the Roman Empire to an end, which finally breaks down the political barrier between the Eastern and Western dominions of the Latin race, which sees Italy, Gaul, Spain, and Britain overrun and appropriated by the Teutonic race, and the sway of the Church in process of establishment on the ruins of the ancient State.

Henceforth, the story of the Franks will be more definite in its character, and may be pursued with some greater degree of confidence ; for now we shall have to do with a Frank people settled in a Frank land, under Frank kings—with a nation some of whose descendants, living in the same towns, rearing their cattle on the same pastures, were doubtless included amongst the Frenchmen of the France of the Capets.

We have already seen reason for supposing that the true cradle-land of the Germans who were called Franks was the country lying between the Middle Rhine and the Hercynian forest—the same country, roughly speaking, which a German of the present day calls Nassau, Hesse, Unter-Franken, Ober-Franken, and Mittel-Franken, the three last of which correspond (again roughly speaking) with the kingdom of Thuringia in the sixth century. But now it is necessary to subdivide the nation of Franks. We have hitherto regarded them as a conglomeration of German tribes, extending eastward almost as far as the confines of the Boii, and westward as far as the Limes Germanicus and the Rhine. We must proceed to draw a distinction between the Franks of the west, the protagonists of the war against Rome, and the Franks of the east, from whom the others were frequently recruited. The conglomeration or confederacy had made a single nation; the organised nation tended at once towards a rivalry of its organic parts.

Thus in the fifth century we come, in the meagre accounts of the historians, upon Franks of Thuringia and Franks who were not Thuringian. It will give a broad notion of the truth, approximately correct, if we say that the Thuringians were the Franks who stayed at home, whilst the Western or non-Thuringian

Franks are represented by those who poured westward across the Rhine, in the last and most successful of the Frank invasions, under Clodion and Merowig, and founded the Merovingian realm in Gaul. It is shortly after this juncture—that is to say, in the lifetime of Childeric and Clovis—that we find the rivalry spoken of above developing into open hostility.

Of Clodion, or Hlodion, who was perhaps the father of Merowig,[1] and at any rate his predecessor in the chieftainship of the latest immigration of Western Franks into Gaul, we know little but what is told us by Gregory of Tours; but this Roman bishop of the sixth century was almost a contemporary of Clovis, and his testimony on the point is acceptable in itself, in addition to being the best that we can get. According to Gregory, "Chlogion" (for that is how he writes the name), "a man of the highest rank in his nation, is stated to have been king of the Franks. He lived in Dispargum, a fortified place, which is on the borders of the Thuringian land. Now, in our own territories, that is towards the south, the Romans continued to occupy the country as far as the river Loire." Clodion, the writer goes on to say, drove the Romans out of Camaracum (Cambrai), in the year 445, and occupied the surrounding country up to the bank of the river Somme.[2]

We are face to face with a number of interesting questions which are sure to challenge any one who concerns himself with the history of the Franks.

[1] "There are some who say that King Merowig, who was the father of Childeric, descended (de stirpe fuisse) from Clodion."—*Gregory of Tours.*

[2] See Note at the end of this Chapter.

What relation did the Merovingian family and their comrades of the fifth century bear to the Franks who had already been settled between the Meuse and the Scheldt, whom Julian, as we have seen, describes as the nation of the Salians? What is the meaning of the word Salian, which is at least as doubtful in its application as the word Frank? Why were some of the Franks at Brabant, or other Germans settled on the left bank of the Lower Rhine, called in their own language Lite, and in Latin Læti? And, starting with the passage just quoted from Gregory of Tours, where was the Dispargum from whence Clodion came?

In spite of Gregory's statement, which appears to be fairly precise, subsequent history has left the origin of the Merovingians in doubt. Some writers have said distinctly that they came from the Low Countries, and that they were Salian Franks, descended from the settlers in Brabant whom the Emperor Julian describes as Salians. But if they came from Dispargum, on the borders of Thuringia—where the father of Clovis sought refuge on his expulsion from Tournai by his *leudes*—they were not Franks of the Lower Rhine, and not Salians on that score, though they may lay claim to the term for other reasons. There is an element of doubt as to the exact position of Clodion's Dispargum; and it will be interesting to see whether the German scholars who are making a special study of the archæology of the Roman ramparts which enclosed the Agri Decumates will be able to throw any additional light on this not unimportant historical problem.

In some historical maps there is a Dispargum

placed between the principal forks of the Scheldt, on what authority it is impossible to say. Grässe, in his "Orbis Latinus," gives us two localities: (1) Duisburg, in Rhenish Prussia; and (2) Disburg, or Burg-Scheidungen, in Thuringia. Now there is a town called Deutz, formerly known as Duisburg, a short distance from Cologne on the right bank of the Rhine, and in the zone of the old Limes Rhenanus, which the Romans at their strongest kept clear of German occupants. The German name of Duisburg then or later given to it might represent Duicziburgum, or Tuiscoburgum, the hold or fort of Tuisco, the war god. Similarly there is a Duisdorf on the left bank of the Rhine, not far from Bonn. It is possible that Duicziburg was shortened into Duisburg, Latinised into Disburgum, and thence corrupted into Dispargum. But Gregory would scarcely have described this place, even on hearsay, as "in termino Thoringorum"; for there is no evidence whatever in history that such a phrase as "termini Thoringorum," or Thuringia, was at any time applied to a district of the Belgian lands.

Again, there is a town called Dieburg, in Hesse, on the road between Darmstadt and Aschaffenburg, twelve or fifteen miles to the south-east of Frankfort-on-the-Main. It would have been within the Roman ramparts, and its position, though not in Thuringia, is in the borders of the Thuringian land. The ramparts were broken both before and after the time of Probus; and it is as likely as not that an ancestor of Clodion was amongst those who broke them. However this may be, Dieburg and Disburg may very possibly be two different forms representing the place which Gregory called in Latin Dispargum, but which Germans in their own language called Burg-Scheidungen. Now Scheidungen, which appears in Low-Latin writers as Schidinga, would mean *divisio*, or more correctly *secessio*. We do, in fact, find Divisio used as a proper name for the same place which the Germans called Burg-Scheidungen, a town of division or secession.[1]

The adjoining sketch-map shows the position of Dieburg in relation to the surrounding countries,

which are here represented with their modern names and boundaries.

[1] Such a form as Divisio-burgum is certainly conceivable. Dufresne quotes a passage from a charter of Archbishop Wylbrand of Magdeburg, dated 1236:—" Equidem præfati præpositus et capitulum emerunt in Glouch moliendinum cum curia attinente, pomerium etiam adjacens et salictum, cum omni utilitate et provenientibus ejus, ab ejusdem fundi principio usque deorsum ad locum qui Divisio Latine, et Scheidinghe vulgariter appellatur." The identification of the Dieburg mentioned above with Gregory's Dispargum, and with a border town of the Western Franks, is made with some diffidence, but it seems to be most in accordance with the various indications.

If, then, we recognise here, with some approach to confidence, the origin of the Merovingian dynasty, and consider Dispargum to have been a frontier-burg between the Eastern and Western Franks in Germany, we may go on to ask ourselves the further question, whether the name of Salian Franks belonged equally to the eastern and western branches, or specially to either of them. In considering this question there are certain points of departure which require to be kept in mind. The first is that we have no more probable or satisfactory derivation for the name of Frank than the statement that it was given to the Rhine-and-Main Germans from a word in the "Attic" or Chattan language (that is, in a German dialect), to indicate their character as fighting men. This, at any rate, may show that the Western Franks, Chattans and others, whom S. Remy called by implication Sicambrians, were the first to receive that name, which afterwards spread to the eastward, and again to the northward, being carried and localised along and across the Rhine, and in the Low Country between the Rhine and the Scheldt. Then we have the unquestionable fact that the Franks who were permitted by Julian, and by Probus and others before him, to remain where they had settled, in the Batavian and Tungrian (Toxandrian) lands, were called by Julian and others the Salians, or Salian Franks. Why Salian? What were the limits of the Salians? And what distinction, if any, are we to draw between Salian and Riparian Franks?

In face of the difficulties created by the loose application of the names of Frank, Salian, and

Salian Frank, to German warriors and settlers in a zone extending from the mouths of the Rhine to the Roman ramparts, thence along the banks of the Main and its tributary the Sala (Saale), and to the furthest limits of Thuringia, it is impossible to claim these titles exclusively for any particular subdivision of the Teutonic van. All that can here be attempted is to sum up the conclusions which appear to be most reasonable and probable.

(1) The original Franks were the representatives or successors of the Sicambrian League which opposed itself to Julius Cæsar. They included the Catti or Chattans, from whose dialect the name was drawn, and whose homes lay outside the middle section of the Limes Germanicus. This view is supported, amongst other reasons, by the disappearance of the separate tribal names of the Sicambrians, Chattans, and Hermundurians about the time when the name of Frank came into ordinary use. And from the Sicambrians and Chattans the new name was gradually extended throughout the zone which has just been described.

(2) The name of Salian Franks was then given, for the purpose of further distinction, to the Franks who inhabited the country bordering on the ramparts and the Hercynian forest, in which rise two rivers called Sala or Saale, one of them flowing with a very sinuous course to the south-west, into the Main, through the land of the Chattans, and the other flowing northwards, between the lands of the Cheruscans and the Semnones, to empty itself in the Elbe. If this be so, the Thuringian Franks might be called Salian, as

well as the Western Franks whom Clodion led to Cambrai and Tournai; but it is equally probable that the name was taken solely from the tributary of the Main, and that it properly belonged to the original Franks, first known as Chattans and Hermundurians.

(3) The Riparian Franks (considered apart from the Salians on the left bank of the lower stream) were those who were settled on either side of the Middle Rhine, a little before and after the time when the Western Franks under Clovis were establishing themselves in the greater part of Gaul. Their name is especially preserved in the Riparian code of German law, which has various points of distinction from the Salic and other codes. They had a *rex crinitus*, a long-haired king, of their own, until Clovis annexed their country towards the close of his reign.

(4) The Salians spoken of by Julian may have been Chattans by origin, as were their neighbours, the Batavians. In that case they may be looked upon as the earliest Salian Franks who obtained settlements in Gaul, occupying the country which is now Brabant. The view is supported by their easy coalescence with the Franks under Clovis, and by the apparent absence of rivalry and hostility between the two sections. There is no necessity or reason to derive their name of Salians from the river Issala or Yssel. Such similarity as the two names present is a mere coincidence.

(5) As for the terms Læti and Lěti, which were applied to the Tungrian and other North-western

Franks at least as early as the middle of the fourth century, it would perhaps be impossible, with any explanation, to feel satisfied that the difficulties connected with them had disappeared. Ammianus, as we have seen, tells us of Læti who, in 356, found their way as far as Lyon, and were repulsed by Julian; the Code of Theodosius (438) mentions the Læti in the Roman army; and the Riparian Code speaks of *lætica terra*, which was the land held by Læti on condition of military service. Was this word "Læti" anything more, originally, than a military nickname, bestowed by Roman soldiers on their foreign comrades, just as they had nicknamed other Germans Franci, Petulantes, and perhaps Burgundi, and as Romans of an earlier day had divided the Gauls into Togati, Comati, and Braccati? That is perhaps the only supposition on which we can accept any connection between Læti and Lĕti. It is possible enough that Germans who paid no tribute to Rome applied the contemptuous term of *lete* or *lite* to their race-fellows who consented to pay tribute to, and fight for, the Italian masters of Gaul, and that Roman soldiers, hearing the term, made a pun out of it, and called the more or less contented and lucky settlers *læti*. The explanation of the German term is simple enough. In the various German dialects, as Thierry [1] has said, *lite*, *lide*, *lete*, meant a man of low rank—a *letzte* man, or, in English, one of the *least* of men.[2]

We return now to Clodion, and to his expedition from Dispargum to Cambrai. He took the town

---

[1] "Considérations sur l'histoire de France," c. 5.
[2] The tax which they paid was called *lidimonium*.

and occupied the neighbouring country as far as the river Somme, possibly in the absence of any powerful Roman force. It was not long before the army of Aëtius arrived; but in the meantime the Franks had added to their exploits by capturing Turnacum (Tournai), the chief town of the Nervii (corresponding to the modern Flanders). These victories cut off the Romans from Itius Portus (Wissant), and thus deprived them of the trade route to Britain. No Roman general could sit down under such a blow without admitting that the cause of Rome in Gaul was lost. Aëtius, a Scythian by birth, but a "comes rei militaris" and a consul of the empire, was by no means inclined to submit. He came up with Clodion's Franks near the town of Helena, and defeated them (447); but history tells us nothing as to the fate of Clodion himself. All we know is that the Franks were still in Cambrai, Tournai, and Teruenna (Térouanne) in the next generation.

The "last of the Romans," as the admirers of Aëtius called him, was a successful general. In 425 he had rescued Arles from the Goths. In the following years he arrested the progress of more than one German inroad, and defended the Roman colonies on the Rhine. In 434 he measured his strength against the Burgundians under Gundachar, and hurled them back from the Rhine valley into Rhætia. Next year he forced Theodoric to raise the siege of Narbonne, and almost immediately afterwards quelled a new Bagat in the north-west, gaining victories at Tours and Chinon.

But Aëtius found, as one Roman general after

another had found to his cost, that the task of defending the long and exposed frontier of Gaul, of simultaneously fighting three or four enemies already established within their borders, of watching and opposing the constant popular uprisings, of dealing with the high-spirited Armorican confederation, and of repulsing every now and then the piratical attacks on the northern and western coasts, was an impossible one. Whilst he marched southwards again, to the relief of his lieutenant at Toulouse, the Germans once more gathered in force, crossed the Rhine, sacked Mainz, Cologne, Trèves, and other cities, and swarmed over the ill-protected land. It was with, or close in the wake of, these that Clodion had led his army of Franks, keeping himself, no doubt, to the south of Brabant, where his race-fellows had been established since the days of Julian.

Aëtius was prevented from pushing things to an extremity with the Franks by the appearance of another and more formidable enemy, who threatened the whole country with overwhelming ruin, and for a time united many conflicting interests in a common effort of self-defence. An enormous host of Huns — Manchu Tartars, according to some, who had gradually in the past hundred years closed in from Asia upon the rear of the migrating Alans and Germans, and who advanced slowly through Europe in the third, fourth, and fifth decades of the fifth century—entered Gaul in 451. Attila (Etzel) had fairly earned his title as the "Scourge of God." Eighteen years earlier he had dictated terms of peace to the emperor at Byzantium, and during most of the intervening time he exacted from Theodosius II. an annual tribute, constantly increasing, to supplement the booty drawn by his swarm of locusts from the lands on which they had settled.

It is a question how far this Asiatic scourge—one of the most deadly inundations of barbarous humanity known to history—was a propelling cause of the great westward movement of Teutons already mentioned. The Southern Tartars and Chinese are said to have driven out their neighbours in the second century of our era; and the Huns would certainly drive other races before them. Their plan of thoroughly denuding and impoverishing their victims before they pressed on to fresh feeding-grounds might well account for a migration of centuries — extending over more than half a century in Europe alone.

Hideous to look upon—half-shaped wooden blocks, as one writer describes them, and yet more hideous in their unrelenting and destructive cruelty—they had nevertheless found or forced alliance (with the Ostrogoths amongst others) during their forward progress. By their numbers, their spirit and savagery, their unprecedented force of mounted men, and the momentum of their victories, they were for a long time utterly irresistible. The destiny of Attila caused him to turn aside from Italy and force his way into Gaul, which, indeed, offered him at this time a richer prey. This Yellow Terror passed through the Hercynian forest and across the Rhine, devastated the valleys of the Rhine, Moselle, Meuse, and Seine, sacked the towns, and slew all that stood in its path.

At length the city that bore the name of Aurelian (Orléans) checked the advance of the conqueror. Before he could break down its walls he heard of the approach of a vast army from the south, and, knowing that his mounted forces required a more open country in which to move with effect, he fell back to the Catalaunian plains, probably between Troyes and Châlons. The bursting of this black cloud which had hung for so many years over Europe made all the dwellers in Gaul forget their minor enmities. With Aëtius and his "Romans" came Theodoric, king of the Visigoths, and his son Thorismond, Franks under Merowig, and probably Armoricans, all eager to bear their part in this supreme struggle for existence. A hundred and sixty-two thousand men are said to have fallen on the field (June 21, 451); but beyond this fact, and the fact that civilisation triumphed over barbarism, we have the most meagre details of what was unquestionably one of the decisive battles of the world.

Attila fled; Goths, Romans, Franks fell asunder on the morrow of his flight. Within three years Aëtius, Thorismond, Attila, had all died violent deaths; and Gaul was once more the theatre of rebellions, civil war, invasion, and constant assassination.

Merowig died in 457 or 458, leaving the chieftaincy or kingship of the Flandrian Franks—or at any rate of the Tournai Franks—to his son Childeric. The historians are not definite as to Merowig being the son of Clodion, and this is the reason why we have come to speak of the Merovingian rather than of the Clodian dynasty.

But Childeric was certainly the son of Merowig. Childeric began his reign unfortunately, setting his youthful desires on wanton pleasure rather than on the stern delights of war. He was driven from power in the first year after the death of his father, and for a while the Comes Ægidius, successor of Aëtius as military governor of Gaul under the Emperor Majorian, extended his authority over Tournai, as well as over the Gallo-Romans. Majorian died in 461, and Ægidius amused himself with the usurped title of Augustus. He continued, with his headquarters at Soissons, to fight those whom he considered the enemies of Rome, including Visigoths, Franks, and Burgundians; whilst at the same moment fleets of Saxon and Frisian boats sailed up the Loire, probably welcomed by the irreconcilable Armoricans, who never lost an opportunity of striking at their ancestral enemies. So many Britons are said to have come over at this time, fleeing from the Saxon fury, that the Armorican peninsula retained thenceforth the name which it bears to-day.

In the year 463 Ægidius was worsted on the Rhine by a new Frank invasion. The oft-told tale was repeated — "Cologne was sacked," and the Germans, scorning to settle in the walled town, pushed forward across the valleys, and either threw in their lot with the race-fellows who had preceded them, or, if the earlier settlers refused to make room for them, sought new habitations for themselves in the farms and vineyards of the Gallo-Romans.

Whilst the Roman count was fighting the Franks in the east of Gaul, the people of Tournai and Cambrai had grown tired of Ægidius, and had forgotten their grievances against Childeric. Their reason for deposing him, Gregory tells us, was that he had made too free with the families of his chief supporters.[1] But when he was setting forth on his exile he had divided a gold coin with a trusty friend, who promised to do what he could to win back the hearts of his people. "If you send me your half," said the king, "and the two are united again as they were before, I shall know that it is safe for me to return." Then Childeric had gone to the castle of King Basinus in Thuringia; and Basinus would be more ready to receive the son of Merowig when he came to him with a grievance against the Western Franks. Moreover, the young guest found favour in the eyes of the Queen Basina.

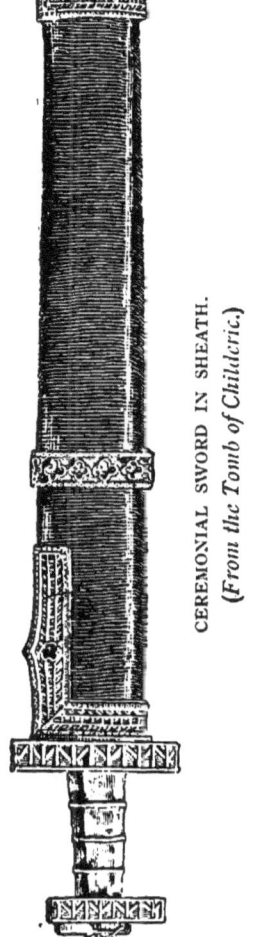

CEREMONIAL SWORD IN SHEATH.
(*From the Tomb of Childeric.*)

---

[1] Professor Kurth ("Clovis," p. 197) suggests a more probable and less personal reason for the temporary exile of Childeric.

One day a traveller from Tournai brought to Childeric a piece of broken gold, and he matched it with his own, and knew that his throne in Gaul was awaiting him. So he set forth at once, and re-entered his kingdom. He had not been many months in Tournai before a gay cavalcade came out of the east; and, behold, it was his friend Basina, the queen. Childeric was surprised to see her—or so we might conclude from the artless tale of Bishop Gregory. "Why have you followed me from far

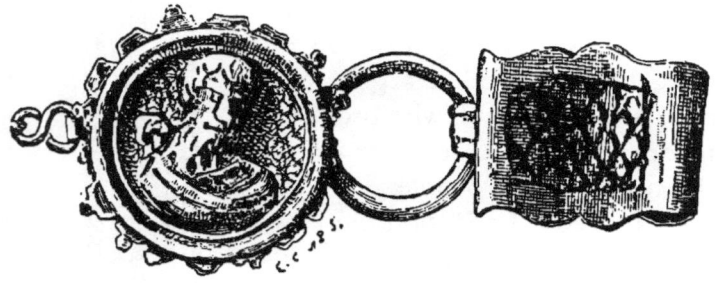

BUCKLE.
(*From the Tomb of Childeric.*)

Thuringia?" he asked her. "I have followed you," said Basina, "that I may live with you, because you are the strongest and most capable of all men. If I knew another stronger than you, I should want to live with him; but I do not." Then Childeric was glad, and made her his queen; and we can easily understand that the jealousies of the Eastern and Western Salians were not decreased by this transfer of allegiance on the lady's part.

Basina, the hero-worshipper, became the mother of

Clovis. Childeric reigned for eighteen years, and died in 481, leaving a boy of sixteen to succeed him. Meanwhile the last possessions of the Roman Empire in the west had crumbled away. Odoacer the Herulian was in Rome; the imperial trappings which Augustulus had scarcely had time to wear were packed off to Constantinople. Gaul and Spain and Britain were in the hands of the new nationalities, and the ancient throne of the Cæsars was vacant for ever.

Nearly twelve hundred years after the death of

MOUNTED TOOTH.
(*From the Tomb of Childeric.*)

Childeric a tomb, evidently dating from Merovingian times, was discovered at Tournai, and identified by the archæologists of the day with that of the father of Clovis.[1] In it were found Frank arms, coins of the later empire, a gold ring, and sundry other ornaments, some of which, if the tomb were indeed that of Childeric, may have been worn by Basina. They were presented to Louis XIV., and kept in the Cabinet des Antiques. Thence a part of the collection, having survived the Revolution, was stolen in

[1] Cf. Jean Jacques Chifflet, "Anastasis Childerici I., Francorum Regis," 1655.

1832, but the remainder may still be seen at Paris, a link of material fact between the fifth and the nineteenth centuries.

NOTE.

This is what Gregory of Tours says of the original Franks in the second book (c. 9) of his "History":—

"De Francorum regibus, quis fuerit primus a multis ignoratur. Nam cum multa de eis Sulpitii Alexandri [d. 425?] narret historia, non tamen regem primum eorum ullatenus nominat, sed duces eos hubuisse dicit: quæ tamen de eisdem referat, memorare videtur. Nam cum dicit, Maximum intra Aquileiam, amissa omni spe imperii, quasi

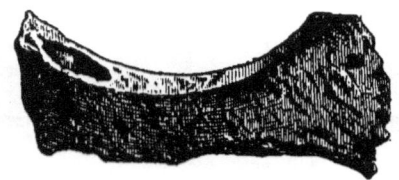

AXE-HEAD.
(*From the Tomb of Childeric.*)

amentem residere, adjungit: Eo tempore Genobaldo, Marcomere, et Sunnone ducibus, Franci in Germaniam prorupere, ac pluribus mortalium limite inrupto cæsis, fertiles maxime pagos depopulati, Agrippinensi etiam Coloniæ metum incussere. . . . Hanc nobis notitiam de Francis memorati historici reliquere, regibus non nominatis. Tradunt enim multi eosdem de Pannonia fuisse digressos. Et primum quidem litora [the left bank] Rheni amnis incoluisse: de hinc, transacto Rheno, Thoringiam transmeasse: ibique juxta pagos vel civitates reges crinitos super se creavisse, de prima, et ut ita dicam nobiliori suorum familia. Quod postea probatum Chlodovei victoriæ tradidere, idque in sequenti digerimus. Nam et in consularibus legimus Theodomerem regem Francorum, filium Richimeris quondam, et Ascilam matrem ejus, gladio interfectos. Ferunt etiam tunc Chlogionem utilem ac nobilissimum in gente sua regem Francorum fuisse, qui apud Dispargum castrum habitabat, quod est in termino Thoringorum. In his autem partibus, id est ad meridionalem plagam, habitabant Romani usque Ligerim fluvium . . . Chlogio autem missis exploratoribus ad urbem

Camaracum, perlustrata omnia ipse secutus Romanos protegit ...
usque Suminam fluvium occupavit."

In saying that the Franks formerly dwelt on the nearer side of the Rhine, Gregory might well have had in his mind such a fact as the transportation of 40,000 Sicambrians from the left to the right bank in B.C. 8. Or he may have referred generally to later expulsions of Franks by Constantius Chlorus and other Roman emperors and generals, implying that Thuringia was the rallying point from which the Franks returned to conquer the land of their temporary sojourn.

I add the commentary devoted to this passage from Gregory by Professor Kurth of Liège, in his elaborate work on "Clovis," because it presents the opposite view to that which is taken in the text. Everything—so far as the origin of Clodion is concerned—as the reader will observe, dates from Gregory of Tours, and the difference of opinion proceeds from different interpretations of the Latin text.

SPEAR HEAD.
(*From the Tomb of Childeric.*)

"The origin of this family is buried in obscurity. It was to a great extent forgotten as early as the sixth century, possibly owing to the mythological character of the tradition in which it survived, and there is now but little hope of establishing any more than that which is preserved for us by the father of Frank history. The highly poetical form impressed on this tradition is indicated in the name which it assigns to the native land of the dynasty, and to the most ancient of its dwelling-places. This country was Toxandria, the land of the Tungri, but the tradition calls it Thoringia, whether because it confounds the name of the Tungri with that of the Thuringi, or for some other undiscoverable reason. In regard to the royal residence indicated by tradition under the name of Dispargum, the most assiduous research has not succeeded in fixing its locality, and everything tends to convince us that the locality exists in poetry alone. At any rate these two names" (of Dispargum and a Belgic Thuringia) "do not appear outside of the popular tales of the Franks. Historians and geographers know nothing of them; they belong to a cycle of legends which gathered about the nation in its infancy . . .

"The *Liber Historiæ*, c. 5, deceived by the name of Thuringia, and a victim to its own craze for geographical corrections, started off on a false scent, and placed Dispargum on the other side of the Rhine. . . Other attempts at identification, far more hazardous" than Duysborch and Duisburg, " have been made ; Famars and even Tongres have been thought of ; but there is no better proof of the impossibility of fixing the locality of this legendary place in the domain of actuality. Let it abide in the mists of fiction ! "

The reader must judge whether a fair interpretation of the text of Gregory does not dispose of the unsupported notion of a Belgic Thuringia, and confirm (in this respect) the *Liber Historiæ*.

VIII.

KING CLOVIS.

WHEN Clovis came to the throne in Tournai, the only part of Gaul which still remained under Roman organisation and authority was the district governed by Roman counts in Soissons. It ran from the boundaries of the Burgundian kingdom in a north-westerly direction to the Channel coast, between the Seine and the Somme. On the west it was bounded by the Seine and its tributary, the Yonne—with an insecure supremacy on the left banks of those two rivers; and its eastern limits, beginning with the upper course of the Meuse, crossed the Aisne and the Oise to the mouth of the Somme.

The Franks had already four kings in Gaul. (1) Siegbert ruled over the Riparian lands, which lay along the Rhine from Coblenz and Cologne towards the sea, and included Tolbiac and Tongres; (2) Ragnacar was king of Cambrai, the first of Clodion's conquests; (3) Clovis ruled at Tournai, on the Upper Scheldt, over a country partly corresponding to the province of Hainault; and (4) Cararic was ruler of the last-formed kingdom of Térouanne, lying between Tournai and the Somme.

The Allemans had by this time subdued or made terms with the colonists in the Decumates Agri, and towards the end of the fifth century they penetrated as far as the Moselle. They had come in the wake of the earlier migrating Franks, as well as by way of the Upper Danube, and occupied most of what is now Bavaria, as well as Würtemberg and Baden, between the sources of the Rhine and the Danube.

The Visigoths, early in the century, had gained a footing in the south-west of Gaul, and, after Atolf had been driven into Spain, their countrymen who succeeded them overspread the whole of Aquitaine, from the Loire to the Rhone, together with the nearer part of the Narbonensian province. Thus they ruled from Bordeaux to the neighbourhood of Tours, Orléans, Clermont, and Arles.

The Burgundians, who had followed the Goths, were settled between Aquitaine and the Alps, stretching southwards from the borders of the Alleman lands as far as the river Durance, a tributary of the Rhone which cut them off from the sea.

The possession of Narbonne, Arles, Marseille, Aix, and the other cities on or near the Mediterranean shore, was often contested, but they also fell at length into the hands of the Goths (A.D. 477).

There remained the north-western section of Gaul, the "third" and part of the "second Lugdunensis" of Augustus, which for many generations had been the general rendezvous of Keltic refugees, fleeing before the southern and eastern invaders. It would be difficult to assign precise limits to the territories north of the Loire which, before the conquests of Clovis, held themselves free of Roman domination, or even of the authority of Ægidius and his son Syagrius, the self-styled kings of the Suessiones (Soissons). Ægidius defeated the Visigoths at Orléans in 463. North-west of Orléans was the country of the warlike Aulerci, and one tribe of this formidable association were the Diablintes, mentioned by Cæsar amongst the "Armoricæ civitates." Roughly speaking, it was to the west of a line running northward from the Loire, through Tours or Jublains to Bayeux (Augustodurum Baiucassium) that the descendants of the original Gauls, tempered by such Romans and Germans as had settled in their midst, asserted their independence in 383, and again in 408, and maintained it up to the time of their alliance with the Franks nearly ninety years later. It was practically the same country which had formed a league against the Romans in 56 B.C., and again in 54 and 52, and which in the intervening centuries had been conspicuous in every effort to shake off the Roman yoke, and in every Bagat of Gallic insurrection.

The Armorican country which subsequently bore the name of Bretagne was somewhat narrower than that which has been described, being limited, approximately, by the present confines of Poitou, Anjou, Maine, and Normandy. The name of Armorica had been given by the Romans to the maritime districts between the mouths of the Loire and the Seine, to represent the term used by the Gauls themselves (*ar mor—ad mare*, that is to say, the seaside). The Gauls had probably given this term to the whole coast, with no exact application to a circumscribed locality. Cæsar seems to use it as applying in the limited sense mentioned above; but the Armorican cities which declared their independence in the fifth century, and finally expelled the Roman authorities, included those lying between the Loire and Garonne. They were prosperous cities, strong, and proud of their immunity as compared with the more exposed inland towns. Some of them carried on a busy traffic with Britain, from whence, in the most distracted periods of British and early English history, they received many immigrants. When Clovis came he recognised the strength of the Armorican cities, and rather conciliated than attempted to conquer them. The consequence was that they gave him valuable aid against the Visigoths and Burgundians.

Such, in mere outline, was the political situation of Gaul in the latter part of the fifth century. The divisions of which we have spoken were but the temporary result of the first general scramble for the fragments of the Western Empire, when the collapse of that empire was admitted by its last defenders. Henceforth, for many years to come, the map of the country changed from year to year. The Allemans and the Visigoths had but the shortest lease of their conquests, the Burgundians were crushed and humiliated, even the realm of Clovis was parcelled out again almost as soon as it had been pieced together, and the independent Kelts, Gallo-Kelts, and Gallo-Britons were constrained to accept a sovereign.

But, after all the changes, it was the Franks who endured, who grew constantly stronger, who built up a law, a church, and an empire.

Meanwhile Clovis reigned in his father's stead, and grew to manhood, nursing the ambitions which had been bred in him, and resolved to be such a man as his mother, Basina, thought she had found in Childeric—not strong, but the strongest. When he came to man's estate he found himself surrounded by kings and confederacies all of whom probably thought themselves as powerful as he. Amongst them was his neighbour on the west and south, Syagrius, king of the Suessiones, the son of his father's enemy Ægidius. On this Syagrius Clovis determined to flesh his new-forged blade. With his kinsman Ragnacar, the king of Cambrai, he invaded the last remnant of Roman Gaul, and won a great battle near the town that is now Soissons. Syagrius took refuge with Alaric II., king of the Visigoths. The Frank demanded his surrender, and Alaric, who was not prepared to defy the young hot-head, delivered the son of Ægidius to his enemy. This was in 486, and Clovis, having slain his captive, added the valley of the Seine to his kingdom of Tournai. Paris fell into his hands not long after Soissons, and by this time, when he was little more than twenty years of age, he had under his command an army on which he could rely.

The typical Frank soldier was a tall, muscular man, well-strung to his work, and inured by constant training in war and the chase. Light of complexion until the weather had tanned his face and arms, with red or yellow hair and moustache—the king and his

FRANK WARRIOR (TYPICAL).

leudes and *antrustions* wearing two long plaits which reached the waist—he must have been as handsomely set-up as he was prompt and vigorous in fight. His close-fitting vest, lined outside with the furred skins of animals, gradually gave way to a coat of mail, under which a short-sleeved tunic hung down to his knees. His leather shoes were secured by long strips which crossed each other round the shins and above the knees; and he carried a lance (originally the *framea*, headed with a flat iron tip, varying in shape), javelins, a battle-axe, a dagger, a double-edged sword, and a round, oval, or straight-edged shield, with its boss drawn out to a point.

Most of the German fighting men were of this stamp, but the event proved that none of them were stronger, braver, or more formidable when their blood was up than the Franks. To say that they were cruel and bloodthirsty is to speak a commonplace. In that respect they scarcely differed from the Romans, who had trained or sharpened their aptitude for war. It was in the Roman army itself that they had learned the arts of discipline, the traditions of soldierly drill and camp-life, which converted a brave man into a hardened legionary. There is abundant evidence that the Riparian, the Sicambrian, the Chattan, the Salian Frank had learned all that Rome had to teach, and learned it better than the Alleman, the Goth, the Burgundian, or the Langobard. They had learned, in short, how to create an army out of a crowd of men. The swarms by whom Cæsar used to find himself surrounded were formidable enough, even when they had nothing to oppose to the Roman legions except their bare bodies and a handful of darts; but when the enervated Italian began to stay at home and fill the ranks with trained barbarians, he was simply creating the instrument which was to destroy him.

Gregory of Tours gives us a striking picture of Clovis and his *leudes*, at the time when the Franks were overrunning the kingdom of Syagrius, which incidentally shows us how the old habits of the raiding barbarian had begun to be controlled and held in hand by the spirit of a disciplined army and the authority of a military king.

About this time, says Gregory, many of the churches had been plundered by the army of Clovis, for he was still sunk in his grievous errors. From one church these enemies of the faith had carried off a bowl of remarkable size and beauty, as well as other beautiful vessels used in the services of the church. Therefore the bishop sent a messenger to the king, beseeching that, if he could not prevail to have any of the other sacred vessels restored, at any rate the bowl belonging to his church might be given back to him. And the king said to the speaker: "Follow me to Suessiones, for there all the treasure which has been taken is to be parcelled out, and, if this vessel falls by lot to me, I will do as the Papa wishes." And when they came to Suessiones, and all the booty had been arranged in the midst, before Clovis and his warriors, the king said to his *leudes*: "I beg only this thing of my brave warriors, that they will not refuse to give me yonder bowl, over and above what falls to me by lot."

And the *leudes* said that they and everything belonged to the king, that he must do and take what seemed good to him, for no man could withstand him. But one foolish fellow, who was greedy and headstrong, raised his battle-axe and smote the bowl, and said, "Nought shalt thou have, beyond whatever the lot may give thee!" And they were all amazed at these words, but the king governed himself. And when he had received the bowl he gave it to the messenger, but he nursed in his heart the memory of that insult. And when the year was at an end he ordered the whole army to assemble for a parade of arms. And as he went slowly round the ranks he came to him who had smitten the bowl. And he said to him, "No man has arms so ill cared for as thou. Neither spear nor sword nor hatchet is fit for use!" And he seized his hatchet and flung it on the ground. And when the man was stooping to pick it up again the king raised his two hands and buried his own blade in the warrior's skull. "Thus didst thou," said he, "to that bowl at Suessiones."

Within the next year or two Clovis took up the ancestral quarrel of the Western Franks—a quarrel which may never yet have come to a violent breach, and which may have amounted to a mere secession of one branch of the Salians from the other branch, to a mere division of the land on the east and west of the Scheidungen-burg. Jealousy there must have been, as a natural consequence, and the jealousy had turned into bad blood when Basina left her husband's castle to follow her "strongest man" into the plains of Gaul. So the son of the errant hero-worshipper sent or led his victorious army, swollen with levies from the Riparian Franks, and attacked the Eastern Salians. We have but a scanty record of this expedition. Gregory of Tours, who possibly knew more about it than he has told us, is mainly concerned with the relations between Church and State in Gaul, and is at this point eager to come to the all-important fact of the conversion of Clovis. Our knowledge amounts to little more than the defeat of the Thuringians, and the addition of their country to the western realm.

How far was this quarrel between Western and Eastern Franks, or between Franks and Thuringians, hereditary? It is impossible to be precise in tracing the pedigree of Franks to Chattans, or of Thuringians to Hermundurians, and it may be only fanciful to refer the reader to a story which Tacitus relates of the year 58. "The same summer a great battle was fought between the Hermunduri and the Chatti, both forcibly claiming a river which produced salt in plenty, and bounded their territories. They had not only a passion for settling every question by arms, but also a deep-rooted superstition that such localities are especially near to heaven, and that mortal prayers are nowhere more attentively heard by the gods. It is, they think, through the bounty of divine power that in that river and in those forests salt is produced, not, as in other countries, by the drying up of an overflow of the sea, but by the combination of two opposite elements, fire and water, when the latter has been poured over a burning pile of wood. The war was a success for the Hermunduri, and the more disastrous to the Chatti because they had devoted, in the event of victory, the enemy's army to Mars and Mercury, a vow which consigns horses, men, everything, indeed, on the vanquished side to destruction. And so the hostile threat recoiled on themselves."[1] Salt and potash are still plentiful in Saxony, to which the Elbe Sala is somewhat nearer than the Main Sala; but it is most probable that the latter river is the one indicated by Tacitus as a boundary between the Chattans and the Hermundurians.

The marriage of Clovis to Clotilda (Chrotechilde), the Burgundian, is compact with romance—and let us understand at once that the future history of the Franks is as full of romance as the most glowing imagination could desire. The romance of the Middle Ages is largely Teutonic or Scandinavian, and, more than anything else, it is Frank, or Gallo-Frank and Burgundian, not Roman, not even Gothic or Alleman, or Thuringian, or even Saxon in any large degree, but by great preponderance Frank and Norse.

Gundachar, king of the Burgundians, son of Athanaric, whom the Christians had had no cause to love, was converted in 430. He had suffered at the hand of Aëtius, as well as of Attila; but, after he had embraced Christianity (though in its heretical form), and after the defeat of Attila, he established his dominion in the south-east of Gaul. He left four sons, Gundobald, Godegisil, Chilperic, and Godomar, whereof the two elder brothers were sorry rogues, even if judged by the standard of their time. Gundobald slew his brother Chilperic, tied a stone round the neck of his wife and drowned her, and would have

[1] "Annals," xiii. 57, Church and Brodribb's translation.

STATUE OF CLOVIS (XII. CENTURY).
(Formerly in the Church of Nôtre-Dame de Corbeil.)

slain her two daughters if they had not been hidden by their friends. Emissaries of Clovis saw the maiden Clotilda, and told their master of her beauty, whereupon the king of the Franks demanded her in marriage. Gundobald, who by this time was king, and had recently extended his dominions to Aix and Marseille, dare not deny his powerful neighbour. Now Clovis already had a son Theodoric, who was the child of a pagan wife, but when he saw Clotilda he loved her very deeply, as all his acts sufficiently show.

Clotilda was very young when she was married; but, however young she may have been, she was a good Christian, and she made up her mind to proselytise the king of the Franks. Fortunately for the Church, although she sprang from a family of rank Arians, she was an Orthodox Christian—a fact easily accounted for if the friends who rescued her from her uncle were themselves Orthodox. Now there was an Orthodox bishop of Tournai. There had been a bishop of Paris, under the archbishop of Sens, for a century or two; but the archives of the bishopric of Tournai date the first appointment in 487, and the second in the following year—that is to say, at the moment when Clovis was reducing the kingdom of Soissons. Clotilda's first son was Ingomer, and she had him baptized at Tournai, as likely as not by Bishop Eleutherios. Almost immediately the child sickened and died. Clovis reproached his wife with her confidence in the God of the Christians. "You have often told me," he said, "that my gods can do nothing for me—that they are but wood, or stone, or iron. Your God you think all-mighty, one that hears and answers those who believe in him. You took our son and caused him to be baptized in the church of the Christians, and behold, it has killed him. My gods are angry, and yours cannot help us." Clotilda answered him like a saint. "I bear up against my sorrow," she said, "because I believe in the wisdom and goodness of the true God. Ingomer is with the whitest angels in heaven."

As for Clovis, he was engrossed at this time in a fruitless effort to subdue the Armoricans, who made as good a stand against him as they had made against former enemies—for a coastwise people is rarely subdued until battle has been waged by sea as well as by land. About the end of 495, or the beginning of 496, Clotilda had her second boy. Of course he was christened, just as Ingomer had been, and she called him Chlodomer. As bad luck would have it, Chlodomer sickened too; and Clovis began to storm again, saying that the God of the Christians was worse than useless. But Clotilda told him that she was praying for the child; and she prayed, and he recovered.

The king was dubious, but not convinced. Full of joy at the recovery of his son, he set out on his expedition against the Allemans, at the head of a large army of Franks, who were not all his own particular subjects. At any rate he was accompanied by Siegbert, ruler of the Riparians, who held his court at Cologne, and who in this

STATUE OF CLOTILDA (XII. CENTURY).
(Formerly in the Church of Nôtre-Dame de Corbeil.)

battle was dangerously wounded in the foot. The campaign was by no means easily won, though Clovis was successful in the end, and the South Germans were finally driven out of Gaul. Clovis pursued them into their own land, and his victory was so complete that they did not care to try conclusions with him again.

It was at a critical moment of his chief engagement with the Allemans near Tolbiac that Clovis, finding himself hard pressed, raised his eyes to heaven, as Gregory imagines the scene, being pricked to the heart and weeping sore; and he said: "Jesus Christ, whom Clotilda declares to be the son of the living God, who art said to give help to those in trouble and victory to those who trust in Thee, I earnestly pray for Thy succour. If Thou wilt grant me the victory over these foes, and if I behold the strength that this people who are called after Thy name declare that they have found in Thee, then I will believe in Thee, and will be baptised in Thy name. For I have called on my gods, but they are far from helping me, so that I think they have no power at all, seeing that they do not aid such as render them obedience. Now do I call on Thee, with good will to believe in Thee, so that Thou save me from mine enemies." And whilst he was yet speaking, the Allemans lost their courage and fled.

When the conqueror returned to his home, and told Clotilda that he had called upon her God in the day of battle, that his prayer had been heard, and that he was ready to be baptised, there was great rejoicing. It was determined to have an imposing ceremonial, such as, even in those days, the bishops in their handsome and well-found churches were able to provide. The church at Tournai was not fine enough; moreover Tournai was not sufficiently central. It was different with Reims, the old capital of the Remi, already important before the Romans came, and especially important to them as the strongest place westward of Trèves, when Augusta Treverorum was the capital city of Northern Gaul. Reims, as the ecclesiastical writers say, was the metropolitan bishopric of Western Belgica, the diocese created by Diocletian and adopted by the Christian Church; whilst Tournai, Cambrai, Térouanne and Soissons were amongst the eleven sees subordinated to it. Here there was a venerable bishop, Remigius or Remy, the seventh of his line destined for canonisation as a saint. It was therefore at Reims that Clovis, by direction of the Church, was to be baptised. All the bishops in his dominions were apparently summoned to attend; the church was richly decorated and censed; there would be a magnificent spectacle for a people who loved magnificent spectacles, and gay processions in the streets, both religious and military. For Clovis was attended by three thousand of his picked soldiers, who were to be baptised on the same day, the first sheaves of the harvest which the Church now set itself to reap.

Bishop Remy had the dignity of his order, as well as the bearing of the saint and the imagination of the poet. Gregory gives us no more than the opening sentences of his address—or perhaps this was all that he said to the fierce young warrior who strode up to the font, stripped of his mail and his casque, and clad in a long tunic of white:— " Mitis depone colla Sicamber: adora quod incendisti, incende quod adorasti " — "Worship what you have burned, burn what you have worshipped." And so the most powerful *rex crinitus* of the Western Franks became a professing Orthodox Christian —won over by his personal interest, no doubt, but also by his hour of agonising prayer on the field of Tolbiac, and, perhaps most of all, by the love and the adroitness of Clotilda.

THE BAPTISM OF CLOVIS.

By the cruel irony of coincidence, Alboflede, the

sister of Clovis, who was baptised at the same time with her brother, died not many days afterwards. It is to be hoped that the king did not see in this misfortune, as he saw in the death of Ingomer, the avenging wrath of the gods of his ancestors. Apparently a little before this time, the other sister of Clovis, Augofleda, was married to Theodoric, king of the Ostrogoths, a tolerant Arian in religion, and naturally more attracted than his brother-in-law to the civilisation of Rome.

It may or may not have been the firstfruits of his conversion that, in the following year, Clovis offered terms of alliance to the Armorican cities. No doubt he found himself partly dependent upon them for supplies of various kinds, and recognised the difficulty of their complete subjugation. Moreover he had other designs in hand; for it was evident that he nursed the ambition of ruling over the whole of Gaul, and the Burgundians and Visigoths were already in constant dread of his attack. But, before we deal with the remaining years of the life of Clovis, it will be well to glance at the position now held by the Gallican Church, and by the Christian Church in general, for this will assist us to understand the narrative which follows.

IX.

CONQUESTS OF CHRISTIANITY.

THE baptism of Clovis, which implied the general conversion of the Franks to Christianity, set the crown on a century of striking successes for the Western Church. The Goths had been partially Christianised in Moesia, and their migration into Gaul had established a State in the south-west of that country which acknowledged and protected the new faith. The Burgundians in the south-east were also Christians. The Gallo-Romans had mostly followed the line taken in the preceding century by the Christian emperors, and, though since the time of Constantine there had been more than one Augustus who either clung openly to the pagan creed, like Julian, or treated Christian and pagan with impartial indifference, the Christian religion was rapidly extending, and the secular *imperium* had practically given place to the spiritual. The Kelts readily embraced the faith of Christ; there was a bishop of Nantes in the third century, though Rennes, the chief town of Brittany, was behind its sister-city in this respect. The Armoricans traded with Ireland, and early in the fifth century S. Patrick, a missionary bishop from the Breton Church, crossed the seas and (so the fable runs) converted a new kingdom.

Humanly speaking, the success of the Church in building up its great authority, not merely over monarchs and people, but also between different monarchs and different peoples, was due in a large measure to its perfect organisation in the midst of so much that was disorganised. The bishops and their clergy knew their own minds, and their ambitions were directed, as a rule, to a single object, external to themselves, whereas the organisation of the State constantly varied, and the ambitions of Cæsars, *duces*, prætors, *comites*, and fiscal officers were frequently, if not usually, centred in their personal interests. Thus, both on spiritual and on secular grounds, it was inevitable that Christianity, implanted in the decaying empire, should strike its roots deep in the soil, and grow with phenomenal rapidity.

So rapidly did it grow that already in the fourth and fifth centuries, before the last Augustus of the imperial State had worn the purple and laid it aside, the Christian bishops afforded many striking examples of that august imperiousness which distinguished the popes and bishops of a later day. None of these instances is more striking than the story of the penance of Theodosius the Great. Theodosius was associate emperor with Gratian, and afterwards sole Emperor of the East; he defeated the Goths in 382, and the usurper Maximus five years later. Whilst he was living at Milan, in 390, some local trouble broke out at Thessalonika, and a few soldiers were slain by the rioters. The emperor sent an armed force, who would of course be mainly barbarians, with orders to stamp out the disaffection. The citizens were tempted into the circus by an exceptionally brilliant spectacle; and, when the place was as full as it would hold, the soldiers secured the entrances and slaughtered all the spectators, to the number of seven thousand or more. Theodosius made no secret of his responsibility for this act of retribution; but when he went to worship at the church of Ambrose, the archbishop of Milan, Ambrose met him in the porch, and refused to admit him except as a penitent. So Theodosius (who had doubtless been warned by the archbishop of what he intended to do) put off his imperial robes, assumed the white garb of penitence, and openly confessed his sin before the congregation. As a penance he was excluded from communion for a period of eight months. Thus, and thus early, did the Christian Church assert the supremacy of its authority over the most mighty potentates.

The gradual assertion of the spiritual dominion over the hearts of Romans and barbarians alike, the great part which was played by men like Leo of Rome, whose eloquence and personal dignity sufficed to deliver the capital of the empire out of the hands of Attila and his Huns, the conversion of ruthless warriors like Clovis, combine to impress us with a sense of the sublime confidence and inspired courage of these leaders of a faith which was still young, still despised by perhaps a majority of intellectual men, and barely at this time recovering from the last of the general persecutions. It is true that there was often much subtlety united with the confidence and courage by which these victories were obtained. It was the vision of an angel by Leo's side which had turned the superstitious heart of Attila; it was a coincidence

ALTAR TRAY AND CHALICE.
(*Enamelled gold, fourth and fifth century; found near Châlons.*)

interpreted as a miracle which had persuaded Clovis that the God of Clotilda would fight his battles for him. But the builders of the Church were Italians, who had not ceased to be Italians when they became Christians; and it must be admitted that the means which they sometimes adopted to extend the frontier of the faith remind one rather of the pagan whose cunning had always supplemented his physical prowess, than of the guileless disciple of Christ.

We have been speaking of the ecclesiastics who concerned themselves, by choice or necessity, with the tortuous ways and methods of statecraft, with kings and warriors who were not to be won for the new faith by mere admonitions, or even by the championship of civil and social rights. It was by such means that the humbler converts had been won, and still continued to be won. The slavery of the slaves, the sufferings of the poorest taxpayers, the misery of the unsettled and fugitive population which filled the ranks of successive Bagats, were a soil prepared beforehand for the husbandry of the Christian preachers, and their harvest was already great when the first barbarian king underwent the rite of baptism. It was the bishops, as we have said, who secured from Valentinian the appointment of the *defensores;* it was to them, as being ever ready to hear and to advise, that all who had grievances arising out of the abuse of the civil powers naturally brought their complaints.

Socially, spiritually, and intellectually, the Gallic Church stood prominent in the Christian commonwealth, long before the conversion of Clovis. Just as Roman letters and the pagan culture had been cherished in Gaul, from the older Province to the northern sea, from the birthplace of Ausonius to the home of his maturer years, even when they languished at Rome and in Middle Italy, so the

Church in Gaul was stronger and purer, and more free from widespread heresies, than any other of the Western Churches. From the Eternal City, as Hadrian had called her in the palmy days of empire, from Rome thrice sacked, and often menaced with destruction, the bishops repeatedly appealed to the civil power in Gaul for the defence of the Church against her foes. Thus Sidonius, bishop of Clermont, who died in 488, addressed a Latin poetical epistle to Euaric, king of the Visigoths, urging him to go to the protection of Rome during the visitation of the Vandals.[1]

The conversion of Clovis, after his earlier victories had been achieved, and when the probability of still greater conquests must have been apparent to all observers, naturally inspired the then bishop of Rome, Gregory the Great, with definite hopes of championship from the young and vigorous nationality of the Franks. Clovis was hailed as "rex Christianissimus." Avitus, bishop of Vienne, in what was now Burgundian land, wrote to Clovis excusing himself for not having attended the ceremony of his

---

[1] Gregorovius, "History of the City of Rome in the Middle Ages," bk. iii. ch. 1.

" Eorice, tuæ manus rogantur
Ut Martem validus per inquilinum
Defenset tenuem Garumna Tibrim."

A century later we find Pope Pelagius II. writing to the Bishop of Auxerre : "We believe, not without profound acknowledgment of the providence of God, that your rulers agree in the profession of the orthodox (Nicene) faith with the supreme authority of Rome (' Romano imperio ')—to the end that He might raise up neighbours and supporters for this city, whence that faith was ordained to spread abroad. . . ."

baptism; and he ended in this strain: "This alone I beseech you, that you will spread amongst the nations around you the light which you have received. Sow the seeds of faith from the garner of your heart, and do not hesitate to send missions to other states, that they may advance the cause of that God who has so greatly exalted you. May you shine for ever, by your crown on those who are present with you, by the glory of your name on those who are absent. We sympathise with your joy, and, so often as you fight in those lands, we conquer."

Whilst these half-converted Teutons fought their way to a fuller civilisation and a purer Christianity, the sympathies of the Church were inevitably with the Orthodox rulers, and against the unorthodox. For it was clearly understood in those days that the orthodoxy of the Church could only be established by force of arms; that the faith as they saw it at Constantinople and at Rome, the faith in the equal godhead of the three Persons of the Trinity, which Arius had denied at Alexandria, for which Athanasius had contended against Arius, and which the Council of Nice had confirmed and defined in 325, would perhaps never be perpetuated unless Rome could enlist the strongest nationalities in her service, and unless she was bold enough to bid them draw the sword, and shed the blood of the heretics. Rome saw, with a clearness of intellectual vision which did more than anything else to establish her predominance amongst the Christian Churches, that the temptation to say, "There is only One God, and the Holy Ghost is His emanation, and Jesus is only His prophet," would evermore be almost irresistible to simple minds. But at the same time she saw that, in that case, these

TOMB OF S. REMY.
(*At Reims : Renaissance*).

same simple minds would go on to conclude that God was vague and impersonal, that Jesus was only human and therefore fallible, and that his philosophy was as open for discussion as that of Plato. Therefore, thirdly, Rome saw that the only chance of maintaining the saving faith in Christ unimpaired and effectual for all ages was to establish at once, and once for all, the full doctrine of the Trinity in Unity —that God is One, that Christ is one with Him, and that it is a blasphemy to speak of the procession of the Holy Ghost from God, and not from Christ also.

This was the foresight of Rome, and this is her distinctive part in the building of the Christian creed. For a long time, for nearly two centuries, the issue between Arianism and Roman orthodoxy was in doubt. To the beginning of the sixth century it must have appeared to many that the gospel as interpreted by Arius, as accepted even by Councils which had not yet been discredited, would eventually prevail. The danger apparent in Africa seemed to be even greater in Northern and Western Europe, for the Germanic nations were almost unanimous in favour of the heresy. The Goths adopted the views of Arius, and so did the Burgundians and the Vandals. The earlier Teutons, as Tacitus tells us, had had the notion of one original god, with human attributes, though they held that Tuisco sprang from the earth instead of from heaven. They more easily grasped the idea of divine unity than of divine triunity. However this may have been, it is necessary to remember that the invaders who overran or governed Southern Europe in the fifth century, so far as they were of European origin—Odoacer, Theodoric, Alaric, Gaiseric, Gundachar—were Arians, whilst the Churches of Greece, Italy, and Gaul were Orthodox. It was not without influence on subsequent events that Athanasius in his banishment lived and taught at Trèves, where Hilary of Arles was amongst his disciples. For when Romanised Gaul was overrun by the barbarian hosts, she won this victory in her defeat for Christianised Rome, that the strongest nation of Europe became an Orthodox Power.

As we have already seen, these European invaders —we may exclude the Huns and other Asiatic races from consideration—were by no means intractable when they had secured a settlement in Roman or Romanised lands. They adopted Christianity, they respected and imitated the Roman civilisation, some more readily than others, but all of them sooner or later. The Goths especially grew comparatively mild and tolerant in a few generations, and began to apply themselves to the arts of peace. But if the ancient animosity between Roman and Teuton was dying out, the old fighting instincts of the Central and Western Germans, continually reinforced or stimulated from the north, by no means tended to disappear. The enmities were modified in some respects, and became more sectional in their manifestation, but they gained in intensity what they lost in extent. In the period of transition which we are now considering, the translated nations, having no longer a common Roman enemy to contend against, contended with each other; and they fought, not as of old, for their liberty, but for one form or other of the Christianity which they had embraced.

This is an important fact in the history of the Franks. They came into Gaul, it is true, well-equipped for the part which they had to play, the most keen in war, the most resolute in purpose, the most ambitious of rule, amongst the German peoples. They had been the foremost opponents of Rome for five centuries, they were the first settlers in Gaul, and they were superior in arms, as the event proved, to all their competitors. But from the end of the fifth century they had an additional sanction and encouragement in the favour of the Orthodox bishops, which counted for a great deal even in the time of Clovis, and for incalculably more in the next two or three centuries. Meanwhile it is evident that the conversion of the Franks brought even a greater gain to the Roman and Gallic Orthodox Churches than it brought to Clovis and his subjects.

A recent historian has said that "the motives which induced Clovis to accept baptism and to profess faith in the Crucified One were of the meanest, poorest, and most unspiritual kind. Few men have been further from that which Christ called 'the Kingdom of Heaven' than this grasping and brutal Frankish chief, to whom robbery, falsehood, murder were, after his baptism as much as before it (perhaps even more than before it), the ordinary steps in the ladder of his elevation." There is much truth in the remark; but the measure of the truth is only to be estimated when we have decided upon the true historical scale of measurement. It would be idle to compare Clovis, as a man of arms, with anything higher than the typical fighting Frank of his age and race, or, as a Christian, with anything more fit for the Kingdom of Heaven than the Burgundian bishop who wrote to him, on the morrow of his conversion: "So often as you fight, we conquer." To fight was his virtue; to grasp fresh territory was his noble ambition; to rob and to slay were his ancestral mode and tradition of warfare. A greater crime than all these was falsehood and treachery. We shall see that Clovis is accused of both these things by a man who was almost his contemporary, and who had every reason to take a lenient view of his conduct.

In any case it is clear that Clovis did not suffer by his repudiation of the Teutonic deities, and he was quite entitled to think that the God of the Christians gave help to true believers. The channels through which that aid reached him were Clotilda, the Orthodox bishops, and the Councils which they were constantly holding throughout the country, wherever there was a trouble to allay, or a quarrel to compose, or an incipient mutiny against the authority of the Church to overawe. The bishops could raise wars, secure allies, and restore peace; the clergy could check popular and servile discontents, look after the sick and the poor, make the women more gentle and serviceable, conciliate the Gauls and the Romans, and even facilitate the collection of the taxes. Certainly Clovis had ample cause for satisfaction. All he had to do was to fight as his father fought, to add victory to victory and kingdom to kingdom, and to do honour to the God of Clotilda.

X.

THE SUBJECTION OF GAUL.

CLOVIS, as we have seen, offered terms to the Armorican cities in 497. The cities accepted these terms, and recognised the rule of the Franks, just ninety years after they had declared themselves free of the Roman military and civil authority. Yet it is doubtful whether they would have accepted the new authority, however easy the conditions, if it had not been for the good offices of their bishops.

Whose was the master mind at this crisis amongst the Orthodox bishops of the Western Church, whether Remigius, or Avitus of Vienne, or Gelasius of Rome, or Anastasius who succeeded Gelasius, and wrote a letter of congratulation to welcome Clovis into the fold, is not quite clear. Nor is it clear whether the bishops suggested to Clovis, or he suggested to them, that Arian heretics like the kings of the Burgundians and the Visigoths could not be allowed to establish themselves permanently between the sacred city of Rome and the champion whom God had raised up for her in the north. Such ideas must have occurred simultaneously to the bishops and to Clovis, for they were in the natural line of development of the ambitions of both.

But it is not likely that either side would think of hurrying forward on a career of conquest in advance of suitable occasion and pretext. About 495 Theodoric, king of the Ostrogoths, who ruled at Ravenna and held sway over Rome, had married Augofleda, the elder sister of Clovis. Ostrogoths and Visigoths continued to live on terms of mutual amity, and it would have been perilous, as well as impolitic, to precipitate a quarrel with either of these nations. But Theodoric himself was not well disposed to the Burgundians, and it was understood beforehand that war was inevitable between Clovis and the uncle of Clotilda.

Gundobald, as already said, had murdered the father and mother of Clotilda. His brother Godegisil, bearing this in mind, and thinking it wise to make terms for himself with Clovis at the expense of Gundobald, sent a secret messenger to the king of the Franks, offering to be his man. "If you will help me," he frankly said, "against my brother the king, so that I may either kill him or drive him out of the country, I will pay you every year such tribute as you may decide upon." Here, then, was the pretext or occasion for which Clovis had waited; and, in the last year of the fifth century, he prepared an expedition, and led his army southwards.

Then Gundobald sent to Godegisil and said: "Come and help me, for the Franks are moving, and they have made up their minds to seize our lands. Let us therefore be as one against our enemies, lest they should make us suffer what others have suffered." For Gundobald and Godegisil were already at rivalry; but Gundobald did not know that his brother had written to the Frank. And Godegisil answered, "I will bring an army and help you."

So Godegisil came to his brother; and the army of the Franks, which had waited for the arrival of the traitor, came into touch with the Burgundians, and there was a great battle. And Godegisil suddenly turned round upon his brother, and Gundobald saw that he had been betrayed. He fought bravely for a long time, but his army was cut to pieces, and he himself escaped with difficulty to Avenio, which we call Avignon. Then Godegisil triumphed as if he had been the conqueror; but Clovis followed Gundobald to the valley of the Durance, for he saw that he was too brave an enemy to leave behind him.

Now Gundobald had a friend in Avenio, by name Aredius, who seems to have been a Gallo-Roman, and was certainly a witty and resourceful man. And the king opened his heart to Aredius, and said: "Vallant me undique angustiæ, et quid faciam ignoro" —"My enemies close me in on every side, and there is no way out of my difficulties." Aredius listened to him, and bade him not despair, "for I," said he, "will go to the king of the Franks, and will take care that he shall destroy neither you nor your country. Only promise to do what is necessary in your own interest." And Gundobald promised.

Then Aredius went to Clovis, and said he had come from the luckless Gundobald, and wished to devote himself for ever to the service of the conqueror. The Frank eagerly welcomed his new adherent—for he was just the kind of adherent that a Teutonic king always welcomed, and perhaps rarely secured, amongst the Roman inhabitants of the conquered lands. Aredius was "jocundus in fabulis, strenuus in consiliis, justus in judiciis, et in commisso fidelis;" and, when he had made his impression as a good companion and a teller of capital stories, he ventured one day to give the fierce barbarian a little common-sense advice. "This Gundobald," he said, "is shut up in the town, which is very strong. You are not making much headway against him, but your army is eating up the crops, and destroying the vines and olives. Why not impose a tribute on him, and leave this rich country to supply part of the money which must come into your hands?" The Teuton king was persuaded—as nearly every Teutonic leader could be persuaded by a plausible Roman. He sent to Gundobald to demand ransom, and a yearly tribute, which the Burgundian readily promised; and Clovis withdrew his army from the Rhone country. But Gundobald did not keep his promises; and perhaps Aredius was specially careful, after that, not to fall again into the hands of Clovis.

Gundobald recovered his army and his kingdom,

and hunted down his brother Godegisil at Vienne, and put him to death. Then we are told that he "established a milder code of laws for the Burgundians, so as to prevent their magistrates from dealing harshly with the Romans." This is the Burgundian code known as the *Lex Gondoboda*, or *Loi Gombette*—one of the famous barbarian Codes which go far to prove, as indeed we already know from Tacitus, that the name of barbarian must not be too indiscriminately applied to the Teutonic races.

If the records of the time were not so disappointingly thin, we should be able to reconstruct the situation as it now stood with far more confidence and precision. But the few writers who deal as contemporaries with the events under consideration paid no attention to dates, and did not attempt to make their narrative reasonably continuous. One is almost tempted to think that a man like Gregory of Tours, who clearly had something of the instinct of a historian (though without any historic style), must have had more method in his work than is apparent in his "History of the Franks," and that he or some one else cut out many passages from the account as he originally wrote it. It is easy to understand that he would think it no part of his duty to report all the consultations and conclusions of the Orthodox bishops in regard to their policy towards the Arians, or to their manipulation or direction of Clovis. But he rarely mentions the national or provincial Councils of the Gallic Church, at which the relations of the Church and the States were doubtless (more or less formally and openly)

A GALLIC COUNCIL.
(*An Eighteenth Century Suggestion.*)

brought under discussion, although these Councils were held every few years, and sometimes year after year. It is not by any means improbable, it may rather be looked upon as a matter of course, that the Gallic bishops, in their keen anxiety to deliver the country from heresy, and to make the most of their new instrument for this purpose, gave the Arians ample cause to think that a crisis was approaching, and that a deliberate attempt would be made to deprive them of the freedom of belief and worship which they had secured under the Gothic and Burgundian kings.

It so happens that we have no record of a Council in Gaul between that of Arles in 475 and that of Lyon in 500. The explanation may be that the peacemakers were for a time in the ascendant, and that negotiations were being patiently carried on with the object of bringing about an agreement between the Orthodox and Arian bishops. At any rate, the two parties met in council at Lyon in the last year of the century, four years after the conversion of Clovis; and it may even be that the summoning of this council of conciliation led Clovis to put a lame conclusion to his war with Gundobald, and thus to lose the political fruits of his victory. If the Burgundian war had come after the failure of the Council—for it did fail—it is most unlikely that Clovis would have suffered Gundobald to ride off with a promise, and Burgundy to slip out of his hands.

Conciliation had failed. The Arian States knew that the Orthodox bishops would never meet them on the point of doctrine, and would never rest so long as there was a chance of weakening or destroying them. They were nervous, for a twofold reason, about the growing power of Clovis; but against Clovis they were able to set the strong man of the south, who from Ravenna overawed both the feeble emperor at Constantinople and the feeble authorities at Rome. Moreover, they had the tactical advantage of occupying an unbroken zone of Arian power and influence, extending from the Danube to the western sea, and from the Mediterranean to the Loire, between the Orthodox ecclesiastics in the south and the Orthodox Franks in the north. It was, indeed, a formidable confederation, and it speaks much for the awe which Clovis had recently inspired that even Theodoric, the master of Italy, half of Gaul, and a large part of Spain, could not feel any confidence in the issue without making special efforts to detach the Eastern and Central Franks from the headstrong convert of Reims.

The first five years of the sixth century were consumed in preparations, deliberations, and patient watching for opportunity—Clovis in the meanwhile striking another blow at the restless Allemans. The strategy of the Arians, seeing that they undoubtedly expected an attack from Clovis, is not what one would have looked for in Theodoric and his allies. Alaric had assembled his army in the north-western corner of Aquitaine, away from his capital, and as far as possible from his father-in-law, on whom he relied for assistance in case of need. It is true that he did his best to gain time, and to avoid giving Clovis the pretext for which he seemed to be waiting. He even asked Clovis for a friendly interview, which took place—the time, more important than the place, is not mentioned—on an island in the Loire, near to

AMBOISE IN THE SIXTEENTH CENTURY
(*The Meeting-place of Clovis and Alaric.*)

the modern Amboise. There they ate and drank together, and vowed friendship, and parted, as Gregory says, "pacifici."

In 506 two things happened in the south of Aquitaine, at places not very many miles asunder, which stood to each other almost certainly in the relation of cause and effect. Quintian, bishop of the Ruteni, living in the town which is now called Rodez, fell into disfavour with the citizens because he was ready, or because they thought he was ready, to welcome the rule of the Franks. He being Orthodox, whilst the majority of the citizens would probably be Arians, such a suspicion might easily occur during the excitement caused by an immediate expectation of war. Alaric was at this time with his army at Poitiers. The affair at Rodez came to an open dispute, and Quintian was privately warned that there was a plot against his life. So he escaped with a few priests, and betook himself to the neighbouring territory of the Arvernians, where he was welcomed by Bishop Eufrasius, who gave him "houses and fields and vineyards," saying that the Church of the Arvernians was quite rich enough to support two bishops. Now, it was in the same year 506 that a council of the Orthodox Church was held at Agde, a coast-town on the other side of the Cévennes; and, whether the Council was held before or after the disturbance at Rodez, it does not seem to be a violent supposition to conclude that there was a connection of some sort between the two events. The significance, in that case, would be much the same, whether the Council met at Agde because of the troubles that had arisen in Rodez, or whether the Arians at Rodez were excited by reports brought from Agde, where Quintian would in all likelihood have attended the gathering of the clergy. If the Council, which met on September 11th, came after the ill-treatment of Quintian, there

RUINS OF MARMOUTIERS.
(*Residence of S. Martin of Tours.*)

would be much exasperation amongst the Orthodox Christians; and the incident would not be without effect on the proceedings of Clovis.

"And so," Gregory abruptly says at this point,

"Clovis the king said to his *leudes:* ' It goes very much against the grain with me that these Arians should hold any part of Gaul. Let us go forth with the help of the Lord, and overthrow them, and make their land our own.'" The summons was greeted with joy, and preparations were made for an advance.

In the spring of 507 Clovis led out his army, and marched through the country round about Tours, on the way to Poitiers. The character of the compact between Clovis and the Church was rendered very manifest in this campaign. The king issued strict orders that his army was to touch nothing whatever, except grass for the horses, during its progress through the country which had been governed by the holy Bishop Martin. The Teutonic warrior was on his way to champion the cause of orthodoxy, and miraculous appearances were vouchsafed to him, so that he and his men were convinced that they were under the special protection of Heaven. Bearing in mind his experience in the battle of Tolbiac, Clovis pledged himself to a pious recognition of the Divine favour if victory should be vouchsafed to him; and thus it was an army with the spirit of crusaders which finally came in sight of Alaric, in the Vocladensian Plain (near the modern Vouglé). The Goths were the first to attack, and the battle was obstinately fought; but it ended in the rout of the Arian host, and the slaughter of Alaric by his ruthless enemy. Clovis had a narrow escape from death at the hands of two Gothic lancers, but the speed of his horse or the strength of his mail sufficed to save him.

Pushing southward without delay, he took the rich

seaport of Burdigala (Bordeaux), which was one of the chief centres of academic learning as well as of trade in Gaul, and, marching along the right bank of the Garumna, secured Tolosa, the capital of the Visigoth kingdom. In the following year he besieged Carcaso (Carcassonne), between Toulouse and Narbonne.

The dominion of the Visigoths in Aquitaine, excluding the Pyrenean and maritime provinces, was now practically wiped out. Less than a hundred years had passed since Atolph, brother-in-law of the earlier and greater Alaric, had made his first entry in the Narbonensian province, and barely ninety since Tolosa became the capital of Visigothic Gaul. The Visigoths left but faint traces of their occupation; yet here again we have to make a significant exception in regard to the codification of the law. Apparently one of the last acts of Alaric II. was to nominate a commission of bishops and Roman jurisconsults, who were charged to summarise the principles and practice of Roman law. They based their labours to a large extent on the code of Theodosius, published in 438, which reduced into a comprehensive summary the *jus privatum*, the law of administration and government, the criminal law, the fiscal laws, the laws of procedure and local administration, and the ecclesiastical law. Some modification of these maxims was introduced by the Visigothic commission, mainly for the purpose of alleviating their severity and strengthening the principle of impartiality. The "Breviarium" of Anianus, as it was called, after the name of the president of the commission, survived in the courts of Gaul and Spain for several centuries.

The conquests of Clovis in the south were now checked by the Ostrogothic king. Theodoric, as we have said, had been anxious to prevent the war between Clovis and Alaric, even to the extent of appealing to the other Teutonic and Arian nations to take common action for the preservation of the Visigothic kingdom. The rapidity of the movements of Clovis in 506 had anticipated anything that could have been done in this sense; but, even apart from that, it was not likely that the Eastern or Riparian Franks would conspire against the ruler of Tournai and Soissons in order to play the game of the Goths in Italy and Gaul. Another reason which accounts for the failure of Theodoric's earlier plan is that Gundobald the Burgundian, whose interest was certainly to propitiate Clovis rather than to give him further cause of offence, was now in league with the Franks; whilst Theodoric himself was much absorbed in his quarrel with Anastasius, which made it difficult for him to quit Ravenna for Gaul, or even to dispatch an army to the assistance of his son-in-law. So much, however, he did contrive to do, sending his general Ibbas to oppose the Franks under his namesake Theodoric, the eldest son of Clovis. The combined forces of Theodoric and Gundobald were gradually reducing the whole of Southern Aquitaine, when at last the intervention of the Ostrogoths became effectual, and the Franks and Burgundians, in the absence of Clovis, were defeated by Ibbas. The greater part of the Narbonensian province, east of the Cévennes,

DIPTYCH OF SIVIDIUS OF TOURS. (Consul, 488.)

was restored to Amalaric, the son of Alaric, whilst the older Roman province of Gaul was added to the dominion of the Ostrogoths. It was not long before the mutual enmities of these three kings, Clovis, Theodoric, and Gundobald, were patched up by a common understanding. Clovis was confirmed in the possession of his conquests down to the borders of Gascony and Septimania, including the city of Toulouse; and his thoughts now reverted to the north and east.

Meanwhile he appears under a new and extraordinary guise, as a Consul if not as an Augustus of the Roman Empire. The titles, or at any rate that of consul, were conferred upon him by the aged Emperor

Anastasius, in recognition of his victory over the Visigoths; for Anastasius, involved as he himself was in the Monophysite controversy, seems none the less to have been moved to show honour to the champion of the Trinitarian principle against the Arian heretics, who was at the same time at enmity with the masterful ruler of the Ostrogoths. Clovis evidently took huge delight in his new dignities, his Roman robes and his somewhat farcical diadem. The fierce barbarian rejoiced with childish glee in the toys which the emperor had sent him, and his courtiers were ready to fall in with his humour by addressing him as consul or pro-consul. Many of the ancient forms and traditions of Rome were kept alive at Constantinople with punctilious exactitude, and it may be that the consular rank was bestowed on Clovis by virtue of his temporary possession of the old maritime province of Cisalpine Gaul.[1]

It was apparently at this time that Clovis, brought nearer to Roman ideas by his conversion, by twelve years of association with the Orthodox clergy, and now by his consulship, bethought himself how Julian, Valentinian, and Gratian had dwelt at Lutetia on the Seine. Thither, at any rate, he moved his family and his court; but Paris was not yet destined to become the capital even of Western Francia. Clovis lived and died there; and though he had begun his reign as a Frank of the Franks, and a determined enemy of Rome, he now delighted in the imitation of Roman customs, dressing in purple robes, writing to his

[1] See T. Hodgkin, "Theodoric the Goth," p. 222, *note* (Putnam's Sons).

brother-in-law to send him a *citharœdus* in order that he might have music at his banquets, and appointing his commission of learned men to revise the Latin version of the old Salic Law. Was it in any sense on a Roman pattern that he modelled his dealings with his brother Franks during the last few years of his life? He had no sooner become a dignitary of the Roman Empire than he prepared to strike down his actual or possible rivals for the supremacy of the Franks.

It is no part of the duty of one who relates a story from historical sources either to defend the character of his actors or to moralise over their evil deeds. At the same time, it is not enough to repeat in bald terms the bare statements even of contemporary writers. The historian who writes long after the transaction of a particular group or series of events is often better qualified than a contemporary to estimate the significance of facts and the character of individuals; just as it is easier to observe and describe the proportions of a building from the outside than from the inside, or the characteristics of a landscape from a distance than from the midst of it. What is necessary is that we should regard the central figures of history, not merely as man-slayers, or as founders or destroyers of states, but as creatures of their time helping to create the times which succeed them, and as instruments working to certain ends under certain conditions. Neither aspect should be left out of sight; but it is unquestionably more important to place a character accurately amidst its historical surroundings than to discuss its goodness or badness in comparison with men and women of the present day.

Clovis was fierce, formidable, and generally unrelenting, but he carried out, with no greater cruelty than that of civilised Roman conquerors, the ambitions cherished by his Teutonic ancestors for four or five centuries. He availed himself of the treachery of Godegisil, but he was easily persuaded to spare Gundobald. He accepted Christianity with mixed motives, but certainly under the influence of a pure and loving wife. He was ruthless in the slaughter of Alaric; but Alaric, since his pledge of friendship, had failed to protect the Orthodox bishops in Aquitaine, had assumed the offensive, and called in the aid of Theodoric. We know that the enemies of Clovis hated him, whilst his neighbours suspected and feared him; but all that we hear of him as a brother, a husband, and a father, is without exception good.

Full of faults as Clovis may have been, violent, gusty, unscrupulous in pursuing his larger ambitions, we are scarcely prepared by what has gone before for the record of his last two years. This is what Gregory of Tours has to say about it :—

Whilst Clovis was resting at Paris he privately sent word to Cloderic, son of Siegbert the Lame, who had fought on his side at Vouglé—as Siegbert had fought with him against the Allemans—suggesting to him that his father had grown old and decrepit, and that if he should happen to die the wealth which had been accumulated by Siegbert, as well as the kingdom of the Rhinelands, would in the ordinary course fall into the hands of Cloderic. So much as this, no doubt,

Clovis might have said, without any sinister purpose, in answer to a question as to his own wishes and intentions concerning the succession. But Gregory takes the darker view, saying that Clovis sent his message secretly in order to stimulate Cloderic to action.

However this may be, Cloderic resolved to be king without further delay. One day Siegbert rode out of Cologne and crossed the Rhine, intending to spend the afternoon in the "Burconian" wood—that is, the wood of Duisburg, about two miles from the right bank of the river. As the midday heat came on, he rested beneath an awning, and, whilst he slept, the assassins hired by his son came in and slew him. Cloderic then sent word to Clovis, saying, "My father is dead, and his treasures are mine. Send trusty men, to whom I may give whatever you desire." And Clovis sent messengers, who asked Cloderic to show them the treasure; and, whilst the murderer was stooping over a chest of gold, they stabbed him in the back. When Clovis knew that the son had paid the penalty of his crime he came to Cologne, and addressed the *leudes*, denying his responsibility for the two murders, and suggesting that the Franks of the Rhinelands should accept his protection. The proposal was received with acclamation, and he was forthwith raised upon a shield and saluted as king.

Now came the turn of Cararic, who ruled over the Northern Franks between Teruenna and the sea. Clovis accused Cararic of holding back in the war against Syagrius, and of playing him false in his struggle against the Gallo-Romans. Having secured the persons of the king and his son, he degraded them in the old Frank fashion, on which he had improved after embracing Christianity, by shaving their heads and devoting them to the religious life, in token that their days of warriorship were ended. The son consoled his father by saying that their hair would grow again, and that they would be avenged; but the words were reported to Clovis, who ordered his captives to be slain, and added their kingdom to his own dominions.

Ragnacar, the king at Cambrai was the next victim. In this case the task of Clovis was all the easier because the vices of Ragnacar and one of his favourites had excited the disgust of his subjects, who made little or no resistance to the invader, but delivered their king into his hands. Ragnacar was led bound into the presence of Clovis, who, feigning indignation, demanded of his prisoner, "Why have you disgraced our race by suffering yourself to be bound? It would have been better for you to die." And, suiting the action to the word, he smote Ragnacar on the head with his axe, and slew him. Then, all his relatives having been removed, he publicly lamented, as Gregory tells us, that he was "left as a stranger amongst strange people, without a kinsman to stand by him if misfortune should befall him." Either the bishop, or the bishop's corrupted text, with an utter absence of consistency, suggests that Clovis was only seeking to ascertain if any of the Franks would claim to be a member of his family, so that his work of extermination might be complete; though in connection with the same events we are assured that every day God cast down his enemies, and added increase to his kingdom, because he walked before Him with an upright heart, and did what was pleasing in His eyes.

Soon after these events Clovis died at Paris, and was buried in the church of the Holy Apostles, which he and the Queen Clotilda had combined to build. He passed away, says Gregory, in the fifth year after the battle with Alaric; and the days of his reign were thirty years, and the span of his life was forty-five years. Queen Clotilda, after the death of her husband, came to live at Tours, and there she abode all the days of her life, rarely visiting Paris, but rendering Christian service at the basilica of S. Martin, with all modesty and benevolence.

XI.

CHARACTERISTICS OF THE FRANKS.

THOUGH we may not yet speak of France as a kingdom created by the Franks in Gaul,[1] at any rate we have the Franks exercising dominion in the land

[1] A Roman, of course, might at any time give the name of Francia to the land where the Franks were found. So Claudian ("De Laudibus Stilichonis," i. 236):—

> " Provincia missos
> Expellet citius fasces quam Francia reges
> Quos dederis."

But Francia is not France, even when it is found in Gaul. Claudian uses the term vaguely as an equivalent for the Franks, but especially for the Franks in Germany. Hieronymus, writing about the same time, at the end of the fourth century, speaks of "Francia antiqua" in reference to the country between the Rhine and the Danube, subsequently known as Franconia, in a limited sense of that term. Eumenius, in his panegyric on Constantine, had employed the word Francia for Gaul, which was afterwards known as "Francia interior," "Latina," and "Occidentalis." Some writers speak of Neustria as "Francia Nova," and of the country partly dividing Neustria from Austria as "Francia Media." Germany, on the other hand, was known at times as "Francia Magna," or "Orientalis." As late as the end of the twelfth century, the chronicler Godfrey of Wittemberg, under the date 881, wrote: "Arnulfus totam Franciam Orientalem quæ hodie Teutonicum regnum vocatur, id est Bavariam, Sueviam, Saxoniam, Thuringiam, Frisiam et Lotharingiam rexit."

from which they were never to be expelled, and which they never wholly abandoned. Their laws, their customs, their characteristics, were now planted in Gallic soil, and bore fruit, not only from the original sap, but also in some sense from the sap of the stocks on which they were grafted. Kelts, Teutons of the pre-historic settlements—whom we have included under the name of Gauls—Romans, Gallo-Romans, Britons, Gascons, even Goths and Burgundians, were all concerned with the Franks in compounding the nation to which the last-mentioned people gave their name, but not their language, and to which all contributed in varying proportion their physical, domestic, and intellectual qualities. Let us interrupt for a moment the progress of our story of events in order to take a rapid survey of some of the more conspicuous national characteristics of the Franks.

The confederated tribes whose border-wars with Rome had welded them into a distinct people, and prepared them for definite nationalisation, cannot in the truest sense be said to have assumed a national type until they were both settled as regards territory and governed by the administration of a settled law. So far as settled territory is concerned, we have seen that Franks had been established in Brabant from before the time of Julian, more than a hundred years before the occupation of what was afterwards called Flanders, Artois, and Northern Picardy. These earlier Frank settlers, it is true, were bound to Rome by an obligation of military service, an obligation which they doubtless discharged so long as Rome was powerful enough to enforce it. But at any rate they were settled ; the institutions of a settled people had time to strike root, and the laws of their ancestors [1] were brought together, written down, and consistently applied in the administration of justice. Then, at length, there would be a community of interests under a single impersonal authority, which would deserve to be called a nation.

At what time this bringing together of the Frank laws in a written code took place, it would be impossible to say. The Salic Law, such as we find it in the most ancient Latin translations, is specially attributed, in one of the titles, to the nation of the Franks living between the Carbonarian forest (partly corresponding with the Ardennes) and the river Ligeris (Lys).[2] Some take Ligeris here to mean the Loire. But there was never a time at which the

---

[1] " De minoribus rebus principes consultant, de majoribus omnes, ita tamen ut ea quoque quorum penes plebem arbitrium est apud principes pertractentur. Coeunt, nisi quid fortuitum et subitum incidit, certis diebus. . . . Considunt armati. Silentium per sacerdotes, quibus tum et coercendi ius est, imperatur. Mox rex vel princeps, prout ætas cuique, prout nobilitas, prout decus bellorum, prout facundia est, audiuntur, auctoritate suadendi magis quam iubendi potestate. . . . Licet apud concilium accusare quoque, et discrimen capitis intendere. Distinctio poenarum ex delicto. Proditores et transfugas arboribus suspendunt, ignavos et imbelles et corpore infames coeno ac palude, iniecta insuper crate, mergunt. Diversitas supplicii illuc respicit, tamquam scelera ostendi oporteat, dum puniuntur, flagitia abscondi. Sed et levioribus delictis pro modo poena ; equorum pecorumque numero convicti mulctantur. Pars mulctæ regi vel civitati, pars ipsi qui vindicatur, vel propinquis ejus, exsolvitur. Eliguntur in iisdem conciliis et principes qui iura per pagos vicosque reddunt. Centeni singulis ex plebe comites, concilium simul et auctoritas, adsunt " (Tac., "Germania," xi., xii.).

[2] See tit. 47 (" Lex Salica, the Ten Texts . . ." by J. H. Hessels. Murray).

recognised possessions of the Franks could be described as lying between the Ardennes and the Loire. The description is just conceivable as applied to the dominion of Clovis alone, immediately before and after his marriage—which, to be sure, was not an unlikely time for the translation of the ancient code into Latin. But elsewhere the text speaks of the

EARLIER FRANK SETTLEMENTS IN BELGIAN GAUL.

Franks as being governed "per proceres." This expression may have been left standing by the carelessness of the translator. The date of the translation, however, is not a question which lends itself to confident statement.

Now the country between the Ardennes and the river Lys is the district which may be regarded as the third zone of Frank settlement—Batavia [1] being the first, Brabant the second, Hainault the third, and Flanders the fourth; and the time of settlement was, roughly speaking, between the concessions of Julian to the Salians in 358 and the invasion of Clodion in 447. All these settlers would, as a matter of course, have their own customs and laws, if not identical yet closely similar for all the Franks and their most neighbourly allies. In intervals of peace the chiefs and their *leudes*, the men of religion and counsel, would meet together, to administer, or build upon, or, if necessary, collect, the laws of their ancestors.

The fact of our finding the earliest copy of the Salic code with a defined application to the third zone of settlement does not, of course, in any way prove that the code originated with the Franks of Hainault, or that the Salic law was in a special sense the law of the Belgian Salians. The code comes down to us as that which was in force under the Merovingian dynasty, and the identity of the laws observed in Hainault with the laws promulgated by Clovis is enough in itself to show that they were the common laws of the Western Salian Franks, extending from the Scheidungen-burg, on the borders of Thuringia, to the mouths of the Rhine, Scheldt, and Somme, and afterwards over a great part of Gaul.

It is fair to conclude that, early in the fifth century, there was a Salic, or Salian, code wherever there was a strong Salian chief ruling over a defined territory,

[1] That is, the first known settlement of Chattans. Constantius Chlorus is said to have cleared Batavia of its Chattan settlers in 288; but that is scarcely to be taken in an absolute sense.

and that all these codes were fundamentally one and the same. In any case the laws of the Franks, as of other Germans, existed in their own tongue before they were translated into Latin for the benefit of the Gallo-Romans, and of the Latin clerics who would naturally assist in expounding them. Grimm, indeed, was of opinion that the Salic law itself came into existence in the fifth century, being composed in Latin by jurists who would necessarily use many indigenous words in a Latinised form. But, as Mr. Hessels points out, all the material for such a composition would be in existence beforehand, so that the work of these jurists, whilst it probably amounted to a codification, must also have been in the nature of a translation, article by article, and perhaps phrase by phrase. "Due allowance being made for the legendary character" of statements concerning the origin of the code, "we may fairly infer from the Prologues that, in the tradition of the Franks, their Salic Law dated from a period considerably anterior to the fifth century, and had remained essentially the same, notwithstanding such modifications and additions as became necessary in course of time."[1] A Latin version before the acceptance of Christianity by the Franks need not create much surprise or difficulty for those who consider that war had not been the only mode of interchange between the Roman and the Teuton. There had been a traffic of thought and culture, as well as of merchandise, even across the Lower Rhine; and amongst the Franks there would certainly be many who understood the Latin tongue,

[1] "Lex Salica," as above.

and some who had consulted the law of Rome. There had been Roman captives and settlers in Germany, as well as German captives and settlers in Gaul; thousands of German mercenaries in the Roman army must have returned to their native land after acquiring a Roman tongue; and many generations of trade and intermarriage must have contributed to a set of conditions which made a Latin version of the law a thing to be desired.

It will be interesting to glance at some of the more characteristic features of the Teutonic law prior to the year 500, and of the national customs and institutions from which their written laws had been evolved. The most characteristic features in any body of law will be found in its method of dealing with offences committed by individuals against the interests of the community, resolving itself into various forms of vindication or punishment, and into a system of alternatives allowed by the community for the avoidance of punishment. Such alternatives to punishment are the first signs of mitigation in the law, based as it naturally is, in the first instance, on the cruelties of total or partial suppression. Now the root-fact of Teutonic law in this secondary phase of mitigation was the institution of *wehrgeld*, or money paid in redemption of crime. And a further characteristic of Teutonic law was its clear conception of the double character of crime. Wherever there was an offence against an individual, it was recognised that there was also an offence against the community; and the administrators of the law were not content—as was generally the case amongst the Romans—to punish on behalf of the community without regard to the damage suffered by the individual. In fact, the vindication of the individual (when crime touched an individual) was always the most prominent idea of Teutonic punishments. The redress of the injured person under the authority of law was a substitution for the natural right of private vengeance; and the Teuton saw that the vindication of individuals was a vindication and a defence for the State. This simple intuition gave a distinct character to Teutonic law, which has counted for much in the national developments of the Teutonic race. There was amongst the Teutons a systematic scale of wehrgeld, based not only upon the nature of the crime, but also upon the status of the injured person; and the system itself introduced a further mitigation by the fact that individual sufferers had a stronger motive than the State for accepting a pecuniary indemnity for a wrong inflicted upon them. In most cases the offender had to pay a fine to the royal treasury (known by the name of "fredum," or peace-making), as well as to indemnify his victim. When the parties concerned were slow in coming to an agreement, the judge intervened to hasten the settlement; and he also had the power, in circumstances of special aggravation, to double or treble the stipulated payment.

Wehrgeld differed, as above said, according to the status of the injured person. Amongst the Franks, the highest class after the king was that of the king's *leudes* and nobles, the latter, under the Merovingians (and before their time) being *criniti*, or families entitled or accustomed to wear their hair long; and after them came the *antrustions*. Of the Leti, or Lites, settled on the land, we have spoken elsewhere. Below them were the slaves, and amongst the slaves there was a varying estimation of value, decided according to their worth in the eyes of their masters. The payment of wehrgeld did not, at any rate in the earlier periods, apply to offences against the king, or to public crimes.

IRON SAUFANG.
(*Cologne, sixth century.*)

Another institution of the Teutons arising out of the commission of crime was that of the *urtheil*, or ordeal, which was the judgment or detection of the criminal by means of an appeal to the deity, which was naturally resorted to in the absence of personal witnesses. It was, in this older and less superstitious sense, a sort of sacrament and act of faith, employed with all sincerity in the belief that God would judge between the wrongdoer and his victim when human means failed to provide a remedy. The Church not only sanctioned this form of ordeal, but also added to its solemnity by requiring that the parties concerned —that is to say, the victim and the person suspected of the crime—should attend mass and communicate. Then, in the case of ordeal by boiling water, which is mentioned in the Salic Law, the priest blessed the water, and a ring or a stone, suspended by a cord, was immersed, three times in succession, at increasing depths. The person called upon to undergo the ordeal had to draw out the ring or stone, and his arm was afterwards wrapped in bandages for three days. If, at the end of that time, his flesh had not recovered its ordinary appearance, his guilt was held to be proved.

Ordeal by cold water, which survived for many centuries as a test of witchcraft, required that the arm of the suspected person should be bound to his leg, and that he should be thrown into a pond, his guilt being declared if he floated instead of sinking.

The ordeal of the cross was, in effect, a trial of endurance between two suspected or mutually accused persons, who had to stand with extended arms whilst divine service was proceeding; and the one who first dropped his arms stood convicted.

Ordeal by hot iron consisted in holding a heated bar in the hand, or walking barefoot over hot iron bars or plates.

In ordeal by fire, the person submitted to the test

had to walk, with the consecrated host in his hands, between two adjacent fires.

Another form of decision in contested cases was to employ the Gospels after the manner of the *sortes Virgilianæ*. The book was opened, and an oracle was drawn from the first sentence of the page exposed.

Ordeal by single combat involved the loss of a hand by the defeated combatant; or, in the most serious cases, he was buried alive. This, and the ordeal by cold water, survived longer than the other forms. Charles the Great forbade the ordeal of the cross as tending to profanity.[1]

The law affecting slavery amongst the Franks—concerning which something will be found hereafter, in the fifteenth chapter of the present work—again contrasts favourably with the severity of Roman institutions. The manumission of slaves, which, especially after the adoption of Christianity, was a frequent operation in an epoch and in a country which knew more than one or two modes of reduction to the state of slavery, was effected in various ways, described in the Formulas preserved for us by Marculfus, a monk of Frank origin, who wrote in the seventh century, and therefore dealt in particular with the Merovingian age. Enfranchisement *per denarium* was the most formal and symbolic of these methods. When a master was prepared to liberate his slave, he took him before the count of his district, to whom he announced his intention.

[1] See Lalanne, " Dict. Historique de la France," under the word "ordalie."

Thereupon the slave produced a coin, and offered it to his master as a sign that he wished to purchase his freedom. The master, not receiving the denarius, but striking it from the hand of his slave, signified that he was willing to complete the contract, and at the same time to forgo the price. A *carta denarialis* was then drawn up by the order of the count, and delivered to the former slave as evidence of his emancipation; and the latter (as indicated in the Riparian law) assumed or resumed the condition of a free-born man.

Another mode of enfranchisement (traced back to the Chamavians) was *per handtradam*, when the slave was surrounded by a ring of twelve persons, one of whom was his master, and this master took the slave and passed him outside the circle—a written charter being subsequently given, as in the case previously described.

Yet another mode of enfranchisement amongst the Franks was by the master's last will and testament, when, as Marculfus says, the owner liberated all his slaves "for the remission of his sins and the salvation of his soul." But this case of emancipation was regarded as inferior in kind to the other two, for it did not confer the complete civil rights acquired by those who had earned their freedom before their masters came within sight of death.

XII.

THE SONS OF CLOVIS.

THE death of Clovis was followed at once by the subdivision of his realm amongst his four surviving sons, the oldest of whom, born of his first wife, before his marriage with Clotilda, would be about twenty-five, whilst the youngest could scarcely have been more than thirteen years old.

If Clovis had had one son instead of four, the history of Gaul would have presented a very different aspect. Clovis, if only for a moment, had been virtually an emperor. Kings in subjection to him ruled parts of the dominion which he had conquered; the Allemans and Burgundians were tributary, though in two different senses; the Franks of the Lower Rhine were content to hold their lands intact, acknowledging Clovis as the head of the Salians; his sway over Aquitaine was confirmed by treaty with Theodoric, and by formal recognition from Constantinople. All this was enough for empire, if there had been an emperor. Clovis assumed the title of Augustus but he died at the moment when he had set the coping-stone on his edifice by overthrowing the kings at Cologne, Cambrai, and Tournai. Then came the division of territory and authority indicated below, which made all talk of empire impossible.

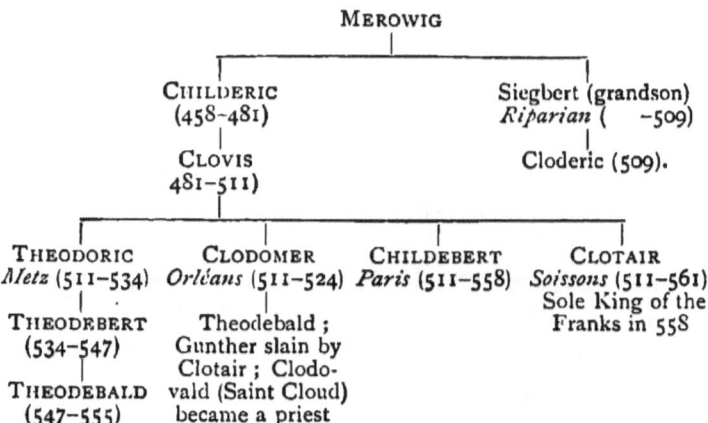

It might almost be concluded from this subdivision of the Frank dominion that the custom of division by lot had been modified on this occasion, in order that Theodoric, the oldest of the four brothers, might receive the kingship of the Riparians, as being already a tried soldier, because it was in the east that fighting was most likely to occur in the near future: and, indeed, the riverain districts were disturbed immediately before and after the death of Clovis. Theodoric had been well treated and trusted by his father, and doubtless by Clotilda also, though he was not her son. The queen probably had something to say in arranging the succession of her infant sons, and it may have been she who drew the capitals near together, and advised that the city of Paris itself should be neutral ground, a centre of amity and counsel, to which none of the sons of Clovis might come at the head of an army. Clotilda lived until 545, and witnessed many of the victories, quarrels, and crimes of her children.

The map on the next page roughly shows the possessions of the Franks in Gaul, on the death of Clovis. The apportionment of this territory amongst the sons of Clovis would be made rather by an enumeration of towns than by a detailed tracing of boundaries, where there were no marked natural features.

The kingdom of *Metz* included Metz, the capital, Cologne, Trèves, Châlons, Troyes, Tolbiac, Clermont, Rodez, Cahors, Albi, Toulouse.

The kingdom of *Orléans* included Orléans, the capital, Chartres, Le Mans, Angers, Tours, Bourges, and Auxerre.

The kingdom of *Paris*, or *Sens*, included Sens, the capital, Melun, Meaux, Evreux, Rouen, Rennes, Vannes, Nantes, Poitiers, Saintes, Bordeaux.

The kingdom of *Soissons* included Soissons, the capital, Laon, Amiens, Cambrai, Térouanne, Tournai, Limoges.

Theodoric, it will be seen, had the march-country, which served as a bulwark to the other three. Clotilda's oldest son had the smallest kingdom; Childebert nominally ruled along the whole of the Armorican coast; whilst Clotair, who turned out to be the fiercest and most grasping of the four, and who survived his brothers and succeeded to all their possessions, held sway, in the first instance, over the old Frank land, between the Seine and Waal, the Meuse and the sea.

There was just half a century between the death of Clovis and the death of his youngest son, Clotair; and it was, upon the whole, a period of continued conquest for the Franks. An early invasion of Northmen from

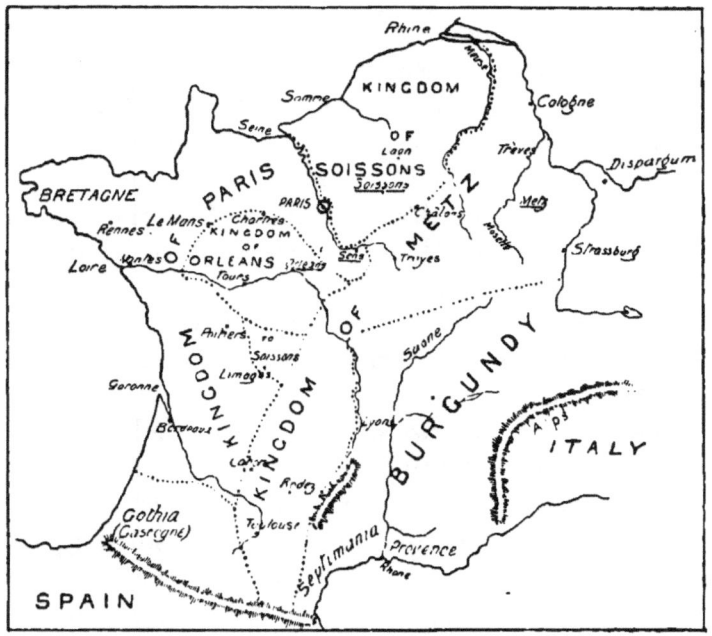

GAUL AFTER THE DEATH OF CLOVIS.

the Cimbric chersonese was successfully opposed—apparently by the energy of Theodoric. In 516 the old Burgundian, Gundobald, the nominal tributary of Clovis, passed away, and left his kingdom to Sigismond his son. Clodomer of Orléans, aided by Clotair and Childebert, either found or picked a quarrel with

Sigismond, invaded Burgundy in 523, and again in 524, carried the king and his family to Orléans, and there slew them. Towards the end of the war, however, Clodomer lost his own life; and Clotair, now about twenty-six years of age, combined with his elder brother, Childebert of Sens (Paris), to murder two of the sons of Clodomer, and to appropriate his realm. The youngest son, Clodovald, was saved by his grandmother, and in good time cut off his lengthening locks, and served the Church, by which he was subsequently canonised.

Clotilda, too, of whom we may here take leave, was to be canonised after her death. Little but what is very good is related of her by the historians; and, making every allowance for the natural disposition of ecclesiastical writers to deal tenderly with one who rendered great services to the Church, her acts were ever those of a virtuous and true-hearted woman. The two grandchildren who were murdered by their uncles had been taken out of her charge against her will, and she bitterly mourned their death. She caused the poor little bodies, Gregory tells us, to be laid side by side on a bier, and followed them at the head of an imposing funeral procession, with many dirges, to the basilica of S. Peter, where they were buried in one grave. It is doubtful, in spite of what Gregory writes, whether she had counselled Clodomer's attack on the Arian Burgundians. If she had, the advice cost her very dear; for not only was the attack unsuccessful, but it caused the violent death of her cousin Sigismond and his family, of her son Clodomer, and of her grandsons Theodebald and Gunther.

Gregory is enthusiastic in his praise whenever he has occasion to speak of her. Queen Clotilda, he says, was honoured by all for her good qualities and her greatness of soul. She gave alms every day, prayed through the night, lived a pure and holy life, and endowed churches, monasteries, and other sacred places, giving with open and lavish mind, more like the handmaid of the Lord than an earthly queen. "The kingship of her sons, the craving tendencies of the age, the constant seductions of her position, were powerless to corrupt her. Her very lowliness raised her to the height of grace."

Meanwhile Theodoric, leaving the west to the vigorous hands of his half-brothers, had been turning his attention to the other side of the Rhine. The Thuringians, who had not been thoroughly subdued by Clovis, and had even contemplated an alliance with Theodoric the Goth for the defence of Aquitaine, were naturally all the stronger for the withdrawal of the Western Franks. The eldest son of Clovis, whose sphere of kingship of course extended eastward to the ancient seat of his ancestors, would have no lack of pretexts for, and opportunities of, attacking the Thuringian king. He called his brother Clotair to his aid, and, whilst Childebert continued to pursue the political objects of the dynasty in Gaul, Theodoric and Clotair advanced in the old familiar highway of the Franks, and reduced the Thuringians to submission (528). In the following year Clotair married Radegund, the daughter of the conquered king. Once more a princess of the Eastern Franks acknowledged her "strongest man" amongst the enemies of the

Thuringian house. The immediate fate of the Main valleys, and of the uppermost valleys of the Danube, vaguely known as Bavaria to the chroniclers of the time, was decided simultaneously with that of Thuringia, and the Western Franks asserted their dominion as far eastward as the Upper Elbe, Augsburg, and possibly the banks of the river Inn.

Childebert, at the request of his brother Theodoric, overran, in 530, the revolted province of Auvergne, of which Clermont was the principal town, and brought it into subjection. Thence he turned southward in the following year, penetrated almost to the walls of Narbonne, expelled from Gaul the Visigoth Amalaric, and shortly afterwards received a cession of territory from another grandson of Theodoric the Great, the Ostrogoth Athalaric, the young and ill-fated son of Amalasuentha.

One object, if not the principal one, of Childebert's expedition against Amalaric was to avenge his sister Clotilda, who had been married to the king of the Visigoths—an Orthodox Christian to the Arian, the daughter of Clovis to the son of Alaric. The marriage had been a failure, and the young queen, complaining of Amalaric's cruelty, had asked her brother to come to her rescue. In one sense Childebert was too late; for, though he defeated Amalaric, who fled as far as Barcelona, and was there slain, the unhappy queen died on the journey home, and was buried by the side of her father in Paris.

On the return of the two brothers from Thuringia, they aided Childebert to complete the conquest of Burgundy, which was effected in 534. Godomar, the brother of Sigismond, fought in vain for his kingdom, and lost his life in the struggle. As he was the last male heir of Gundachar, Burgundy would now naturally fall to the heirs of Clotilda. In the same year the eldest son of Clovis ended his not ignoble life, and his son Theodebert reigned in his stead.

It is likely enough that Theodebert had no great confidence in his uncles, and at any rate he was soon at war with them. One of his first acts was to come to an understanding with the Greeks of Marseille and with the Ostrogothic king Vitiges, who had married the sister of Athalaric (536). Childebert and Clotair not unnaturally took this amiss, and threatened their nephew with vengeance. Theodebert vacillated. He sent a force of Burgundians to aid Vitiges, who, after failing in his long siege of Rome, was now expecting at Ravenna the return-siege of Belisarius. That did not prevent Theodebert from taking advantage of the misfortunes of Vitiges in Italy to invade Provence, and inflict defeat both on the city of Marseille and on the weak force of Ostrogoths who opposed his progress. In this way the old Roman province fell into the hands of the Franks; and the Emperor Justinian, severing the last figment of a tie between the Roman Empire and its conquests in the West, renounced whatever claim he may have had upon the land of Gaul.

One hears comparatively little of the Frank womenfolk amidst these narratives of the warlike deeds of their fathers and brothers. Procopius, in his history of the Gothic war in Italy, tells a story of Totila, who twice made himself master of Rome—how he fell in love with the daughter of Theodebert, and asked her hand in marriage. It had happened that the victorious Goth, on his first entry into the Eternal City, had allowed it to be sacked, pulled down one-third of the walls, and threatened to turn it into pasture for cattle. Belisarius had appealed to his enemy to spare what long ages had built and cherished; and Totila had listened to the old general, who was then supposed to be at the point of death. He contented himself by carrying off the Senate, and driving out the inhabitants; but he had no sooner left the city than Belisarius re-entered it, and defied the efforts of the Goth to recover it. And when Totila asked Theodebert for his daughter, the grandson of Clovis replied that he could not regard as king of Italy, or think him likely to become king of Italy, a man who did not know how to hold Rome when he had conquered her, but allowed the city, half-destroyed, to fall again into the hands of the enemy (547).

Fortune favoured Totila with the chance of responding at once to the challenge of Belisarius and to the reproach of Theodebert—perhaps, also, of deserving and winning the hand of Theodebert's daughter. Rome was retaken. Totila found the city barely inhabited, stricken with poverty, though full of hoarded grain, and all the open spaces covered with fields of wheat. " To repopulate it he recalled Goths as well as Romans, even senators from Campania; and, providing for their needs, gave orders that everything which had been destroyed in his first conquest should now be restored. He then invited the people to the Circus Maximus, and the last chariot races

VOTIVE CROWN OF KING SUINTILA.
(Gold and Precious Stones :—" *Suintilianus Rex offert.*'
Early seventh century.)

which the Romans saw"—the same Romans who saw the last consul of Rome—" were those given in farewell by a Gothic king."[1]

Theodebert did not withdraw his taunt, for he died in the year in which he made it. He, too, had dreamed the German's dream. His ambition had lured him into Italy. If he had lived he might have made common cause with Totila, or even turned his arms against him. Six years after his death we read of Allemans and "Franks," under Lentharis and Bucelin, who devastated Sicily and Southern Italy, as well as the northern Adriatic shore, and who were ultimately defeated by Narses. But these were not the Franks of Theodebert. They seem to have come southward through the land of the Allemans, and were associated with Goths and Huns.

Childebert and Clotair, in the meantime, had made a disastrous expedition into Visigothic Spain, whence they were forced to retreat empty-handed. For the next few years they had sufficient to occupy them on their eastern frontiers, where the Saxons had replaced the Franks as the most aggressive German power, behind whom the pent-up swarms of the Danes and other Northmen were already pressing for an outlet. They had enemies within, as well as without their borders; there were revolts on which history has dwelt more lightly than on the wars which made for greater political changes. And there was an enemy which fought not with hands, but with the finger of God—the terrible recurrent plague, which, bred in the East, and propagated in the track of the invader, and

[1] Gregorovius, "Hist. of Rome in the Middle Ages," bk. ii., chap. vi.

on a thousand battlefields, decimated Western Europe in the latter half of the sixth century. From 542 onward there was scarcely a year without some more or less deadly visitation of the *lues inguinaria*. Gregory, Procopius and his continuator, Paul Diaconus, and other contemporaries, abound in gloomy details.

"Confined to no season, and spreading without contact, it seized alike on men and animals. The frenzied imagination heard in the air the braying of trumpets, saw the mark of the destroying angel on houses, and stalking in the streets the demon of pestilence himself, or ghosts (φάσματα δαιμόνων) who imparted death to those they met by a blow. The consequences were not always immediate, but generally followed in three days. The stricken died, overpowered by sleep or consumed by fever. . . . Gregory assures us that men with their own eyes beheld arrows shot down from heaven, apparently piercing their fellow-men. Fear gave birth to visions." [1]

Half a floating poison, half a nervous disorder, this earlier Black Death may be regarded as both effect and cause of some of the most ghastly human tragedies which stained the annals of the time.

Theodebald, who succeeded his brother Theodebert in the kingdom of Metz, died without issue in 553, and Clotair entered into his possessions. With them he inherited the duty of defending the whole of the German marches; and an immediate war with the powerful Saxon confederation taxed his energy, and was not always waged with success. If he had not

[1] Gregorovius, bk. iii., ch. 1.

been so well engaged at home, he might have directed another expedition to Thuringia, which was at the mercy of the unruly mixed hordes—Allemans, Huns, Goths, so-called Franks—who constantly harassed the dwellers on both sides of the Danube, and some of whom had recently been ejected from Italy by Justinian's martial eunuch. In addition to his Saxon war, Clotair had to face the menaces, and even the attack, of his brother Childebert, who does not seem to have acquiesced in his appropriation of Metz. But in more ways than one the ruthless modes of self-aggrandisement which had been adopted by the youngest son of Clovis had to be expiated in his riper years. On the death of Clodomer, Clotair had married his brother's wife, Gondeucha, though he had caused two of her three sons to be murdered. It is easy to imagine a direct chain of cause and effect which made the son of Clotair and Gondeucha rebel against his father. For five years (555–60) the open breach continued, and during the latter part of this time Chramnus secured an asylum and practical aid amongst the sturdy Bretons. He even contrived to raise an army, in alliance with Cenober, whose name recalls some of the most heroic enemies of Julius Cæsar. But Clotair defeated this army at Dol, took his son prisoner, and burned him with all his family.

That is almost the last scene in the life of this bloodthirsty Frank. Childebert of Paris had died childless in 558, and thus the last quarter of the dominions of Clovis passed into the hands of Clotair. He did not live long to enjoy his full splendour as sole king of the Franks, for he died in 561, not many months after taking his brutal vengeance on Chramnus.

Clotair, like Clovis, left four sons, who immediately divided their father's compact realm. The chief political changes of the next hundred and ten years are shown in the table on the opposite page.

DESCENDANTS OF CLOTAIR.

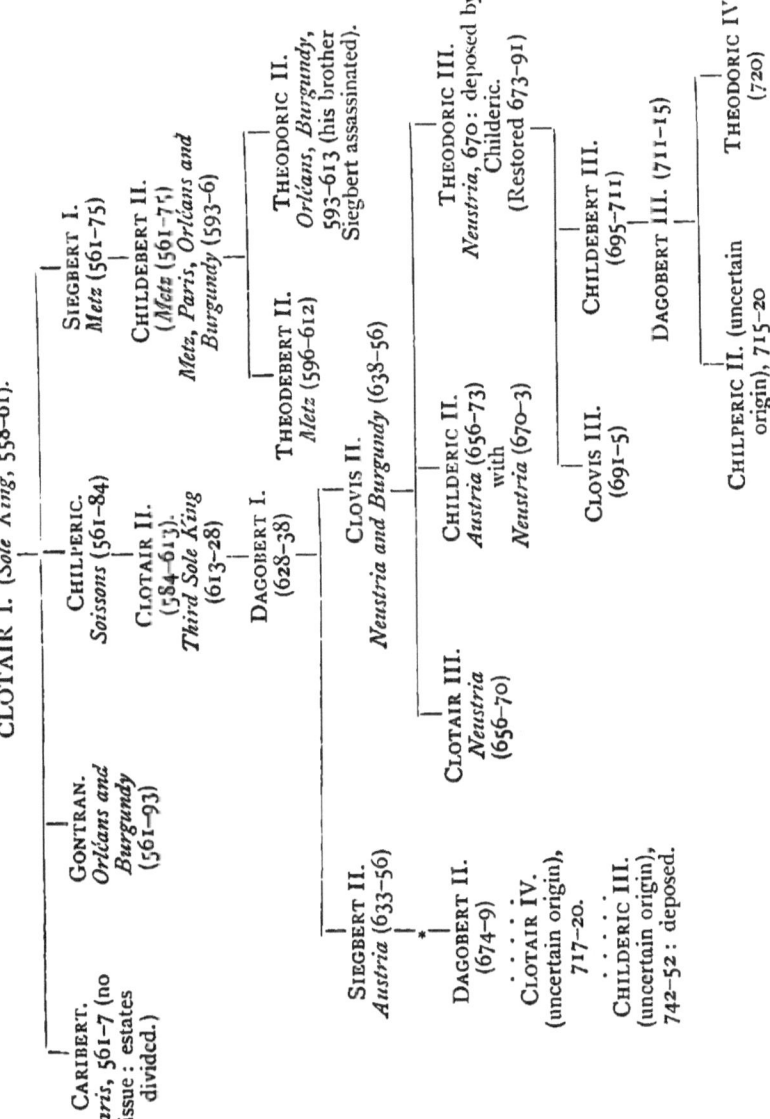

XIII.

THE SONS OF CLOTAIR.

THE subdivision of the realm of Clotair was made, as was usual (though not universal) with the Franks, by lot. Speaking approximately, Caribert received what had been formerly known as the kingdom of Childebert, Gontran the kingdom of Clodomer, Chilperic the kingdom of Clotair, and Siegbert the kingdom of Theodoric.[1]

It was not long before Siegbert was forcibly reminded that he occupied the post of greatest danger and honour, for a new generation of Huns, descendants of those who had ravaged Europe under Attila, invaded the borders of his territory in 562. He repelled the attack, but his absence in the east

---

[1] Gregory says: "Inter se hi quatuor . . . divisionem legitimam faciunt: deditque sors Chariberto regnum Childeberti, sedemque habere Parisios: Guntheramno vero regnum Chlodomeris, ac tenere Aurelianensem: Chilperico vero regnum Chlotaris patris ejus, cathedramque Suessionas habere: Sygiberto quoque regnum Theodorici, sedemque habere Remensem." Reims, it will be noticed, takes the place of Metz as capital of the north-eastern kingdom; but if a Frank instead of an ecclesiastic had been giving an account of the matter, he would probably have written Metz, not Reims. Siegbert is more associated with Metz than with Reims.

was sufficiently prolonged to enable his treacherous brother Chilperic to encroach upon his dominions. When he returned he found it necessary to drive Chilperic out by force of arms; and, though he succeeded in doing so, he had henceforth on his western borders an enemy for life—an enemy whose malice was made more deadly by one of the most venomous women encountered in the pages of history.

There came one day in 566, into the land of Austria, and to the court of King Siegbert, two beautiful daughters of the king of the Spanish Visigoths, by name Brunhilda and Galeswintha. Brunhilda was the bride of Siegbert, and for nearly fifty years she was destined to play a sinister part in the country of her adoption. Now Chilperic in the meantime had married Audovera, who, to her misfortune, had a seductive and intriguing maid called Fredegonda. Audovera had borne her husband three sons, Theodebert, Merowig, and Clovis, when she fell a victim to a cruel plot of Fredegonda, and was repudiated by the king. Chilperic, though already on intimate terms with the traitress, married his sister-in-law, Galeswintha; but from this defeat Fredegonda plucked a barbarous victory, for within a year the king's daughter was strangled, and Audovera's maid sat on the throne of Soissons.

Brunhilda and Fredegonda are fit heroines for the most sanguinary of the Teutonic sagas, in which they appear much distorted, and amidst different surroundings, but with a manifest parentage of fact and suggestion. They were mortal enemies, and it would be hard to say which was the more implacable; but perhaps Fredegonda's crimes were the most fiendish and unprovoked.

Caribert of Paris having died in 567, his kingdom was divided by his three brothers; and this was a new cause of enmity amongst the sons of Clotair. For a while, their internal quarrels were checked by invasions of Lombards and Saxons, who were successively expelled by Mummolus, the Count of Auxerre, and a general in the service of Gontran, at the head of a Burgundian army. Siegbert, in the meantime, had made terms with the Huns, in the year of his marriage with Brunhilda.

Ever since the murder of Galeswintha, her sister had been urging Siegbert to make war on Chilperic, and to avenge her on the hated Fredegonda. Hostilities broke out in 573, and Chilperic sent his eldest son, Theodebert, to hold that part of Aquitaine which had fallen to the lot of Siegbert. The latter, who found both his brothers, as well as his nephew, arrayed against him, called in large armies from the other side of the Rhine. Theodebert was defeated and slain in Aquitaine, and, Chilperic being driven back in the north, Siegbert allowed himself to be proclaimed king of his brother's dominion. At this point (575), the women come once more to the front.

Chilperic was beaten, and could no longer rely on his army. His capture, or at any rate his expulsion from his kingdom, was imminent, when Fredegonda persuaded two unhappy youths, whom she armed with poisoned daggers, to assassinate the victorious

Siegbert at the moment when he was raised on the shields of his soldiers, and saluted as king of Soissons and Paris. This turned the tide of failure; for almost everything depended in those days upon the presence and energetic direction of the king. Chilperic's *leudes* gathered round him again; Siegbert's friends were paralysed; the auxiliaries fell away; and Fredegonda had the satisfaction of securing the persons of Brunhilda and her children.

The widowed queen had not been long in durance when she found a friend in Merowig, the second son of Audovera, who contrived her escape. In gratitude, or under stress of circumstances, Brunhilda married Merowig; but their union was short, for the son fell into his father's hands, and, at the instigation of Fredegonda, he was put to death. Fredegonda's thirst for blood seemed to be stimulated by each new crime. In 580 she secured the death of Clovis, Audovera's third son, of Audovera herself, who, as Gregory tells us, "died a cruel death," and of certain other sons of Chilperic, who might not have been considered as out of the line of succession merely because they were not legitimate. In this way she made a clear path for her own son, Clotair; and shortly afterwards, in 584, there followed what was perhaps the inevitable sequel of such a series of achievements, the assassination of Chilperic, at the town of Chelles, by the woman to whose insatiable cruelty he had ministered for eighteen years.

In the meantime Chilperic had been fighting with his brother Gontran; and he had so ruthlessly taxed and oppressed his subjects that they rose in rebellion against him in Brittany and at Limoges. In 580 his excitable soul was subdued by a terrible outbreak of the plague, by an earthquake, by a destructive overflow of the Loire, and by the attitude of the bishops in their Council at Braisne, near Soissons—where the Merovingians had one of their royal residences (see p. 306). He solemnly burned his more tyrannical decrees; but the contrition does not appear to have made any permanent change in the character of his misrule.

Gontran of Burgundy was as warlike as any of the sons of Clotair. Some of the greatest victories of the Franks of Burgundy had been gained by Mummolus, already mentioned; but Gontran himself conducted one or two successful campaigns against Chilperic. He also conquered Gundobald, an illegitimate half-brother, who was backed by Didier, the duke of Toulouse, and raised the standard of revolt near Orléans; and after one defeat he overthrew Reccared, king of the Visigoths, at Carcassonne.[1] A black stain seems to rest on the character of Gontran in connection with the death of Mummolus; but the circumstances are too much in doubt to render a judgment on this point in any way safe. He behaved admirably to his nephew Childebert, the son of Siegbert and Brunhilda, whom he protected, adopted as his son, and, being childless, nominated as his successor. Nevertheless, in some of his acts he showed himself true to the Merovingian type. Tired

[1] It was this Reccared who, with his subjects at Narbonne, turned his back on the Arian heresy in 587; and a Council of the Gallic Church was held at Narbonne in 589, apparently in the vain hope of arranging terms between the old and the new converts.

of, or incensed against, his wife Marcatrude, he put her away, and married one of her attendants, Austrachilde; and, when his two brothers-in-law took him to task for his cruelty to their sister, he killed them both. Four years later, Austrachilde fell sick and died, whereupon Gontran gave orders that her physicians should pay with their lives the penalty of their failure.

Childebert, whilst still a boy, marched at the head of an army against the Lombards in Northern Italy. We even read that the Emperor Maurice sent him from Byzantium a subsidy of fifty thousand sous of gold,[1] with a letter in which he spoke of the ancient amity of the Franks and Rome: " Priscam gentis Frankorum et Ditionis Romanæ unitatem." Childebert lost two armies in the vain attempt to drive out the Lombards. In 593 Gontran died, and Brunhilda's son became King of Paris, Orléans, and Burgundy, as well as of the eastern realms of his father.

Two women now governed, or attempted to govern, the fortunes of the race of Franks. Fredegonda, the queen-mother of the western kingdom, was approaching her fiftieth year when Gontran died, and Brunhilda's son held for a moment by far the larger part of Francia. It was not for this that Audovera's tirewoman had unsexed herself in her early youth, betrayed her mistress, duped her royal lover, strangled her Spanish rival, poisoned the daggers for her brother-in-law, used her husband as an instrument for the murder of his own sons, hired cutthroats to rid her of Chilperic, and

[1] The Frank sou (solidus) of gold weighed 73·5 grains.

assassinated the bishop of Rouen when he reproached her for her crimes. We shall look in vain through the pages of history for a woman capable of more deliberate, sustained, and successful murders than those by which she carved her path to the throne, advanced the cause of her husband so long as it suited her that he should live, removed every possible rival to her son Clotair, and transferred the crown from father to son as soon as Clotair had reached what in those days was regarded as the age of militant manhood.

The alliance of Gontran and his nephew Childebert was probably conceived, in part, as a measure of defence against the treacheries of Fredegonda. The succession of Childebert to the united kingdoms of Orléans, Burgundy, Metz, and two-thirds of the patrimony of Caribert, would unquestionably be looked upon by Fredegonda as an injury and a menace to Clotair. And her spite at the aggrandisement of Brunhilda's son would be none the less keen because Childebert was high in favour with the Church, which she herself had grievously offended.

There was, however, no necessity for Fredegonda to wait for pretext or opportunity of fighting. Brunhilda, on her side, had studiously nursed her vengeance against the murderess of her sister and her two husbands. She was the guardian of her son, and exercised in his name many of the functions of royalty, living most of her time at Metz, and entirely failing to keep the confidence or goodwill of Childebert's *leudes*. She quarrelled also with more than one of the prominent ecclesiastics, and, like Fredegonda in this respect, made enemies of the principal men in the kingdom. The war between Metz and Soissons, in 593–6, was fought mainly in the latter country, and the invaders had the worst of it throughout. It was virtually the private war of the two queen-mothers, and the younger woman triumphed.

So far the fates had fought for Fredegonda; but she was not destined to witness the full realisation of her ambitions, and to see the whole Frank nation united under the sceptre of her son. It is doubtful if we ought to add the poisoning of Childebert (575) to the long list of her achievements. At any rate the son of Brunhilda died by poison on his return from a campaign against the Bretons, as he was preparing to take his place at the head of the invading army between Soissons and Laon. Discouraged by the death of their king, the eastern army lost the battle; and the *leudes*, refusing to continue a war in which they had probably never been enthusiastic, withdrew to their own country.

It was at this moment, or very shortly afterwards, that Fredegonda died. She died, so far as we know, a natural death; but in that age, with such a woman, at such a crisis of far-reaching hatred and revenge, all forms of death are conceivable. When, sixteen years later, Brunhilda, an old woman verging on her eightieth year, fell into the hands of Fredegonda's son, and, after three days of continuous torture, was bound to an unbroken horse and dashed to pieces, many of the Franks must have thought that her violent death was a fitting close to the career of the Gothic princess who had wrought so much evil to their race. To this extent the drama of Brunhilda's life is more complete than that which centres in the life of Fredegonda. History, so lavish of her tales of blood, sometimes capriciously drops her curtain over the last scene of a moving tragedy, without satisfying the interest which she has aroused.

Though the ill-starred Brunhilda survived her enemy for so many years, they were years of diminished power and influence, but not of diminished malice. Her quarrels with the *leudes* of Childebert, interrupted for a moment by the war with Soissons, came to a head after the murder of her son and the triumph of Fredegonda. Those two events seem to have deprived her of all self-control and caution. The duke of Campania (Champagne), who lived at Troyes, and was one of the strongest subjects in the kingdom of Metz, aroused the fear and rancour of the defeated queen, who held the *leudes* responsible for the disasters of the last few years, as they held her responsible both for the war itself and for the consequences which followed from it. In 598 Duke Wintrion was assassinated by the hirelings of Brunhilda. From that time her position became untenable; she was compelled to flee from Metz, and took refuge with her younger grandson Theodoric II., a boy of twelve, who ruled in Burgundy. The elder son, Theodebert II, sat on the throne of Metz. Both were loyally served by their *leudes*, and Clotair, who seems to have been quite ready for the *rôle* of usurper, was driven back as he advanced along the Gâtinais plains, between the Loire and the Yonne.

The brothers now turned their attention to the south-western corner of Gaul, the old Novempopulania—the original Aquitania—which had been left by Clovis unsubdued. It had recently been overrun by the Vascons from Northern Spain, who had never owned the sway of the Visigoths. Theodebert and Theodoric mastered the country without much difficulty, and appointed a duke to govern it (602). From that time forward this interesting country, which includes Navarre and Béarn, and the Basque descendants of one of the most obscure of the Asiatic migrations, has followed the fortunes of the Franks and of the French.

But whilst the kings were building up their father's realm, their grandmother was still plotting mischief and weaving disaster. Brunhilda had so far secured an influence over the Burgundian clergy that in a synod in 603, held at Châlon on the Saone, they deposed and banished the bishop of Vienne. Didier returned to the see a few years later, only to be assassinated by order of the relentless old woman. Worse than this, she sowed dissension between Theodebert and his brother, the latter of whom was encouraged to make war upon the king of Metz. It was not until 610 that the sons of Childebert opposed each other in the field. Theodoric was successful in two battles, fought at Toul and Tolbiac; and he crowned his victory by slaying Theodebert and his family. Pushing on to Metz, he enjoyed there for a few months the triumph of his trebled kingdom, and there he died (613).

Clotair soon arrived on the spot at the head of his

army. Brunhilda encouraged a part of the forces which had followed her grandson to make a stand on behalf of his illegitimate son Childebert; and, no doubt, she did her best to avoid falling into the hands of Clotair. But the son of Fredegonda, now fairly entitled to the sole dominion of the Franks, swept

REALM OF THE FRANKS UNDER CLOTAIR II. (613).

aside the partisans of Childebert, seized the unhappy creature whom the atrocities of his own mother had tortured into a malevolent fiend, and stamped her out of existence with barbarous cruelty.

Clotair II. was the third king of the Franks who exercised sole dominion over the conquests of his race in Germany and Gaul. He did not exercise it long. Even before his death in 628, he made his eldest son Dagobert king of the eastern half of Francia. Clotair thus practically recognised the broad distinctions existing between the comparatively unmixed Germans who lived in the Oster Ric, or Reich, and the amalgam of Kelts, Romans, and Franks, who inhabited the country which Germans learned to call the Frank Reich, whilst the Gallicised Franks accepted the Latin form of Francia, France. The continuator of Gregory's history transforms Oster Ric, dropping the guttural, into Austria, wherein both of the German words are more than half concealed. From the time of the third partition of the Frank realm—which, as we have seen, took place during the life of Clotair II.—it is correct enough to speak of the eastern and western halves as Austria and Neustria. The frontier between the two was not rigidly fixed. When Clotair assigned Austria to Dagobert, he retained Soissons, Paris, Orléans, Burgundy, Provence, Aquitaine. On his death, Dagobert was king both of Austria and of Neustria, though a kingdom made up of Provence and Aquitaine was for three years under the rule of his younger brother Caribert. As a rule, the old kingdom of Burgundy fell within or followed the fortunes of the Neustrian State. In 633 Dagobert followed Clotair's example in making his son Siegbert, at the age of three, nominal king of Austria, a still younger son, Clovis, being styled king of Neustria (with Burgundy). This anticipation of the heirship was probably an attempt to avoid some of the evils which had followed participation by lot.

The idea of empire, it will be observed, was of slow growth in the minds of the Franks. Indeed, the eastern and western empires of Rome had not supplied them with many arguments in favour of a centralised government of widespread dominions, nor was the organisation of their provinces and towns, especially outside of Gaul, sufficiently advanced to encourage a military ruler to try an experiment after the Roman model. Of course there had been local organisation in Gaul, both within and without the Church, before the Goths, Burgundians, and Franks overran the country; and the local subordination which had guaranteed a large measure of public order for settled communities was not likely to be destroyed by the invaders, since to them it guaranteed revenue as well as order. Apart from the dislocations of actual war, and such capricious or punitive dispossessions as the invaders would have recourse to when they appropriated land for themselves and their followers, the old state of things would be continued for all who paid their taxes, rendered their services, distributed their merchandise, or plied their trades. Some landowners would contrive to hold their own; some cities would escape the destructive flood and preserve their municipal privileges. And we know that, at any rate so far as the names and fashions of the Roman *duces* and *comites* were concerned, the Franks accepted them willingly enough. It is impossible to feel much confidence as to the precise duties of the Frank dukes and counts, or as to the precise limits of their authority, though we know that these duties were at different times military, civil, and judicial, and that the titles were of wide geographical application. We read in the sixth and seventh centuries of dukes of Champagne, Toulouse, and even Aquitaine, counts of Brittany, Laon, &c., lords or seigneurs corresponding to the old senatorial landowners, and to the *leudes* of the Frank courts, with others of inferior wealth and standing, and patricians (especially in Provence) who owed their titles of honour to Byzantium, but were recognised as being of noble rank by the Frank kings whose subjects they became.

XIV.

THE MAYORS OF THE PALACE.

From the beginning of the seventh century the history of the Franks includes more and more frequent mention of certain honourable and influential persons associated in the government of the country, to whom it is now necessary that we should devote special attention. These are the Mayors of the Palace.

The Major Domus, or Magister Palatii, was a functionary appointed during the last century and a half of the Merovingian dynasty to exercise authority in the palace and household of the king. The term itself was borrowed from the old imperial *régime*. The office, under the Franks, was the creation of circumstances; the officer, who would be able to relieve a strong king of some of the more irksome of his duties, would be indispensable when the king was fighting at a distance from his principal palaces, or when he was a minor. It would be necessary that his authority and his administrative power should extend over the *leudes;* and thus he would inevitably be, from the beginning, the most important man in the kingdom, after the king. It cannot be said with certainty who was the first Frank Mayor of the Palace, or under what circumstances he was appointed. The office doubtless existed before the Latin name: the most influential of the king's *leudes* may have discharged such functions as those just mentioned soon after the house of Merowig was established at Soissons, or, at any rate, soon after Clovis extended his kingdom to the western sea. Whether the Mayor increased in authority step by step from small beginnings, or—as is more likely—was established by the *leudes* as a check on the abuse of power by the king and his family, at all events we first hear of him at a time when some check of this kind was absolutely necessary.

It seems probable that the simultaneous presence of the two queen-mothers, Brunhilda and Fredegonda, in the two palaces of Metz and Tournai, and the extraordinary part which they played in the affairs of the Franks, did more than anything else to call the office into existence, or to give it its special importance. Certain it is that the strong line of Mayors of the Palace in the seventh and eighth centuries led ultimately to the downfall of the Merovingian dynasty. Both Fredegonda and Brunhilda had been seriously embroiled with the *leudes* of their sons or grandsons. The Franks were well accustomed to the counsels and even to the strictures of their women; but, as the Salic law excluded women from succession to estates, so the fighting men and the court officers, the judges, administrators, and clergy, would be sure to watch with jealousy, and seriously to resent, the endless intrigues and disastrous machinations of the queens. Fredegonda was more than once in danger from the *leudes* at Tournai. Brunhilda's quarrel with the *leudes* at Metz came to a crisis, as we have seen, by her compassing the death of Duke Wintrion of Champagne, and being driven out of the country in the following year (599).

During the minority of Childebert, about the year 575, the Major Domus was in no sense the king's creature and instrument, or his appointed representative with the *leudes ;* he became rather the representative of the aristocracy at the court, and the overseer of the king. In this change the power of the aristocracy was making itself felt, though the innovation was strenuously resisted by a monarch here and there, and doggedly opposed by the queen Brunhilda, until her party was defeated, and she herself was captured by Clotair. Clotair, as we have seen, united the Frank kingdoms under his sway, but even he was forced by the Austrian and Burgundian aristocracies to promise that he would not interfere in the elections of the Mayors of the Palace. He swore, moreover, to Warnaher, Mayor of Burgundy, and Rade of Austria, not to dispossess them of their offices. According to a chronicler, Clotair was a "patient" monarch, and he seems to have played his cards with considerable success. On the death of Warnaher, in 626, he asked the Burgundians if they would elect a new Mayor. This invitation, as Clotair had doubtless anticipated, they declined, asking that they might be allowed to treat separately with the king. The return to the old system, however, brought about a state of aggravated anarchy and disunion much more serious than the internal dissensions which existed at the same time in Austria, where the continuance of the mayoralty formed a kind of national balance of powers.

Clotair II. died in 628, and was succeeded by his son Dagobert. Dagobert contrived to keep his brother Charibert out of his inheritance, and in 630 was in full enjoyment of authority. But the aristocracy was distinctly against him, though the prudence of Pepin of Landen, the Mayor of Austria, restrained them from openly breaking with the king. At length, under pressure of an invasion of the Slavonians (633), Dagobert agreed to recognise a separate government for Austria, and he nominated as king his three-year-old son, Siegbert II., with Grimoald, son of Pepin, and Otho to manage the kingdom, while Pepin was to live in Neustria.

Dagobert was one of the most kingly monarchs of the Merovingian line, and the little that we are told of him creates the desire to know considerably more. He revised and promulgated the laws of the Franks, and was a patron of the ecclesiastical scholars and artists of his day. He fought many battles, most of them successfully, headed an expedition into Spain, suppressed a revolt of the Gascons, and broke the growing power of the kings of Brittany. Amongst his ministers were S. Audoenus (Ouen), his chancellor, and S. Eligius (Eloi), his "magister nummorum," a famous worker in gold, who designed and adorned many thrones (including that of Dagobert), tombs (including that of S. Germain, bishop of Paris), and other details of church and palace architecture, with the taste of a true artist. Though he had never

REPUTED THRONE OF DAGOBERT.
(*The Work of S. Eligius; restored by Suger in the twelfth century.*)

been ordained, Eligius was made bishop of Noyon; he founded several abbeys, and was long held in peculiar reverence. To swear by Saint Eloy, as Chaucer tells us, was held a venial oath for nuns and friars. He seems to have been an artist in words as well as in gold, and left behind him a number of popular homilies. His life was written by his friend S. Ouen, and is preserved for us in the "Spicilegium" of the Benedictine bookworm Achéry.

Dagobert's death in 638 marked the beginning of a series of Merovingian *rois fainéants*, lasting for about a century. Dagobert himself had shown something of the earlier Merovingian force in an attempt to impose Christianity upon the Frisians, and he founded the first Christian church at Utrecht. Ega, who had been appointed by Dagobert guardian of his infant son Clovis, now became Mayor of Neustria, whilst Pepin returned to Metz. In the following year Grimoald, on the death of his father, secured the position of sole Major Domus of Austria, though only after considerable trouble from Otho, described as the "bajulus"[1] of Siegbert, who was slain in 642 by a partisan of Grimoald's. Some years later Grimoald caused Dagobert, son of Siegbert, to be shorn and sent to Ireland, while he set his own child, Childebert, on the throne. The mass of the people, however, refused to recognise this act, and finally both father and son were slain. Grimoald met the fate of many prescient persons who are too eager to assist the natural course of evolution. He had

---

[1] That is, "baillivus de palatio"—a different office from that of "magister de palatio," or major domus. Some have regarded "seneschal" (seniscalcus) as a quasi-Teutonic equivalent of "major domus." But it is unnecessary to look for such an equivalent. Latin was freely used at the Frank court before the office was created.

anticipated coming events by something like a century.

The table on the opposite page (which should be compared with that at the end of the twelfth Chapter) shows the descent of the hereditary mayors of the family of Pepin of Landen, who were the ancestors of the Carolingian Franks. Landen is a town of Liège in Belgium, close to the present border of Brabant, and about thirty miles due west of Tongres.

Siegbert of Austria died in the year 656, and Erkinoald, who was then Mayor of Neustria, succeeded in making Clovis II., and after him his son Clotair III., sole king of the Franks.[1] When Erkinoald died in 657, Ebroin was elected Mayor by the Neustrian vote. But the union of the kingdoms did not long remain firm, for in 660 the Austrians demanded that Childeric, second son of Clovis, should be sent to Metz, and Wulfoald was elected Mayor. Ebroin made violent struggles to maintain his position, until he was finally slain in 681.

In 673 the Austrians recalled Dagobert from Ireland, and made him king. He was disinclined to play the part of *roi fainéant*, and an insurrection, headed by Pepin of Héristal, the nephew of Grimoald, and his cousin, Duke Martin, ended in his death. In 679 the Merovingian monarchy virtually disappeared from Eastern Francia. From the year just mentioned Austria was governed by an aristocracy headed by the cousins, of whom Martin, however, was slain in the next struggle with Neustria. Pepin had better

[1] See the genealogical table, p. 179.

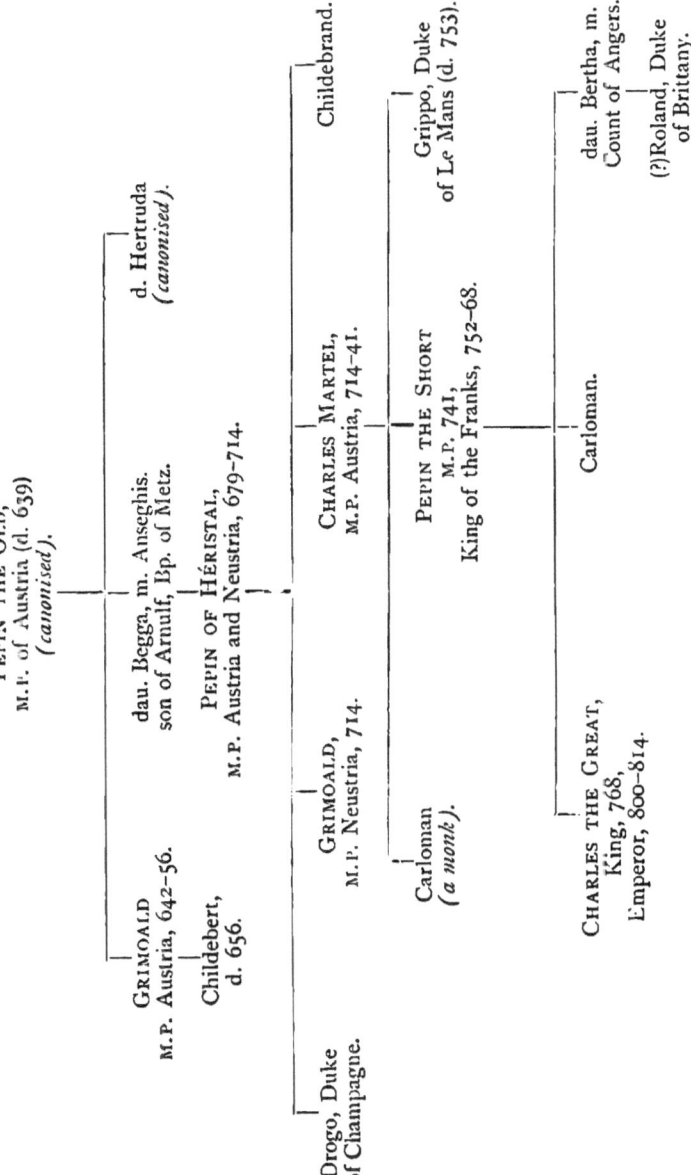

fortune, and, after the death of Ebroin, he practically ruled both countries. He continued to recognise Theodoric as king, while taking on himself the government of Neustria, the control of the royal treasures, and the supreme command of the army. Under the title of Mayor of the Palace he governed until his death in 714. After this event, Neustria broke into open revolt. Pepin of Héristal's widow, Pletruda, cast his natural son Charles (Martel) into a dungeon, and set out for Neustria with a force drawn from the *leudes* of Pepin and Grimoald, apparently designing to govern under cover of the name of the young Dagobert III. The Neustrians, however, cut this force to pieces, and the Austrians were for a time in great danger. Charles, fortunately for them, managed to escape from his prison, and rallied round him the Austrian army, with whose aid in 717-9 he utterly crushed the Neustrians, and was then recognised as Duke of Austria. According to Fredegarius he had enthroned Clotair IV., of whose parentage we are ignorant, and who did not survive the fourth year of his nominal reign at Metz.

Charles began at an early age to display those qualities of impetuosity and sustained force, both in fighting and in the exercise of government, that were to earn for him the title of Martel. He never accepted defeat, but, like his grandson after him, struck again and again until his purpose was accomplished. Scarcely had he triumphed over the Neustrians when it became necessary for him to turn his attention to his German neighbours on the east. Still maintaining the hereditary Merovingian puppet on the throne—Theodoric IV., a boy of seven, succeeding Chilperic II. of Neustria in 720—he played in every other respect the part of king, and in particular led the armies of the Franks to victory against their enemies. Saxons, Bavarians, and Allemans successively felt the weight of his heavy hand. Fresh troubles arose and were quelled in Neustria. Aquitaine, never yet wholly restful under the sway of its conquerors, defied the son of Pepin more or less openly for several years. In the Frisian lands, in Burgundy and Provence, this greatest of the Mayors reasserted the supremacy of the Franks, and confirmed the power which the effete Merovingians were no longer able to wield.

But the crowning triumph of Charles Martel was gained over the encroaching Saracens, who in 730 began to pour into Aquitaine, and who soon overran Gascony and Septimania. Odo, the Duke of Aquitaine, was now only too glad to appeal to the warlike Mayor of Austria. Charles led an army across the Loire, and found the Saracens advanced as far as the plain country lying to the north of Poitiers. Here, in October, 732, he overthrew them in a famous victory, and turned the tide of infidel conquest in Western Europe. The Saracens fled southwards again, but they continued to hold Avignon, Narbonne, and other towns on the Mediterranean seaboard. As soon as Charles had settled other difficulties on the north and east of the Austrian kingdom, he marched once more against the Moslems, took Avignon in 737, and drove the Saracens from the neighbourhood of Narbonne. He was now the acknowledged champion of Christendom, and Gregory III. sent an embassy from Rome, soliciting his aid against the Lombards. It cannot, however, be said that Charles was popular in his character as a champion. He levied toll of those whom he assisted, as conquerors have frequently found themselves compelled to do; and his *leudes* are said to have been enriched at the expense of the Church.

Both Pepin of Héristal and his warlike son renewed the attempt of Dagobert to subdue and Christianise the Frisians. Charles Martel so far succeeded that Radbod, the Frisian duke, consented to undergo the rite of baptism. But Radbod admitted a qualm of conscience at a fatal moment. Standing with one foot in the font, he suddenly turned round to the presiding bishop, Wolfran, and said, "Where are my ancestors who have gone before me?" "They are in hell," said Wolfran, "with other infidels." "Good," said Radbod, as he withdrew from the water; "I had rather feast with my forefathers in the halls of Woden than live in heaven with those fasting little Christians of yours" The chance was gone, and Charles had to do his fighting over again. He defeated Poppo, the son of Radbod, in 750; but it remained for Charles the Great to bring the double work of subjugation to an end.

Charles was not destined to see Rome, nor yet to work out the problem of kingship in Austria. He died in his fifty-second year (741), leaving three sons, Carloman, Pepin, and Grippo. During the next few years Carloman and Pepin signalised their accession to the government of Austria and Neustria by repeating the achievements of their father in Allemania, Bavaria, Saxony, and Aquitaine; whilst Childeric III.—another puppet of unknown parentage, the last of his family—had been brought from a convent and crowned king of Austria. In 747 Carloman assumed the cowl, and the authority of Pepin (distinguished from others of his name as Pepin le Bref, owing to the shortness of his stature) was recognised throughout the Frank dominions.

It has been suggested by some writers, though on insufficient evidence, that Childebrand, the younger brother of Charles Martel, was the ancestor of Hugues Capet, the first King of France.

In 752 Pepin considered that the fitting moment had arrived for setting the crown of Francia on his head. Childeric was of so little account in his kingdom that no strong opposition was to be feared from him or his friends; but there was more reason to hesitate over the jealousy which might be aroused on the part of the Frank aristocracy. It is possible that encouragement had already been given to the ambition of Pepin by the ecclesiastics, by the memory of Pope Gregory's appeal to his father, and by the growing perplexities of Pope Stephen. At any rate the last of the Mayors could reckon on the powerful influence of the Church. And so the fateful step was taken; Childeric was hustled off to another convent, and Pepin became King of the Franks.

We may note, before concluding this chapter, what Sismondi has to say in his "History of the French" concerning the origin of the Mayors. Fredegarius, or a writer to whom this name has been given, speaks of the election of a Mayor during the minority of Siegbert I.; but, as Siegbert was never a minor, Sismondi concludes that the chronicler was thinking of Childebert II. (561–75), and that at any rate he is to be trusted as proving that the Franks, not later than 575, elected their own officers to represent their interests at the court of the king. "The nation sometimes dispensed with the election, but, when it did nominate a Mayor, it was for the purpose of subjecting the nobles to discipline," when the king was not yet, or no longer, able to control them.

Sismondi goes on to say that "a name translated from one language to another has been the cause of a long-lived error about the functions of this officer." He believes that a confusion arose, and was allowed to grow up, between the "mord-dom," or judge in cases of murder, and the "Major Domus," or chief domestic officer of the court. Gregory, in fact, calls Waddon, manifestly an officer of the latter kind, major domus. Bandegisil, bishop of Le Mans from 581 to 586, is also named in Gregory's chronicle under the same title, though he would certainly not have been elected by the Franks to control the *leudes*.

The fact remains that, as early as the sixth century, the title of Major Domus was given to the controlling, popularly elected officers—to the officer mentioned by Fredegarius, to Duke Wintrion or Quintrion, elected after the death of Chilperic of Soissons, in 584, and to a similar officer elected by the Burgundians after the death of Gontran, nine years later.

XV.

ROME APPEALS TO THE FRANKS.

BEFORE we follow the history of the Franks under the Carolingians it will be well if we turn aside for a moment, and glance at the position of affairs in Italy, at the increasing temporal and spiritual authority of the Roman Church, and at the waning influence of the Byzantine Empire in the concerns of Western Europe.

We have already seen how Narses, who came to Italy in 582, on the mandate of the Emperor Justinian, triumphed over the last efforts of the Gothic invaders, and hurled back the hordes of Allemans, Bavarians, Franks, and others who followed in their train. The long agony of Rome and Italy, assailed in succession by so many ruthless foes, had left the land too feeble to resist another and a fiercer visitation. The Langobards, who in the general shifting of the German tribes had for some time found a temporary home in Pannonia, now poured through the passes of the Rhætian Alps, and overran the country whose name of Lombardy still bears witness to their presence. Alboin, who crossed the frontier in 568, had in a few years fixed his seat at Pavia; and it was against his successor that the gallant Childebert, urged alike by emperor and pope, vainly contended between the years 584 and 590. The Lombards made good their footing, and withstood all attempts to expel them. The empire was now but weakly and formally represented in Italy by the Exarch of Ravenna; though correspondence was still maintained between the popes and the emperors, with little practical outcome. The very names of the former Roman government were rapidly passing away: consuls and senate had ceased to exist, *consulares* and *præsides* were no longer appointed under the Exarch Longinus (567), and there was no further significance in such terms as those of the præfecture of Italy or the vicariates of Italy and Rome. Nevertheless in the seventh century *judices* were still appointed under the supervision of the bishops, and the military terms of *duces*, *magistri militum*, and *tribuni* continued to imply much the same thing as they had signified for centuries past.[1] But in Italy, as in Gaul, the dukes assumed with their territorial titles an element of fixity which tended steadily towards hereditary transmission.

The Lombards seized practically the whole of Italy. Only Rome, Ravenna, and other ports to which succour could more easily be dispatched, maintained or purchased immunity from the ruthless barbarians. It has been said that necessity had made the bishops of Rome her advocates, and was soon to make them her rulers. At all events the Eternal City had at this

[1] Cf. Gregorovius, bk. ii. ch. 7.

time no leadership or protection except such as was furnished to her by the Church. The first of the Gregories more than once turned back the besieging Lombards by using the all-prevailing "silver spears" with which the patrimonies of the Church supplied him—for Christian Rome was already a wealthy temporal, as well as a spiritual, power, though her wide domains had not yet acquired the political authority of a State.

This Gregory it was who sent Augustine on his mission to England; and he and his successors never ceased to labour for the conversion of the Lombards to the Orthodox faith. With scanty help and sympathy from the exarchs at Ravenna—on whom, as representatives of the imperial power, the popes at this time depended for the ratification of their election —Rome continued her faithful struggle against the barbarians. After her ineffectual efforts to expel the Lombards from Italy by the aid of the Orthodox kings, she waged throughout the seventh century a spiritual war, alike against the barbarism and against the heresy of the half-converted Arians. Early in the eighth century, in the pontificate of John VII., Aribert the Lombard restored to Rome the estates of which the first invaders had robbed her; and henceforth the countrymen of Alboin may be regarded as an Orthodox and a civilised nation.

Yet in the next generation we find the Church of Rome, with its rapidly developing temporal authority, opposed to two rival powers, either of which in the preceding century she would have found it impossible to withstand. Under Gregory II. Rome was virtually at war with the Emperor, Leo the Isaurian, and with the Lombard king. Liutprand, aiming at a kingdom of united Italy seized Ravenna and advanced against Rome; and once more the wealth of the Church and the diplomacy of its spiritual head availed to save the Eternal City. A second time, in 729, Liutprand approached the walls of Aurelian, and a second time, more dramatically than before, Gregory raised the sacred symbol of his authority, and put his enemy to flight.

The awe of the Lombard was soon dissipated; for, seeing a new energy in Gregory III., who opposed his schemes with new intrigues and alliances, he made a third advance upon Rome in 739. It was now that the Pope, fortifying his belief in the divine authority of the Church by an appeal to the sword of the faithful, bethought him of the conqueror of the Saracens, and invoked the aid of Charles Martel. He wrote two letters to the son of Pepin, entreating him to defend the Holy Church, his spiritual mother. But the appeal was in vain. The Franks may not have cared at that time to attack their Teuton race-fellows, or may not have been convinced that the quarrel of Rome with a Christian king was either sacred or just. It is doubtful whether Charles would have changed his mind if he had lived. Both he and Gregory passed away in 741; and Liutprand, after disarming Gregory's successor by a not very honourable treaty—whereby the Pope abandoned his former allies—died in the following year. It was the year of the birth of Charles the Great.

Nine years later, towards the close of the prosperous

pontificate of Zacharias, Ravenna once again fell into the hands of the Lombards. Astolf, pursuing the ambitions of his predecessors, expelled Eutychius (751), declared himself successor to the Byzantine exarchs, and demanded the submission of Rome. The threats of Liutprand were repeated; Rome was in imminent danger of siege and massacre; no aid could be expected from the emperor, who had been unable to prevent the extinction of the exarchate. In these dire straits, Pope Stephen II. appealed (753) to the son of Charles Martel, who had recently assumed the title of king. Pepin welcomed an invitation which chimed so well with his own needs. Stephen travelled to Paris, and there, at S. Denis, consecrated Pepin, his wife, and his two sons; whilst Pepin undertook (in the Treaty of Kiersey) to defend Rome against the Lombards, and to restore Ravenna, with the five cities lying further to the south which had formerly owned allegiance to Byzantium.

So the wolf of the Hercynian Forest was called in to protect and nourish the Eternal City, precisely the same number of years after the birth of Christ as had elapsed, when Christ was born, since the foster-son of the Palatine wolf had laid its foundations.

Pepin and his sons received the title of "Patricius Romanorum"; and the honours bestowed by the Pope upon the usurper of Childeric's throne were doubtless considered by the Franks, or at any rate by the most devout Christians amongst the Franks, as an additional confirmation of his right to rule over them. Astolf, who was under no illusion as to the formidable character of the Pope's new champion, prevailed on

Carloman, the monk of Monte Casino, to induce his brother to come to terms. But Carloman travelled no further than the city of Vienne, where he died—as did also the deposed Childeric—in the same year; and Pepin, who had held a council of his *leudes* at the royal palace of Braisne, advanced against the Lombard, and defeated him at Susa and at Pavia. Receiving the eastern cities from Astolf as the spoils of war, he immediately conferred them upon "the Republic of the Romans," by deed of gift. This gift is to be regarded as the foundation of the temporal dominion known as the States of the Church; for such sovereignty as the Emperor had latterly wielded over Eastern Rome was now virtually, if not formally, at an end.

Pepin was every whit as energetic and as warlike as his father had been before him, and as his son was to be after him. He completed the overthrow of the Saracens in Septimania, and of the Germans who had rebelled in Bavaria. He exchanged embassies with the Emperor in Constantinople, inflicted a fresh defeat on the Saxons, and put down with a strong hand, though not without fighting a series of campaigns, the opposition which had been raised against him in Aquitaine by his half-brother Grippo (the son of Charles Martel by a Saxon captive). Shortly after the close of this war, his eventful reign of sixteen years, which laid a solid basis for the victories of his more famous son, came to an end, and the first of the crowned Carolingians passed away.

We have now arrived at a specially interesting crisis in the story of the Franks. Two hundred years in Gaul, with almost undisputed supremacy on both sides of the Rhine, close contact with Roman civilisation, the increase of social ease and legal stability, the life of cities and courts—boons of partial civilisation to which the Christian Church had added its precepts and pomps, its discipline and brotherhood, its amenities and culture—had brought out the best qualities of this vanguard of the Teutonic race, and converted the valiant barbarian into a man of comparative refinement and dignity. The Merovingian Franks, with their cruelty, their truculence, their unrelenting feuds, their unscrupulous and bloodthirsty methods of self-advancement, were giving way, under the Pepins and the Karls, to Franks of equally vigorous self-assertion, but of greater restraint in victory, of less ungovernable fury, of more equable manners, and of a certain instalment of culture. If anything could have saved the world from the worst of its trouble to come, from the submergence of letters, the corruption of Christian faith and practice, the inundation of Asiatic barbarism, and the constant seething of Europe in national and sectional warfare, the young Teutonic nationalities might have effected it. Under Charles in the eighth century, as under the English Alfred in the ninth century, if there was not much settled peace, there was at any rate the encouragement and patronage of learning, with some advance in craftsmanship, art, social comfort and refinements, and the various incidents of civilisation. The growth was more or less continuous in the cities, where it had its root in the old Roman colonies and other settlements, and where from the same stock it was to flower luxuriantly in the Renaissance. But if the growth persisted, it was for a long time choked and starved, so that for centuries the light of learning seemed almost to have been extinguished, and the partial culture of the courts of Charlemagne and Alfred seem to the casual observer like the flame of a candle in the darkness.

The causes of this inevitable relapse are neither remote nor obscure, but they cannot be fully dealt with in this volume. The subject would be too large even for suggestion if it were not important to bear in mind that the Franks, the Angles and Saxons, the Goths and the Lombards, did show themselves, up to a certain point, susceptible of the classical culture, and a polish which, under happier circumstances, might have developed a literature, an art, an orderly system of national and municipal government. But the conditions in which they lived rendered such development partial and transient. Society was exposed to sudden and violent changes. The lives and fortunes of men, their very food and domicile, depended on the physical prowess of those who were free, and on the constant labour of those who were in a state of servitude. There was scarcely a year of intermission, throughout the reign of Charles, from internal or external war. In the forty-five years between his accession and his death, Charles and his sons waged fifty-two campaigns. The Saxon war alone lasted thirty-five years. The Frank Emperor of the West fought in every country of Western, Central, and Southern Europe, and he fought not only with his brother Teutons, but also with the Eastern Huns, the

Slavonians, the Saracens, and the Africans. If for a time he checked the advancing hordes of Asia and Africa, he was not able to raise a durable barrier against them.

When Charles came to the throne—or at any rate three years later, on the death of his brother Carloman—he found himself at the head of a nation which already presented many of the characteristics of what was afterwards known as the feudal organisation. There was, indeed, this grand distinction in the tenure of land, before feudal tenure became a rule, that the estates of the king's *leudes*, and other important and wealthy men, obtained by gift or purchase, were held by an absolute title, in " franc-alleud,"[1] on allodial tenure, and descended from father to son. The owners of allodial estates bore their share of the public burdens, and they followed the king to war, as a matter of course in an age when it was almost the first duty of manhood to fight. But military service was not the exclusive condition of tenure. Treason—and refusal to follow the royal standard when summoned might, of course, be construed as treason—involved the forfeiture of these estates to the king; but it is evident that the conversion of franc-alleud into a tenure-in-chief became a comparatively simple matter.

Military tenure in Gaul, as we have seen, was at least as old as the grant of lands to the Læti, who were German auxiliaries in the Roman army. Such grants were made to other than Germans, and when

[1] Old High German *allod*, Latinised as *allodium*. An equivalent German form was *od all:* hence *adel*, the nobility.

the Franks had established themselves in Gaul their kings very naturally continued the custom. The first Clotair was induced to ordain that an estate which had been held on these terms for thirty years should become the absolute property of the holder. Even such as were already in possession of allodial estates received *beneficia* of land as rewards for particular services, and converted them into absolute property in a similar fashion, thus gradually acquiring broad domains which conferred upon them, virtually or actually, something near akin to the rights of sovereignty. Charles and his immediate successors were strong enough to impose or to restore the military and other duties attaching to the tenure of land, as well as to add stringency to the old German conditions of vassalage; and thus it was that, in the ninth century, the feudal organisation became a potent reality.

In addition to the holders of land, there were, of course, other classes of freemen amongst the subjects over whom Charles was called to rule. Such were the citizens, merchants, and functionaries of a higher order; descendants of urban and rural colonists who had contrived to retain their freedom; vassals of the king and of the greater or smaller landlords; ecclesiastics and men under their tutelage; *capitales*, who paid an annual due for the patronage of others; *lites*, who rendered domestic or agricultural service without being actually serfs; and enfranchised serfs, who passed into one or other class of freemen, according to the circumstances of their enfranchisement.

It is scarcely necessary to add that the serfs, as recognised by the Franks—and the institution survived even to the date of the great Revolution—were not so utterly degraded as the Roman slaves had been. The counter-civilisation bestowed by the Teuton upon the Roman, of which we have already noted conspicuous instances, is nowhere better illustrated than in the treatment which the Teuton accorded to his slave. So far as the observation of Tacitus went, Germans did not employ their slaves in menial duties to minister to their personal ease; each slave had a dwelling and a home of his own; he tilled the land and paid dues to his master, but the rest of his time and labour was his own. He supported his wife and family, lived much in common with freemen, and was able in a large measure to preserve his self-respect. It was a rare thing for a German to strike his slave; and the chief right and defence secured by a freedman was that his former master would thenceforth have to pay a fine for killing him. When the Franks settled in Gaul, it was not amongst the slaves of the Gallo-Romans that the new domination would be most unwelcome.

No doubt an institution like that of serfdom is liable to constant deteriorations. Serfdom in France was never more odious, relatively if not actually, than it was in the eighteenth century; but already in the time of the Merovingians the laws affecting slaves had borrowed harshness from the Roman codes. The beneficence of the Gallic Church, which was constantly exercised in defence of the poor and the wretched, succoured the slaves as it had previously succoured those who were ground down by over-taxation. The clergy preached, the bishops remonstrated and insisted, the annual Councils formulated their demands —which, appealing to Divine authority, were virtually decrees—in the interests of humanity. Churches, abbeys, and monasteries, stood ever open as asylums for the oppressed; and at one of the Councils held at Lyon, early in the sixth century, the bishops were enjoined to excommunicate any master who killed his slave without giving him the opportunity of defence. The public law reinforced the law of the Church. In the time of Charles a slave could not be sold into a foreign country, nor by a Christian to a pagan, nor even at home by Christian to Christian, except under a prescribed form, and in the presence of witnesses.

On the death of King Pepin, the realm which he had usurped and maintained, which he and his father before him had saved before collapsing under the weak hands of the later Merovingians, was once more in danger of falling to pieces. Charles was twenty-six years old: his brother Carloman was a year or two younger; and it is to be remembered that there was now no Mayor to assist the monarch, or represent him in his absence. Both Charles and Carloman were consecrated, the former at Noyon, and the latter at Soissons. There seems to have been a feeling of rivalry between them from the beginning, which soon broke out into an open quarrel. By a strange coincidence the same Duke Hunald of Aquitaine whose revolt had been put down by Pepin and his brother Carloman, and who had retired into a monastery three years before Carloman decided on the same course, now threw off his cowl and sought to avenge the death of his son Waifre, whom Pepin had slain in 768. The sons of Pepin advanced against him, but their association in arms did not continue as long as that of their father and uncle. Carloman withdrew in dudgeon, and left his brother to face the Aquitanians alone. It was hardly less fatal to his career as a king and a soldier than if he also had determined to enter a monastery.

Charles persevered, and won his first campaign. Hunald was taken prisoner; and it may have been due to the magnanimity of his captor that the pugnacious monk was able to escape with his life, and take refuge with Desiderius, king of the Lombards. Shortly after his victory in Aquitaine, Charles married the daughter of Desiderius, by whom he had no child, and whom he repudiated and sent back to her father. By a former wife, Himiltrude, he had a son Pepin, nicknamed Le Bossu, who subsequently rebelled against him.

The queen-mother, Bertha, succeeded in reconciling her two sons. Before they had time to quarrel again, or to give proof that their reconciliation was complete, Carloman died (771); and his Austrian *leudes*, meeting at Cobény, not far from Reims, passed over the sons of their deceased monarch, and elected Charles in his stead. It was another mark of progressive civilisation that the widow of Carloman should be allowed to take her sons to the court of Desiderius at Pavia. Charles, we are told, considered their flight as a matter with which he need not concern himself. Between himself and Desiderius there were now three separate causes of grudging, apart from the political heritage which had descended to Charles from his father — the repudiation of Desiderata by Charles, and the welcome accorded by the Lombard king to Waifre and to the sons of Carloman.

XVI.

CHARLES THE GREAT.

CHARLES was now sole king of the Franks, able to indulge his dreams of ambition—dreams which assuredly were neither few nor humble, though he may not have set his mind from the beginning upon imperial dignity.

From his father Pepin he had inherited a crown won by the sword, which it was necessary that he should keep with the sword. That, in itself, was no light task; but he had also inherited quarrels with most of the surrounding peoples—with the Saxons and Bavarians and Lombards, with the Saracens and the Moors. These quarrels he undoubtedly meant to take up; and behind the Lombard quarrel there was the far-reaching question of the championship of Rome. He, like his father, was a Patricius of Rome; he had been consecrated by the Pope, and he took an early opportunity of sending his two sons, Louis and Pepin, by his third wife the Suabian Hildegard, for the papal benediction.

The most urgent need of the moment was to protect the eastern frontiers against the constant attacks of the Saxons, who, pressed behind by Northmen and Slavonians, were apparently bent on renewing the ancient Rhine war, and wresting from their ancestral allies a portion, at least, of their hard-won possessions. Since the outflow of Saxons, Angles, and Frisians to Britain, the Saxons who remained had extended their name and influence from the Baltic to within a few miles of the Rhine, at its confluence with the Lippe, and from the mouths of the Weser and the Elbe to the borders of Thuringia. Charles was anxious to turn southwards into Italy, but he was unwilling to leave in his rear a nation of so much vigour and pugnacity without fighting the first campaign in what he fully intended to be a definitive and conclusive war.

The campaign against the Saxons in 772 was dramatic in its circumstances, and it illustrated at the outset of his career some of the traits of genius which earned for Charles the title of Great. As a general he was the flower of the Frank race, and displayed their best fighting qualities to perfection: the unexpected and dashing attack, the combination of furious hand-to-hand encounters with an extremely agile recovery, and the annually-repeated expeditions —continued as they had been by the earlier Franks for generations, and even for centuries. There is no reason to doubt that Charles had resolved on war *à outrance* with the Saxons, and that his first campaign was specially calculated to make such a war inevitable. For in this struggle there was something else involved beside the determination of the Frank to hold his own, and to strengthen and extend his boundaries. Charles was by inheritance the chief defender of the Church; he knew how much the Franks owed to the Pope and the bishops, and how the friendship of Rome made for the security of his realm. It was therefore a part of his policy to utilise to the utmost this instrument which Clovis and his successors had found so serviceable. His aim was not only to subdue but to Christianise the Saxons; and he began by striking a blow at their national pride and their national religion. After consulting the general assembly of the Franks at Worms, he crossed the Rhine, marched up the course of the Lippe, laid the land waste with fire and sword, took the fort of Ehresburg, a little above Paderborn, and "threw down the idol which the Saxons called Irminsul." The course of the Lippe skirts the southern extremity of the Teutoburg Wald. It appears reasonable to conclude that Irminsul was the Hermann's Pillar (Säule) set up to commemorate the hero of the Teutons who, seven and a half centuries before, had entrapped and annihilated the legions of Varus, and arrested the progress of Roman conquest in Germany.[1] Whether treated as an idol or not, this pillar would represent whatever was strongest in the collective feelings of the North Germans; and its deliberate destruction by Charles must be taken as showing how completely the king of the Franks had imbued himself with the ideas of Southern and Western civilisation,

---

[1] Some, however, think that it was an idol of Irmin, a national god. A new pillar was set up in its place eleven centuries later.

and how ruthlessly as a Christian he could trample on the sacred traditions of his race.

Almost yearly now, for a generation to come, there was war between the Franks and their neighbours. When Charles did not lead or send an expedition across the Rhine, to carry war into the enemy's country, there was trouble on his own side of the frontier, caused by the raids of the indomitable Saxons. But the king's policy was to attack without intermission. Twenty-three times within thirty years, either he or one of his sons marched eastward against the Saxons, or against the Slavonians behind them, or against the Huns on the Danube. But in the meantime he had his foes to face elsewhere; and in 773 he set out for Italy to assist Pope Adrian against the Lombards.

It has already been said that Charles had married Desiderata, the daughter of Desiderius. He had done so partly at the entreaty of his mother, Queen Bertha, and against the dissuasion and threats of Pope Stephen, who did his utmost to sow dissensions between the Frank and Lombard kings. Charles appears to have treated his unfortunate wife with great cruelty. Eginhard, his biographer, professed to be ignorant of the reason for which she was put away. A later writer [1] declares that the separation was effected on the advice of "priests of the utmost piety," because Desiderata could not provide her husband with a legitimate heir. If it were safe to affirm historical facts on the sole ground

---

[1] Monachus Sangallensis, "Gesta Karoli," c. 17.

of their probability, we might conclude that the same authority which had sought to prevent the marriage by a menace of excommunication and the pains of hell contrived to dissolve it by painting an act of treacherous cruelty in the colours of a Christian duty. Charles married, without much delay, the Swabian Hildegard; and there were many Franks, Queen Bertha amongst them, who blamed the conduct of the king, and lamented the fate of the Lombard princess.

Thirty years after the death of Liutprand, and nearly twenty years after the appeal of Pope Stephen to Pepin, Desiderius came to an open rupture with Pope Adrian, one of his demands being that Adrian should consecrate the sons of Carloman as heirs of their father's kingship. The Pope refused; and in 772, other causes of quarrel having in the meantime come to a head, and Rome being once more threatened by a Lombard army, Adrian sent an urgent summons to the king of the Franks. It was not until the autumn of 773 that Charles set out for Italy. He besieged Desiderius in Pavia, little or no resistance having been attempted by the Lombards; and, perceiving that the capture of the city would be a work of time, he sent for his queen, set up his court, built a chapel, and paid such attention as was possible to the internal affairs of his kingdom. As the Easter of 774 approached before Pavia had fallen, the son of Pepin paid a visit to the Eternal City, where he was received with great pomp as Defender of the Church. He was the first Frank king who had entered the city of the Cæsars; but sixteen years were still to pass before he himself would be indued with the imperial purple.

After a series of the most solemn and impressive ceremonies, after repeated celebrations of the mass at different shrines, with gorgeous ritual, pompous processions, triumphal music, and ascending clouds of incense, after viewing the relics of pagan Rome and the newer but more venerated relics of the Christian saints and martyrs, and after brilliant entertainment of the young monarch as a conquering hero whom Rome herself was prepared to recognise as her temporal lord, Charles was in a mood to which the Pope had naturally desired to reduce him. Adrian treated the subjugation of the Lombards as a foregone conclusion; he addressed Charles as already king of Italy; he reminded him of Pepin's deed of gift at Kiersey, and asked for its confirmation. Charles not only granted this request, but also added to his father's donations, then or subsequently, other cities and provinces. The full extent of his liberality has been much in dispute amongst the historians of the Roman Church; but the question of less or more is one which need not here concern us. The main thing for our present purpose is to realise the position now occupied in Rome by the successor of Hermann, of Marbod, of the proud Sicamber who bowed his neck to receive the chrism of S. Remy. A Patricius from his boyhood, Defensor Ecclesiæ since the death of his father, the king of the Franks was henceforth Dux of Rome and ruler of the Byzantine exarchate. Desiderius accepted the inevitable, and the victor set upon his own head the iron crown of Lombardy.

Charles was beginning to earn his title of Great. The Pope had already bestowed it upon him, and henceforth his subjects learned to speak of him as Charles le Magne. He soon showed that he was no mere pope's man, but a proud and ambitious monarch, who knew how to secure the whole value of his concessions. He did not at once hand over to the Pope all that he had promised, or all that Adrian held him to have promised. For years to come there were difficulties between pope and king on questions of possession, of jurisdiction, and of disputed authority, in which the monarch, with his constantly increasing dominion, took care to maintain a clear distinction between his liberal benefactions as king of the Lombards, as well as of the Franks, and a subserviently weak acquiescence in all the demands of the grasping successor of Saint Peter.

After his return in 774, Charles renewed the war with the Saxons, and was more than ever bent on showing that it was a war waged by a Christian king against pagans, and by Germans who had accepted the light of Roman civilisation and Christianity against their still benighted race-fellows. Missionaries armed only with the cross were allied to the mail-clad warriors of the west. Wherever Charles threw down an image of the dumb, discredited gods of his ancestors, he set up a cross or a church side by side with a fort and a garrison. Too often, when his armies withdrew, the pagans closed in from the rear, massacred the garrisons and burnt the churches; but each advance of Charles was more effectual than the last. The number of converted Saxons steadily increased; and if, as appears probable, large bodies of the enemy submitted to the rite of baptism as a mere device to lull the suspicions of the invaders, there can be no question that the cross and the sword together were gradually prevailing over the outstanding barbarism of the Teuton.

In 776, and again in 780, Charles was compelled to return to Italy, where Adelchis, the son of Desiderius —the latter having retired to a monastery—disputed the authority of his father's conqueror, as well as the authority of the Pope. He found allies in his brother-in-law Arichis, Lombard Duke of Beneventum, who was already in alliance with the Greeks, in the Dukes of Friuli and Spoleto, in the Patricius of Sicily, and even in the Archbishop of Ravenna. The territories of the Pope were thus surrounded and encroached upon, and Charles, who in the earlier year above mentioned had chastised the people of Friuli and Treviso, led his army into Italy for the third time in 780, forced Arichis to acknowledge his supremacy, and had his sons Carloman and Louis consecrated as kings of Italy and Aquitaine—the former receiving the new baptismal name of Pepin, already borne by Pepin le Bossu, son of Himiltrude. Years, however, elapsed before Beneventum was finally reduced to quietude, and Charles, in the meantime, paid his fourth visit to Italy—his third to Rome—in 786.

The Saxon war was continued, in the absence of the king, by his counts and generals. In 777, Charles, who by this time reckoned the banks of the Lippe as included within his dominions, called a general assembly of his people at Paderborn, a little below

Ehresburg, on the right bank of the stream. Thither came not merely Franks, and representatives of the most distant provinces, but (as Eginhard expresses it) "the whole senate and people of the perfidious race" of the Saxons, professing obedience and loyalty. Westphalians and Ostphalians, men of the

SAXON REALM OF CHARLES THE GREAT.

western and the eastern pale of the Saxon confederation, Angrians who dwelt between the two, and perhaps Transalbinians from the other side of the Elbe—though their chief Witikind was not amongst the number—submitted themselves to the king, and declared their readiness to be baptised. "An immense multitude" were accordingly gathered in to the Church, and they were warned by Charles that if they again violated their promise to submit they would forfeit both their country and their liberty. The absence of Witikind was ominous. He was the most energetic of the Saxon chiefs, brother-in-law of Siegfried the Dane, and on terms of amity with the Frisian ruler. Charles might have decided to cross the Elbe at once in search of this dangerous absentee; but his impetuosity drew him in haste to the other extremity of his dominions.

There had come to Paderborn, all the way from Saragossa in Spain, one Ibn-al-Arabi, who solicited his aid against a Saracen foe. Charles remembered the deeds of his grandfather, and was irresistibly impelled to seize this chance of striking a blow at the African invaders of Europe. With the consent of his people he set out in the early spring of 778; and it was not long after his departure that the Saxons, stirred up by the reckless Witikind, fell once more upon the eastern frontier. They had no means of crossing the Rhine, but, as Eginhard tells us, "they laid waste with fire and sword every town and homestead between Diutia (opposite to Cologne) and the confluence of the Moselle and Rhine. They made no distinction between what was sacred and what was not sacred. Their fury spared neither age nor sex, in order that it might be plainly seen that they had crossed the frontier of the Franks not for booty but to gratify their revenge." In the meantime Charles was destined in the same year to experience a still greater calamity.

He had arranged that two armies, one from the

north and another from the south of his kingdom, should converge upon Saragossa, apparently not altogether confiding in the power of Ibn-al-Arabi to place the city in his hands. Marching himself through Aquitaine, and through the dukedom of Lupus, son of the rebel Waifre, he crossed the Pyrenees by the valley of Roncesvalles, whilst the Provençals and the Italians, under Duke Bernard, took the eastern route, and advanced to meet him by way of Barcelona. At first all went well; but Saragossa did not open its gates, and the Saracens, putting aside their own quarrels, combined against the king, and harassed him on all sides. Charles might have been strong enough to beat them, and the enemy showed their respect for him by offering him a large indemnity if he would withdraw his armies. The cost of victory appeared too great; the troops were attacked by disease; and the word had already been brought to the king of the perfidious raids of the Saxons. Charles therefore resolved to abandon the campaign. His retreat was turned into a disaster, not by the Saracens but by the Vascons; whether incited by the treachery of Duke Lupus or by the hope of plundering the baggage-train of the Franks.

Eginhard's account is meagre, but it is the only contemporary version of a story which supplied the later romancers with one of their favourite themes, at a time when every French romancer was singing and adding to the legend of Charlemagne. The Song of Roland became a national epic of France; the Norman-French heard it chanted before them as they faced their foes at the battle of Hastings. Eginhard tells us simply how the Vascons lay in wait on the wooded heights of Roncesvalles, until the main army of Charles had disappeared, and fell upon the rearguard under the king's nephew, Roland, who was in charge of the baggage-train. Every Frank in the rearguard perished; the treasure was carried off, and the marauders dispersed, so that Charles had no one but Duke Lupus on whom he could wreak his vengeance. But the poets fill in the details for us, and describe what none of Roland's warriors had survived to tell. They convert the Vascons into Saracens; Roland, a giant of eight feet, slays all who come within reach of his magic sword Durandal, and sounds a blast on his horn at which the birds fall dead, and which Charlemagne hears many miles away; his friend Oliver fights by his side, with Turpin, the gallant archbishop; a hundred thousand of the enemy are killed, and the fifty Franks who then remained alive are only vanquished by the arrival of a new army of fifty thousand.

Thenceforth, Aquitaine, under the kingship of Louis, was held responsible for the safety of the Pyrenean marches, and waged a long and not always successful war with the Africans in Spain.

XVII.

THE WESTERN EMPIRE REVIVED.

AFTER the return of Charles from Spain, the Saxon war was renewed regularly every year, from 778 to 785. The king led his army in person, each year except 781, when, as we have seen, he was paying his second visit to Rome. In 779, he only went as far as Osnabrück, in Westphalia, where he took vengeance for the Saxon raid of the previous year. He struck first at the west, then at the east, but rarely stopped short of the Elbe. Witikind seems to have been unwilling to meet him, but from his home across the Elbe, or from his second home amongst the Danes, he continued to be the leading spirit of the confederation.

The presence of Charles at the head of his army was always a pledge of victory. Early in 782 an isolated force of the Franks was cut to pieces on the banks of the Weser; and Eginhard relates that Charles, as soon as he heard the news, assembled his army without a moment's delay, set out for the spot where the massacre had taken place, and summoned the leading men of the neighbourhood, from whom he insisted on knowing who were the prime movers in the outbreak. "And as they all readily declared that Witikind was the originator of the crime, but that they could not hand him over because he had fled to the Northmen directly afterwards, no fewer than four thousand five hundred of those who had been induced by him to commit that terrible outrage were delivered up; and there, on the bank of the river Aller, at a place called the Ford (Verden Tuliphurdum), by order of the king, between sunrise and sunset, they were all beheaded. After this notable act of vindication, the king settled down for the winter at Thionville (Theodone villa)."

Three more campaigns were fought before the resistance of Witikind could be overcome. In 785, according to Eginhard, Charles was staying at Ehresburg on the Lippe, the first strong place which he had taken from the Saxons, which he had fortified and adapted as a royal residence. His constant word to the Saxon nation had been that they must choose between Christianity and extinction; and now, as the fighting months had passed away, he resolved to send a peaceful message to Witikind, who was living with his people across the Elbe. The messengers selected were Saxons, and they appealed to Witikind to abandon his struggle against the king, and rely upon his goodwill. Witikind and Abbis, who was with him, remembered all the injuries they had inflicted on Charles and his people, and dare not trust themselves in his hands; but at length, when pledges had been given of their safety, and Charles had sent them hostages in the charge of Amalwin, one of the officers of his court, they came back with the latter to where the king was now sojourning, at his residence of Attigny, in the Ardennes, and were solemnly baptised.

Guizot, in his "History of France," quotes a legendary account of the conversion of Witikind, from a life of the Empress Matilda, written two centuries later, when all that happened in the reign of Charles was surrounded with fable, and when the sober and comparatively trustworthy records of Eginhard were replaced, or were beginning to be replaced, by the pious legends of monks and the imaginative *chansons de geste*. We will take the story as it stands, remarking how the spirit of the age of chivalry, as in the Song of Roland, adorned almost every historic tradition with pictures of single combat and the prowess of knights.

"Now in those days Charles the Great sat on the imperial throne, who was the most Christian of men, a mighty warrior, learned in the law, catholic in the faith, full of goodwill and devotion for all who worshipped God; and on behalf of the faith he made war upon Witikind, as he was ever wont to do on all pagans. One day these two met and determined on a single combat, so that both the armies should render obedience to him who gained the victory. And they met, and fought long and hard; and finally our Lord was aroused by the tears of the Christians, and enabled his faithful warrior to overcome, as his faith entitled him. Then was wrought such a change in the obstinate mind of Witikind that he willingly submitted himself, with his family and the whole army of the pagans, to the power of the king and to the Orthodox faith. And the emperor welcomed him with kindness, and caused him to be baptised by Saint Boniface the bishop, and with his own hand raised him from before the sacred font. And Witikind put aside his errors, and in a spirit of penitence accepted readily the knowledge of the truth. Whereas he had been a zealous persecutor and destroyer of the Church, he was henceforth distinguished as a most Christian patron of churches and worshipper of God."[1]

There were battles still to be fought between Franks and Saxons; and at no great interval of time the Northmen with whom Witikind had been on friendly terms were to take up the ancestral quarrel, and to score a new triumph for the north and east over the south and west. Even before the death of Charles, the first waves of the incoming flood broke upon the coasts of the western empire. But meanwhile the policy and the work of Charles in Saxony, so far as the policy was reasonable and the work practicable, had been accomplished. The backbone of Saxon resistance had been broken; the spirit of paganism had been crushed. The new empire had not yet been formally established when the lines by which empire was to be transferred from the west to the east were already traced out and laid down.

On more than one occasion Charles imitated the policy of some of the Roman emperors and generals, by transplanting whole tribes of pugnacious Saxons from Germany into Gaul, and even into Italy.

It would probably have been a task beyond the energies of Charles himself to attack and subdue the

[1] Pertz, "Monumenta Germaniæ Historica," x. 576.

THE SWORD OF CHARLES THE GREAT
(*Imperial Treasury at Vienna.*)

Northmen—even the Northmen of Denmark and the nearer coasts and islands—as he had attacked and subdued the Saxons. He did not attempt it; and the pacification of the broad zone lying between the Rhine and the Oder may well have seemed to him an ample guarantee against further trouble from the north. He had crossed the Elbe into Witikind's country in 789, and pushed his arms against the northern Slavonian tribes who dwelt on the lower reaches of the Oder. One of the last acts of his reign, more than twenty years later, was to return to the same district at the head of an army, and repeat the lessons of 789, after the Wiltzes had been encouraged in fresh defiance by the growing aggressiveness of the Danes.

Beyond the limits of Saxony and Thuringia, Charles now struck frequent blows at the Slavonians, the Avars, and other Eastern hordes which continued without intermission to obey the historic law of human pressure from east to west. In 787 he was compelled to chastise the Bavarians, who, under their duke Tassilon, contested the king's authority; and Tassilon embraced the fate of many a defeated king and chief when worsted in battle against a champion of the Church—he retreated to the more or less honourable captivity of a monastery. It was at any rate a merciful alternative to the older doom of immediate death. From Augsburg Charles went to Ratisbon, on the Danube, and southwards as far as Friuli, beyond the Drave. In this country, and for a considerable distance along both banks of the Danube, restless masses of Avars and Huns continued to prey upon their more settled neighbours; but by hard and repeated striking, with his own hands or by those of his sons, Charles held them at bay on the borders of his dominions, and prevented them at a critical moment from establishing themselves in Central Europe.

It is unnecessary to enter into details of all these wars, which in a wide semicircle from the shores of the Baltic to the shores of Spain flamed up incessantly on the frontiers of the empire of the Franks. For the Franks had won their empire before the end of the eighth century, and before Pope Leo, the successor of Adrian, added the nominal glory of Roman imperialism to the glory of actual conquest and domination. After an unbroken struggle of more than eight hundred years, the heir of the Sicambrian League gave just laws, and so much of civil liberty as the times admitted, to the subject populations of Germany, Gaul, and Italy.

Charles is more interesting to us as the president of a chivalric court, as a lawgiver, a dispenser of justice, a bulwark of Christianity, a patron of learning, a representative of the first efflorescence of German civilisation, than as a mere conqueror. Without his military genius he could not have had much scope for his political and peaceful qualities; but the flower attracts us more than the soil from which it springs, and the remainder of our story of the Franks may concern itself chiefly with the mark which they made, at the period of their highest development, in the history of human thought and progress. It is necessary, in the first place, to see how Charles, having created an empire, came to assume the imperial crown and title.

Pope Adrian died in the twenty-fourth year of his pontificate, on Christmas Day, 795. Charles wept him, Eginhard tells us, as a son, or as though he had lost a dearly loved brother, and he sent to Rome a marble slab, with Adrian's record in letters of gold, which may be seen in Saint Peter's to the present day. The two men had wrought a great work together, and had recognised each other, without subservience on either side, as leaders of the civilisation of Europe.

Leo III. announced to the king his election to the papal chair, and doubtless asked for his confirmation. The letter no longer exists, but Charles was both Patricius of Rome and successor to the authority of the Exarch. His biographer mentions that Leo asked him to send one of his nobles to receive the oath of allegiance and submission from the Roman people; and therewith the Pope forwarded to the western potentate the keys of Saint Peter's grave and the banner of the city of Rome. The acknowledgment of temporal suzerainty could not have been more explicit and significant. Charles replied by sending Bishop Angilbert with gifts and a letter, promising his continued defence of the Church, and asking for a renewal of the treaty already existing, and a confirmation of his patriciate. Leo conceded to the king more than his predecessor had done; he acknowledged his jurisdiction not only in Italy, and in the exarchate which had been a province of the Byzantine empire, but even in the Roman duchy and in the city.

The recognition of the authority of Charles was so complete, and his temporal power in the west was so free from rivalry on the part of other monarchs, that if the king had specially desired the imperial title in 796 it might well have been assumed by him. But the idea seems to have originated with Leo, and that for reasons which are very easy to understand. Wealthy and influential as the popes had now become, they were not strong enough to stand alone. Even after the destruction of the Lombard kingdom, their neighbours in the south, in Sicily, and beyond the Eastern Alps, could still form combinations full of menace and danger to Rome; whilst Rome, though she could put, and had already put, fighting men of her own in the field, was not in a position to draw the sword precisely as though she had been a temporal and military State. It served the purpose of the Church to have a supreme earthly power identified as her protector, whose authority might stand between her and her enemies, and to whom she could always in the last resort appeal. Leo seems to have perceived this fact from the very beginning of his pontificate, and he took every opportunity of giving prominence to his political relations with Charles. And an opportunity was soon provided for a direct exercise by the king of his sovereign authority in Rome.

Two nephews of Pope Adrian, Paschalis and Theodorus, the former of whom occupied the influential post of Primicerius, whilst the latter was Dux and Consul of Rome, took umbrage at the court which had been paid to the king of the Franks, and stimulated the jealousy of the optimates, amongst whom there had been a strong party opposed to the papal supremacy in temporal affairs. A conspiracy was formed for the deposition of Leo; his person was seized during the ceremonial procession on the feast of St. Mark: he was imprisoned in a monastery, and the conspirators remained masters of the city. Leo had been wounded in the tumult; it was alleged that an attempt had been made to pull out his eyes and cut out his tongue. This news reached Charles as he was setting forth on an expedition to quell a new outbreak of the Saxons. Hearing that the pope had escaped from the cell in which he had been confined, and that he was coming in person to solicit the aid of his defender, the king arrested his march at Paderborn, and sent his son Pepin of Italy, the Count Ansarich, and the Archbishop of Cologne, to escort Leo to his camp.

Paschalis and his friends did not venture to defy the authority of Charles. They sent him an account of their proceedings, brought various charges against the deposed pontiff, and submitted themselves to the judgment of the Patricius. Charles determined that the matter should be tried in Rome. Late in the year 799 he sent Leo back under a sufficient escort and, with him, ten envoys to hold the inquiry and determine as to the truth of the charges on both sides. These envoys were Archbishop Hildebald of Cologne, Arno of Salzburg, Bishops Cunibert, Bernhard, Hatto, Flaccus, and Jeffe, and Counts Helmgot Rotgar, and Germar. It is not without significance that Leo was reinstated in the papal chair as soon as he arrived in Rome. The cause of the nobles had to be pleaded against a pope restored to full authority and against a king whose temporal jurisdiction was admittedly supreme. Neither the substance of their case nor the advocacy by which it was maintained for several weeks has come down to us ; all that we know is that judgment went against them, and that they were condemned to death, subject to an appeal to the king as Patricius.

Charles himself came to Rome in November, 800. He had marched into Italy at the head of an army, part of which was detailed under Pepin to reduce the Duke of Beneventum to submission. The king was received with great pomp, and after a few days he summoned a tribunal of bishops and nobles. The accounts of the proceedings are vague, except that we are told that the bishops declared their inability to occupy the position of judges over their apostolic head, and that Leo purged himself by oath from the charges which had been brought against him. After this, the sentence which had been passed on Paschalis and his fellow-conspirators was commuted into one of exile.

It was a day or two later, on the Feast of the Nativity, that Charles was suddenly crowned by Pope Leo, as he rose from his knees before the high altar of Saint Peter's. The congregation saluted him as Charles Augustus, "crowned by God, the great and peace-giving Emperor of the Romans." The monarch protested, but he was overruled, and the imperial diadem remained on his head.

There is, of course, little ground for surprise in the apparently hurried character of an act which must have been long foreseen and prepared. King Pepin had come back from Beneventum almost as soon as he had reached it, and was present at his father's coronation. Alcuin, Abbot of Tours, the friend and adviser of the new emperor, had hailed him by the

DIADEM OF CHARLES THE GREAT.
(*At Vienna; see p.* 290.)

imperial title before he had set out for Rome. Everything tends to show that the assumption of the higher dignity was a matter of policy which had been considered and determined upon; and at least one ecclesiastical writer, Johannes Diaconus, tells us that the matter was arranged between Leo and Charles at Paderborn. But the desire to avoid difficulties with Byzantium, even if the difficulties amounted to no more than a feeling of jealousy, is amply sufficient to explain the absence of elaborate ceremonial, and the reluctance displayed by the king. According to Eginhard and others, Charles was elected emperor by the Frank nobles, by the Roman optimates, by all orders in the Church, and by the general assembly of the people. In any case the act of Leo was endorsed by the universal assent of the nations ruled over by Charles.

Some well-discussed and intricate problems have arisen out of this coronation of Charles as emperor of the western half of the old Roman Empire. It is perhaps more academic than profitable to consider whether the Pope and the "nations" in Rome had inherited the power of the ancient Senate; whether the imperial authority now vested in Charles was transferred from Byzantium to Rome, or to Aachen; and whether the phenomenon witnessed at the end of the eighth century was, as many have contended, an actual revival and renovation of the Roman Empire. These are considerations rather for a history than for a story, and we need not pursue them further.

So far as our Story of the Franks is concerned, it is manifest that we have now reached the climax of its interest, the true dramatic crisis to which everything that went before contributed, and upon which so much of subsequent history has turned. The Frank stood now at the very summit of contemporary civilisation. Batavian of the north, Sicambrian or Chattan of the south, the men who fought in the van of Teutonism when the Cæsars held the frontiers of Gaul were now undisputed masters of Gaul and Italy. So thoroughly had they enjoyed the fruits of their prowess and ambition that they were identified to-day, and loved to identify themselves, with the Latin empire which they had replaced. It was now their turn to feed the lamp of learning, to impose law and culture, and to stem the fated flood which was pouring in upon them from the north. With a refinement differing in many respects from that of Hadrian and Aurelius, the flower of all the Franks united (or strove to unite) at his court some of the highest ideals of which the human mind had been, or was hereafter to be, capable—the ideals of Greek and Roman culture, of German freedom and domesticity, of Christian grace and altruism, of feudal subordination, and of knightly companionship.

It is important to bear in mind that, although Charles the Great was now Emperor of the Romans, he was not, and did not wish to be considered, a Roman Emperor. If he had listened to those who had advised him to make Rome his capital, the history of Europe might have turned out very differently, whilst the future of the Papacy would scarcely have been less disturbed and distracted. But the emperor was too essentially a Frank to be tempted by the dream of an impossible Roman revival. He did not even restore the ancient palace of the Cæsars in Rome, but took up his residence, so long as he remained there, in one of the ecclesiastical buildings near Saint Peter's. Here he exacted an oath of obedience from the Roman optimates, appointed his legate or *missus* to dwell with the Pope, and confirmed the latter as territorial ruler, under his own supremacy, of the estates of the Church. Meanwhile his son Pepin continued to be recognised as king of Italy.

Though Byzantium had naturally taken umbrage at the coronation of Charles, the usurping emperor of the East, Nicephorus, was glad to conclude a treaty, and formally recognised the western empire. At Rome and at Aachen it was held to matter little or nothing what Nicephorus might have to say on the subject. The latest legitimate emperor, Constantine VI., had died in 797, and his mother, Irene, who was strongly suspected of having caused him to be assassinated, had ruled as empress up to the time of her deposition by Nicephorus. The statesmen and jurists of the West considered the Eastern throne to be vacated, and looked upon Charles as the only emperor. "He was held to be the legitimate successor, not of Romulus Augustulus, but of Leo IV., Heraclius, Justinian, Arcadius, and the whole Eastern line ; and hence it is that in all the annals of the time, and of many succeeding centuries, the name of Constantine VI., the sixty-seventh in order from Augustus, is followed without a break by that of Charles, the sixty-eighth." [1]

[1] Bryce, "The Holy Roman Empire," ch. v.

XVIII.

THE GOVERNMENT OF CHARLES.

CHARLES, as we have seen, resided at different times in many places, and much of his time must have been spent in journeying from one to the other. Apart from his military expeditions, and from his repeated sojourns in Italy, he rarely moved far from the Rhine; but the Rhine was the central highway of his empire, and between Geneva and Nimeguen, Valenciennes [1] on the west and Paderborn on the east, he was frequently in motion. Twice every year he held general assemblies of the great men of the empire, during which he promulgated his laws *(capitula)*, and inquired into the condition of the state. These "March-parades" and "May-parades" were attended by dukes, counts, and laymen of inferior rank, and by bishops, abbots, and other clergy, the laity and clergy sitting and deliberating apart. Held often at Aachen, they were sometimes summoned at Nimeguen, Thionville, Worms, Frankfort, Paderborn, Ratisbon, Valenciennes, Boulogne, and elsewhere. Charles delighted to show that his

[1] Valentiniana, one of the royal residences under the Merovingians.

movements were free and safe in any part of his dominions; and there can be no question that his energetic movements and ubiquity would contribute to the general security.

Two of the emperor's favourite residences, superior to the rest in point of magnificence, were at Ingelheim, a little below Mainz, on the Rhine, and at Aachen (Aix-la-Chapelle), between the Rhine and the Meuse. These, curiously enough, are the two towns mentioned by different writers as the place of his birth. Aachen was of no great importance before the time of Charles. On the direct western road leading from Cologne, the ancient Aquis, or Aquisgranum, must have been at the mercy of most of the German invaders of Gaul; but there was, so far as we are aware, no important Roman settlement at this point, in spite of its springs of tepid water. Charles was attracted to the place, constructed large baths there, in which, we are told, he and his friends could swim to the number of a hundred at a time, built a palace, and set architects and builders at work to raise a costly basilica—the *capella regia* which is to this day commemorated in the distinctive French name of the Rhenish Prussian town. As early as 784 we find Charles writing to Pope Adrian, asking for his concurrence in the removal to Aachen of the decorations of Theodoric's palace at Ravenna. "The palace of the great Theodoric," Gregorovius says, "afterwards the residence of the Exarchs, though falling to decay, still retained its splendid pillars, mosaic pavements, and panels of marble. These treasures were carried away to Germany, there to be used in the decoration of

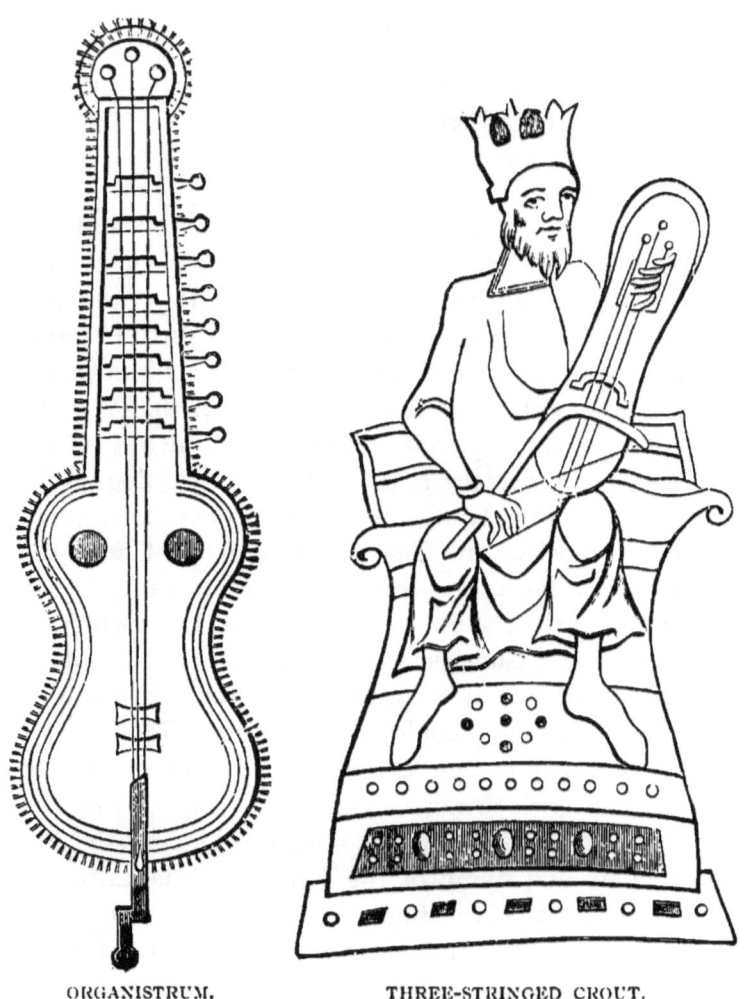

ORGANISTRUM.
(*Ninth century*.)

THREE-STRINGED CROUT.
(*Ninth century*.)

the new basilica at Aachen." Eginhard says that other works of art were brought to Aachen from Rome, as well as priestly adepts in ecclesiastical music, since the king could not procure them elsewhere. Amongst other spoils of Italy, the great equestrian statue of the Gothic king was also removed to Aachen.[1]

The architects employed by Charles to build the

LYRE (*Ninth century*).

basilica, or royal chapel, had a model before them in the church of San Vitale at Ravenna, which had been designed on the plan of the Holy Sepulchre. It is a noteworthy coincidence that, in 801, the Caliph

[1] This statue, described by Agnellus in his history of Ravenna, was "raised on a pyramid six cubits high. Horse and rider were both of brass, 'covered with yellow gold,' and the king had his buckler on his left arm, while the right, extended, pointed a lance at an invisible foe."
—T. Hodgkin, "Theodoric the Goth" (Heroes of the Nations).

Haroun al Raschid, with whom Charles had already exchanged compliments, having dispatched an embassy to him in 797, sent presents to the new emperor in token of his respect, amongst them being a deed of gift of the Holy Sepulchre itself.[1] Already the Patriarch of Jerusalem had remitted to Charles the keys of the sacred edifice, with the "banner of Calvary." The Saracens were steadily encroaching on the doomed empire of the Greeks, and Haroun had laid the Eastern emperor under tribute. This fact no doubt helps to explain the somewhat remarkable action of the caliph; but all the time Charles was striking hard at the infidels in Spain and the Mediterranean islands.

Aachen, then, was not only the frequent residence of Charles the Great and his court, and the meeting place of many of the general assemblies of the Franks, but it was also the permanent seat of empire, the centre from which emanated the imperial edicts and ordinances, whence the *missi dominici* periodically went forth, armed with the emperor's authority, superior to dukes and counts and bailiffs wherever they might come, charged to inspect, to inquire, to dispense justice and to arrange disputes, where money was coined, where the imperial treasures and the public archives and records were guarded.

It would be interesting if at this point we could distinguish more clearly amongst the various national elements of the population over whom Charles extended his sway. There would be representatives of all these nations at the court of Aachen, and the

[1] Eginhard.

names of Charles's courtiers, officials, advisers, and assistants, enable us frequently to perceive that he had his friends and willing helpers amongst the descendants of the Gallo-Romans of the old and the newer Provinces, as well as amongst the Christianised Germans of the north and east. But this does not tell us much about what we should most desire to know—the nature and the extent of the assimilation which had taken place in the last three centuries between the Gallo-Roman and the Teuton. And the absence of any clear indication of a blending of character and feeling, of language and of sympathy, is a proof that the assimilation had not gone far, and that the races had not, and could not have, combined. The Franks had been superimposed upon the Kelts, they had not permeated and transfused them; in Brittany and on the western coast they had not even thoroughly subdued them. The Romans, within something like an equal period of time, had had a larger measure of success, in spite of the probability that Kelt and Teuton were more nearly akin in blood than the Kelt and the Roman. We need scarcely hesitate about assigning a reason for the phenomenon. With the Roman arms came a superior civilisation, intellectual culture and physical comfort, immediate order, adaptive and even sympathetic qualities. With the victorious arms of the Franks there came no peace, no order, an inferior civilisation, an inordinate spirit of plunder, a series of bloodthirsty quarrels amongst the conquerors themselves, little desire or capacity for sympathetic adaptation. This contrast applies rather to the

Merovingians than to the Carolingians; but, before the happy usurpation of Pepin, the mischief had already been done. If Clovis had been a Charlemagne—if the grape had grown upon the thorn—we might conceivably have seen a Gallo-German amalgamation; but in the eighth century this was no longer possible.

In the long wars between Neustria and Austria, though these had been nominally, and perhaps mainly, wars between rival Merovingian kings, the fundamental race-hatreds had had an opportunity of coming into conflict. In the Breton outbreaks, in the long disaffection of Aquitaine, there was unquestionably a strong element of Gallic self-assertion and anti-Germanic fervour. The Gallo-Roman, the Gaul who had rapidly coalesced with the Roman settler, learning his language and adopting his manners, had never been able to accommodate himself to the more brutal and overbearing Frank and Burgundian. And if he could have adopted the manners of the Frank, he would never have risen to the heroic height of learning his language. Perhaps there is no stronger reason, amongst all that can be alleged for the mutual incompatibility of Frank and Gaul, than the radically contrasted genius of their forms of speech. The Frank, when he clothed his thought in words, was broad, full, loud, uncompromising, where the Gaul was mincing, rapid, and ever ready to compromise. The Frank loved his consonants, especially such as he could evolve from the throat outwards; he garnered them every one, and brought them forth with explosive energy. The Gaul took the Latin tongue and proceeded to clip and mutilate it, shedding consonants and syllables, and articulating as little as possible behind his lips, his teeth, and the tip of his tongue. The race which had taken so indistinct an impression of the soft speech of a nation with which it was largely in sympathy was not very likely to assimilate the harsh speech of the cruel and unsympathetic Teuton.

Thus when the Carolingians came to the front, with their ambition for culture, and their devotion to the Christian Church polity, they found a gulf which it was impossible to bridge; and they did not seek to bridge it. The hostility which they encountered in the dukes of Aquitaine and Gascony proceeded, as they knew, from deeper causes than the Merovingian descent of those dukes.[1] One of the first acts of Charles, as we have already seen, was to place his two infant sons on the thrones of Italy and Aquitaine, providing them with astute councillors and administrators, but leaving both Governments to develop a national and almost autonomous State, Italian or Aquitanian, and not forcing upon them a directly centralised rule, like that of North-eastern Gaul and the Rhine lands. With all his Roman learning and Christian fervour, Charles was always frankly German. Even more than his father and grandfather, he recognised that the Frank supremacy had its deepest roots in Eastern Francia, in Austria and not in Neustria, or in Aquitaine, or in Provence, or in Lower Burgundy. He had ascended the throne

[1] Hunald was the great-grandson of Caribert, brother of Dagobert I.

as a German ruler ; his chief determination had been to extend his dominion over the Eastern Germans ; and, when he had been crowned as the successor of the Cæsars, he had never dreamed of centralising his empire further west or south than Aachen. If he looked forward to the time when his vast dominion should break to pieces, he had taken the best means of ensuring that the banks of the Rhine should be the backbone of the dominion of his descendants. By a freak of history, the name of his glorious race— France, Frankreich—was to be assigned, both by Gauls and by Germans, to the country and the nation with which the Franks could never assimilate ; but, in reality, when the ancient races came once more to a parting of the ways, all that was most essentially Frank tended to draw back to the eastward, and that which remained on the west of the Vosges and the Ardennes was essentially Gallo-Roman.

"It is no longer necessary to show," says Mr. Bryce, "how little the modern French, the sons of the Latinised Kelt, have to do with the Teutonic Charles. At Rome, he might assume the chlamys and the sandals, but at the head of his Frankish host he strictly adhered to the customs of his country, and was beloved by his people as the very ideal of their own character and habits. Of strength and stature almost superhuman, in swimming and hunting unsurpassed, steadfast and terrible in fight, to his friends gentle and condescending, he was a Roman, much less a Gaul, in nothing but his culture and his schemes of government, otherwise a Teuton. The centre of his realm was the Rhine : his capitals

Aachen and Engilenheim; his army Frankish; his sympathies—as they are shown in the gathering of the old hero-lays, the composition of a German grammar, the ordinance against confining prayer to the three languages, Hebrew, Greek, and Latin—were all for the race from which he sprang, and whose advance, represented by the victory of Austrasia, the true Frankish fatherland, over Neustria and Aquitaine, spread a second Germanic wave over the conquered countries."

At the same time, Charles was sufficiently cosmopolitan to aim at, and in a remarkable degree to attain, harmonious government, law, and ecclesiastical discipline, throughout the countries which owned his sway. Absolute harmony was, of course, out of the question; but at least there were identical principles which could be applied wherever the Missi Dominici came, and wherever the Church provided channels through which the influence of its earthly defender could operate. The General Assemblies of the Franks were held partly, as has been said, for the promulgation of new laws. The custom had grown out of the folk-moots which were usual amongst the Germanic tribes at the date when written history first takes cognisance of Teutonic institutions; but, whilst the witenagemot in England was being developed amongst the migrated Anglo-Saxons in a more and more popular form, the work of the assemblies of the Franks had tended gradually to narrow itself down to little else than the dictation of the monarch. There is not much indication in the eighth century of what might be called a consultative legislation.

Charles took counsel with his chosen advisers, and laid his new *capitula* before the laity and clergy at the general assemblies; but he was virtually an autocrat, and decided as he wished. This is evident from the account which we have received from Archbishop Hincmar, writing towards the end of the ninth century, on the authority of one of the councillors of the emperor.

In order, as Hincmar says, that the chief men of the empire assembled at the *placita* in March or May "might not seem to have been summoned without reason, the *capitula*, predetermined and arranged, which had been either conceived by himself through the inspiration of God or else specially commended to him since the last assembly, were by the king's authority laid before them for adoption or consideration. And the assembly took these texts, and asked for one day, or two, or three days, according to the importance of the matter in hand, making such representations to the king as they thought fit, and receiving his replies through the palace messengers, whilst no man from without was permitted to come near them, until every point had been submitted to the ears and to the pious consideration of that glorious monarch, and until all concurred in what he with his divine wisdom determined. And in this way they dealt with each of the *capitula*, until all that was necessary at the moment was by the mercy of God transacted.

"In the meantime, whilst this business was proceeding in the absence of the king, he was engaged with the rest of the assembly, receiving their offerings, greeting his nobles (such as were not councillors), exchanging words with those whom he seldom saw, walking with the elders, relaxing his mood with the younger men, and comporting himself in similar fashion towards the ecclesiastics; but ever ready to visit those who were consulting apart, if such was their desire, and to sit amongst them as long as they wished, whilst they with entire freedom mentioned everything which had occurred to them, and candidly informed him of all their discussions, disputes, or friendly deliberations.

"I must not omit to say that, if the weather was fine, the assembly met in the open air, but if not they were entertained in separate halls so that the councillors were kept well apart, and the rest of the assembly found quarters elsewhere, though persons of less consideration were not permitted to mingle with them. But the places appointed for the meeting of the elders (councillors) were divided into two chambers, so that the bishops, abbots, and clergy of higher rank met in the first chamber without associating with the laity. In like manner the counts and other principal personages were early in the day entertained apart from the general body, until the time arrived for the assembly, with or without the presence of the king; and then the councillors assembled as usual, with clergy and laity in their respective chambers, being provided with seats in the order of their rank. But when they had retired from the general assembly, it was for themselves to determine when they would sit together and when apart, according to the nature of the questions submitted to them, which might be spiritual or secular, or of a mixed character. And it was equally in their discretion to call in the attendants when they wished to eat, or witnesses when they desired to conduct an inquiry. So much for their manner of dealing with the questions submitted to them by the king.

"A second custom of the king was to ask whether any one had brought information from the district whence he came, which ought to be reported or discussed with him. This was not merely allowed to them, but even strictly enjoined, so that each one during the interval between the two assemblies was to make diligent inquiry, both within the realm and beyond the borders, into anything which had taken place, from fellow-subjects or from foreigners, from friends or from enemies, and with the aid of intermediaries, without too closely inquiring whence they had their knowledge. The king demanded whether the people in any part, district, or remote corner of the realm were disturbed, and what was the cause of the disturbance; or whether popular complaint had been made, or any grievance had been overheard, which it might be necessary for the general council of the kingdom to discuss; and so forth. And he desired to know whether any conquered nation meditated a rebellion, or any rebellious nation were disposed to submit, or if a nation still unsubdued were plotting against the kingdom, or were disposed to plot. In all such cases, wherever any danger was threatened, he sought out the reason of its occurrence."

This is evidently a very interesting document from

the historical point of view, for it bears witness to a distinct, assiduous, and systematic method, which Charles had adopted before the end of the eighth century, of governing his wide dominions. It was arrived at by grafting autocracy upon the old, popular general assembly of the Franks, and it depended very largely upon the wisdom and assiduity of the monarch. Such is the strength, and the weakness, of all democratic monarchies—of all monarchies, that is to say, which combine popular assemblies with a real controlling or directing power on the part of a monarch. If the monarch is as wise and as benevolent as Charles, all is likely to go well for his lifetime; but too much is staked on the wisdom of an individual, and on the duration of his life. Charles was persuaded that his control, and ultimately his fiat, or the exercise of his will, were better calculated to give welfare and happiness to his subjects than the decision of a popular assembly, arrived at after the excitement of debate, and imposed by the majority (which, under the Merovingians, was exceedingly violent and discordant) on the minority. He being what he was, and his heterogeneous realm still depending for peace and stability upon his sword, it is probable that this persuasion was rightly grounded. At all events his experiment appears to have been as successful as any conceivable form of government which could at that time have been devised.

It is clear from Archbishop Hincmar's account that the General Assembly or Council of the Franks included (1) a Senate ("seniores") composed of distinguished men, divided into the two orders of clergy and laity, with absolutely independent powers of discussion on projects of law introduced by the king, though these may have been suggested and even framed by others. The Senate could deliberate in private, taking as long a time for discussion as they pleased, could interrogate the king, propose amendments, call for evidence, and ask for the king's personal attendance at their sittings; but in the last resort the monarch had power to determine (Hincmar's word is "eligere") as he saw fit. (2) Outside the Senate there were dukes, counts, probably vicars of counts and sheriffs ("scabini"), with other officials, as well as clergy, from all parts of the kingdom, each of whom was charged to report to the king whatever might have transpired in his district affecting the peace and contentment of the realm; and on the strength of these reports, when the matter seemed to require it, a Missus Dominicus might be sent on a special mission of inquiry, with full authority to arrange the difficulty which had arisen. (3) The General Assembly also included others of inferior rank, possibly as a survival of the earlier custom, when all the ranks of freemen were represented at these popular gatherings. They clearly still continued to possess an element of festivity, in addition to their serious concerns of legislation and administration. (4) There would also be the personal *entourage* of the king, including the Chancellor, whose business it would be to provide a record of the capitularies in their final shape, and to affix thereto the imperial seal; with such other advisers and councillors as might not be comprised amongst the "seniores," and yet would not belong to the second category, of those who came from more or less distant parts of the kingdom.

Such, then, was the basis of the personal government set up by Charles the Great, which secured comparative peace and order in the countries subjected to his rule, and did what could be done to reproduce the refinement of Rome and Byzantium. Law, as we have seen, had ever been in a special degree the sanction and protection of the common rights of the Teutonic peoples; and amongst the German codes the Salic law was conspicuous. But with the process of time, and particularly after the constant internecine wars of the Merovingian period, the want was felt of a more modern system, adapting itself year by year to rapidly changing circumstances, and rising from the level of mere fine and punishment, artificial restraints and remedies, to subtler questions of equity, and even to something like a general rule of life for more peaceful and self-respecting men. The Christian equity had to a large extent supplied this need, and the Carolingian kings, who were thoroughly convinced Christians, at any rate in a political sense, sought to embody the ideas of Christianity, as well as the more universal maxims of ethics, in what we know by the name of the capitularies. The practice began at the close of the Merovingian epoch, in the reign of the unfortunate Childeric II.; but it may be safely attributed to the genius and initiation of the Carolingian Mayors.

Between 742 and 921, as many as two hundred and fifty-six capitularies were promulgated by the kings and emperors in General Assembly. Some of them were entirely general, both in character and in their application. Some were specially devised as extensions of particular national codes. Some were primarily intended for the instruction of the political commissioners ordered to represent the authority of the monarch in various parts of the empire. A certain number were domestic in their scope; others were civil or penal; others again, originating no

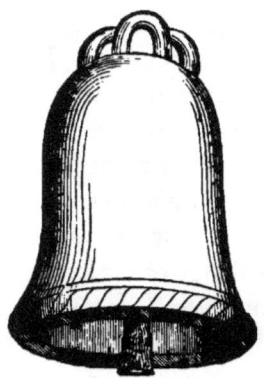

TINTINNABULUM.
(*Ninth century.*)

doubt, with the clerical chamber of the Senate, were canonical or strictly religious. They varied considerably in length. The sixty-five capitularies attributed to Charles the Great include 1,151 separate articles, amongst which are reckoned 87 moral, 293 political, 130 penal, 110 civil, 85 religious, 305 canonical, 73 domestic, and 12 relating to particular incidents. Truth to tell, the Carolingian book of law is void of system and classification. Its contents vary between the definite assignment of a penalty for a definite crime, and the moral maxim which might adorn the commonplace book of a devout and simple-minded man. One is a laconic injunction to be hospitable ; another defines and warns against covetousness ; a third declares that no man is bound to give alms to beggars who will not work ; a fourth bids men beware of venerating the names of martyrs falsely so-called, or the memory of doubtful saints ; a fifth decides that prayer may be effectual in any language.

A large majority of the capitularies of Charles were drawn up after he had been crowned emperor. It was in 802 that he specially set himself to revise or supplement the codes of the subject nations ; and at this Assembly, as Mr. Bryce has pointed out, he put forth a capitulary on the distinction between the oath to the king and the oath to the emperor. All male subjects in his dominions, as well ecclesiastical as civil, who had already sworn allegiance to him as king, were now commanded to swear to him afresh as Cæsar ; and all who had never sworn, down to the age of twelve, were now to take the same oath. "At the same time it shall be publicly explained to all what is the force and meaning of this oath, and how much more it includes than a mere promise of fidelity to the monarch's person. Firstly, it binds those who swear it to live, each and every one of them, according to his strength and knowledge, in the holy service of God ; since the lord Emperor cannot extend over all his care and discipline. Secondly, it binds them neither by force nor fraud to seize or molest any of the goods or servants of his crown. Thirdly, to do no violence nor treason towards the holy Church, or to widows, or orphans, or strangers, seeing that the lord Emperor has been appointed, after the Lord and His saints, the protector and defender of all such."

As no fewer than forty-nine of the capitularies of Charles were promulgated in the last fourteen years of his reign, and more than half of these in the years 801–6, it is evident that his added authority on the assumption of the purple was turned to account for the formulation of a fresh body of institutes in political and domestic legislation.

XIX.

THE COURT OF CHARLES.

ONE of the constant attendants upon the person of Charles the Great, his biographer Eginhard—it is doubtful whether we ought to reckon him amongst the imperial Chancellors—has left us a somewhat minute description of the first Emperor of the Franks. According to this account, Charles "was stout and strong of body, of a lofty stature, yet not beyond just proportion, for his height was certainly not more than seven times the length of his feet. His head was well rounded, his eyes large and piercing, his nose rather long, his luxuriant hair of a flaxen hue, and his face bright and pleasant to look upon. His whole person, whether he stood or sat, was marked by grandeur and dignity; and though his neck was full and short, and his body fat, he was otherwise so well proportioned that these defects passed unnoticed. He was firm in gait, and his appearance was altogether manly; but his refined voice was not entirely in keeping with his figure."

Charles had been brought up by an ambitious

father, and by a mother—Bertha "aus grans pies," celebrated in a thirteenth-century (entirely unhistorical) romance of Adenès the trouvère—who lived until 783, and who, we are told, never had a disagreement with her son, except when he repudiated the daughter of Desiderius. Like most of the Franks, Charles was a warrior before everything, and gave early token of his heroic strength and prowess. But he was a man of thought as well as of action, and his love of learning and letters is beyond dispute. Amongst his earlier tutors and advisers were Archbishop Boniface, of Mainz, who had consecrated his father at the time of the usurpation, Francon and Hithier, who were Chancellors to Pepin the Short, and Peter of Pisa, who taught him to compose fair prose and verse in Latin, which elicited the courteous praise of Pope Adrian.

Prudent and dutiful as Charles displayed himself in most of the relations of life, he was one of those who may be said to have "erred along the line of the emotions." Attractive in his personality, accustomed to secure without much difficulty most of the objects on which he set his mind, there was too much temptation and licence in his position to make it very remarkable that he overstepped the borders of continence. He had in all nine wives, bound to him with or without the sanction of the Church. In his eighteenth year he formed a connection with the beautiful Himiltrude, whom he repudiated in order to marry, at his mother's request, the daughter of the Lombard king, and whose son Pepin he did not formally acknowledge. The romances of a later age have done Himiltrude probably more than justice. The author of the "Croquemitaine" describes her as fairer than all other women. " Her neck was tinged with a delicate pink, like that of a Roman matron in the olden time. Her locks were bound about her temples with gold and purple bands. Her dress was looped up with ruby clasps. Her coronet and her purple robes gave her an air of surpassing majesty." But her beauty availed her nothing when necessities of State intervened, and Charles was called upon to contract a marriage with a view to providing successors to the throne.

The marriage with Desiderata was ill-omened from the first. It was an act of weakness on the part of Charles to yield, two years after the death of his father, to the entreaties of Queen Bertha, and to marry the daughter of a rival monarch, alliance with whom involved enmity to Rome, as well as the sacrifice of ambitions in which he had been trained from his boyhood. Hildegard, the Suabian, to whom he was afterwards married with the full sanction and benediction of the Church, was happy in giving her husband six children :—(1) Charles, who had the title of king of Burgundy, and who died in 811. (2) Carloman, rechristened Pepin, king of Italy, who died in 810, when his kingdom came under the direct imperial government. (3) Louis, king of Aquitaine, who succeeded his father as emperor. (4) Rotrude, whom the Empress Irene wanted to marry her son Constantine, and who died in 810. (5) Bertha, who married the poet Angilbert, her father's secretary, and successively count of the palace to Pepin of Italy and duke of the Western Scheldt lands. Angilbert took the cowl in 790, with the consent of his wife; and he figures in the calendar of the saints. (6) Gisela, the youngest daughter of Hildegard, born in 781, had a motherless childhood, with associations that only accentuated the loss of her mother. She was shut up in a convent by her brother Louis, at the age of thirty-three.

Hildegard retained the affection of her husband until her death in 783, when Charles lost his mother and his wife within the space of a few months. Thereafter he married Fastrada and, on her death, Liutgard, and adorned his court—it can scarcely be said successively—with Maltegard, Geswinda, and others. He had children by several of these, and most of them were provided for by the ever-generous and all-embracing Church—Hugues, a gallant abbé of S. Quentin, who died fighting against the Saracens in 844; Drogon, bishop of Metz; and the abbesses Theodrada and Hiltrude, daughters of Fastrada. Meanwhile the unhappy Himiltrude, who had precedence of all her rivals, was in some measure avenged by her hunchbacked son Pepin le Bossu, who stirred up a plot against his father, and levied war upon him, and whom the Church, still all-embracing, received in 792 as an inmate of the monastery of Pruym.

Our knowledge of the social aspects of the court of Charles is not direct. In tradition and fable there is enough to furnish materials for a detailed romance; but for the facts that can be weighed, and that are entitled to mention in a sober narrative, we depend mainly upon the internal evidence of documents written by contemporaries, on the slight description of Eginhard, and on the letters of Alcuin and others. And from this evidence it is apparent that the court of Charles was a centre of refinement and culture, of noble thoughts and high aspirations. This is true especially of the period during which Charles was in his prime as a king, and in the earlier years of the empire.

Abbot Alcuin was unquestionably the most remarkable man at the court of King Charles, and did more than any one else to give tone and character to his surroundings. He was a member of a Saxon family settled in the North of England, and was brought up at York under Archbishop Egbert, and the schoolmaster Ethelbert, himself afterwards archbishop. Ealhwine, as he then spelt his name, was one of the most brilliant pupils of a school distinguished for its cult of Latin letters in an age when the Latin Church as a whole did little enough for the preservation of the monuments of pagan learning. Ealhwine first assisted and then succeeded Ethelbert as "magister scholarum." He taught Virgil, and he practised himself and his pupils in writing Latin prose and verse. Returning in 781 from Rome, whither he had been to fetch the pallium of the new archbishop, he fell in at Parma with the Frank Defender of the Faith. Charles was seven years younger than Alcuin, and the bright and learned Saxon ecclesiastic—a relation of the S. Willibrod who had preached Christianity to the Frisians, and carried the cross through Saxony in advance of the royal armies—found favour in the eyes of the king. Charles pressed him to come and live at Aachen, and to take in hand the education of his children; and Ealhwine, after returning to York, and handing over his school to a successor, arrived in the valley of the Meuse with a few students who had resolved to follow his fortunes, and a selection from the beloved texts which he and his master Ethelbert had spent many months of travel and much wealth to seek out and secure. He came at first for a term of three or four years, after which he paid a visit to England, and obtained permission from the king of Northumbria to settle permanently in the Frank dominions.

Thus, in the year 782, was set up at Aachen the school of the palace of Charles; and the first pupils were the children of Hildegard, the king's sister Gisela, the king himself, with such of his friends as were studious enough, or courteous enough to exhibit a desire for instruction, Sigulf and the other North-countrymen whom Alcuin had brought with him from York, and doubtless a fair number of persons admitted by the royal favour. Alcuin's method was, of course, oral, and chiefly dialectic. A dialogue between him and the young king Pepin, in which the latter propounds to the magister a series of ingenious questions, remains to this day as an example of early mediæval school work, which combined the master's monologue and the child's exercise of memory with the philosophic argument, or literary theme, of the most advanced students.

We have seen that at Aachen, as in a few other

schools in Gaul and Italy, in Northumbria and
Mercia, in Ireland, and rarely elsewhere in the
eighth century, Latin literature was the groundwork,
or a large part of the groundwork, of mental culture.

CHIMES.
(*From a ninth century MS.*)

There were, of course, the *trivium* and the *quadrivium*,
for which Alcuin made himself in a special manner
responsible: grammar, rhetoric, logic — arithmetic,
music, geometry, and astronomy. The favourite
studies of Charles's " magister scholarum " were

included in the first of these two systems, though he claimed authority to teach in the other also. In a letter to Charles from Tours, where he lived and taught in the later years of his life, he said, "To some I give the honey of the Scripture; others I set myself to nourish upon the fruit of grammatical subtlety. Now and then I intoxicate a student with the wine of the ancient sciences, and a few I dazzle with the brightness and the fixed order of the stars." Charles had caused to be set up at Aachen, whether at the instigation of Alcuin or not, a large planisphere, which might literally dazzle the eye with its brightness; for it was sufficiently valuable for his grandson Lothair to break up into small pieces, at a crisis in his fortunes, for distribution amongst his soldiers.

The scholastic work of Alcuin, as of his master Ethelbert, and the patronage accorded to it by Charles, point to a kind of revival of learning in the eighth century. The schools opened by Alcuin and his disciples were in some instances maintained after his death, by the assistance of royal or other benefactors, so that the effect of the Carolingian revival was not entirely lost; but comparative darkness succeeded as it had preceded the brief illumination which had been diffused by the English teacher and the Frank emperor. It had been a revival, so far as it was scholastic, of the ideas of Cassiodorus, and Augustine, and Boëthius, and of the pagan learning of the schools of the later Roman Empire.

In 796 Alcuin, now over sixty years of age, and

perhaps wearying of the worldly aspects of the court at Aachen, retired to the abbey of S. Martin of Tours, which, with two other abbeys, had been conferred upon him by the king. At Tours he established a school and a *scriptorium*, over which he presided until his death, eight years later. To the end of his life he retained the friendship and esteem of Charles, who had valued his advice on political affairs, as well as on questions of learning and theology. A large number of letters, many of them written to Charles, are preserved amongst his works.

One of the labours of Alcuin at Tours was the correction and reproduction of the service books employed in the churches, and the preparation of other manuscripts, ecclesiastic or scholastic. Whether Charles could write well or ill, he ordered that the sacred books should be examined for the removal of errors, and renewed if necessary. Alcuin therefore opened a *scriptorium*, and employed cunning scribes to write on parchment with loving care and devotion. The result was a school of caligraphy which brought the art to great perfection, and produced manuscripts in what has come to be called the Caroline script, superior to anything yet accomplished, and admired to this day for its clearness and artistic treatment. Alcuin, and perhaps his scribes, came from England and had English models to work upon. It is on these, rather than on Italian, Gallic, and other models that the excellent Caroline hand is based; and the experts tell us that the influence of this hand is manifest in the best of the subsequent scripts, down to the day when the printers began to relieve the caligraphists of their work.

In the school of the palace Alcuin had assumed or accepted the name of Flaccus. The king was known amongst his intimate friends as David—a title sufficiently appropriate in more senses than one; and the king's son-in-law, Angilbert, answered to the pseudonym of Homer. Other men of letters at the imperial court, who were also Commissioners of the king, were Theodulf (who called himself Pindar), an Italian Goth, bishop of Orléans; Smaragde, abbot of S. Michiel; Leidrade, archbishop of Lyon; and S. Benedict of Aniane, whose zeal for the strict observance of monastic rules entitles him to be remembered in association with his namesake and brother-saint, who established the first monastery on Monte Casino two centuries and a half before.

Eginhard, the Bezaleel of the courtly game of make-believe, has been mentioned already as the biographer of Charles. He was still young when the emperor was well stricken in years, having been one of Alcuin's earlier disciples at Aachen. There he afterwards lived as master of public works—the same position that William of Wykeham occupied in relation to Edward III. He was by birth an Austrian Frank, but wrote in Latin, for which he apologises to his readers in the preface to his *Vita Caroli Magni* in these words: "Perhaps you wonder that I, a barbarian, too little versed in the Latin language, should have imagined that I could write in Latin with any elegance or propriety."

He goes on to explain that he only did so in order the more surely to perpetuate the memory of Charles; his thought was not for his own reputation, but for that of his great master. It is fortunate for historians that he was actuated by such motives, for his biography of Charles, as Guizot says, is the most distinguished piece of historical writing between the sixth and the eighth century, the only one, in fact, which can properly be called history at all, inasmuch as it is "not a mere chronicle, but a true political biography, written by an eye-witness of the events described, and that eye-witness one who understood the importance of the events." Eginhard's other works, consisting of letters and annals, do not possess the same literary merit as the Life above mentioned. After the death of Charles, he became the confidential adviser of his son Louis, and died at the age of 73, in the year 844. Raban Maur, archbishop of Mainz, wrote his epitaph, in which he styled him "Vir nobilis, ingenio prudens, probus actu, ore facundus."

A certain literary ability, as well as literary taste and patronage, has been attributed to Charles by his biographers, who may have been disposed to flatter him in this respect, or to attribute to him directly what was only due to his initiation. We are told that he knew Latin well, and even understood some Greek; that he could write good Latin verse; that he studied astronomy, was learned in theological controversies, planned a German grammar, ordered a collection to be made of the old Germanic hero-lays, and re-named the months and the winds in his native tongue. All these things are credible enough, and they would suffice to draw from Alcuin his subtle word of praise:—"If your zeal were imitated by others, we might see a new Athens rising up in Francia, more splendid than the old Athens, for it would be Christ's Athens."

There is less reason for accepting the statement that Charles was the actual author of the four books which bear his name (Libri Carolini), written against the resolutions of the second Council of Nice (787), which declared in favour of image-worship. The Empress Irene brought about this reaction on a point which had helped to alienate the Eastern and the Western Churches. Pope Adrian was well pleased by the change, but the mind of Charles revolted against the encouragement of what he regarded as a superstition. We cannot tell who wrote the Caroline Books; but, in 794, in order to give effect to his convictions on the subject, the king called together a national Council at Frankfort on the Main. By this Council the adoration of images was condemned; and its action drew from Rome a repudiation which does not appear to have greatly troubled the conscience of the Teuton.

Though Charles was, according to his first biographer, "a ready and fluent speaker, able to express himself clearly," it seems doubtful whether he was proficient in actual penmanship—though his signature is a work of art, which almost suffices to prove that he was so. Eginhard, indeed, tells us that he "tried to write, and would keep under his pillow his tablets and writing-book, so as to practise his hand when he had leisure. But he began late

BYZANTINE ENAMEL RELIQUARY.
(*From Mt. Athos. Tenth century.*)

in life, and made little advance." Few laymen at this period, however, could do as much as to sign their names decently : and, even if Charles had to employ an amanuensis, his zeal for the improvement of education, especially among the clergy, cannot be doubted. A letter from him to the Archbishop of Mainz is extant, in which he says : "You are striving with God's help to conquer souls, and yet you are not anxious to instruct your clergy in letters, at which I cannot too much wonder. You see on all sides those who have submitted to your rule plunged in the darkness of ignorance, and . . . you leave them in their blindness." In a general letter to all the bishops and abbés he tells them that "in agreement with our faithful advisers, we have thought fit that, in all bishoprics and monasteries entrusted by Christ's grace to our government, care should be taken not only to live regularly and in conformity with holy religion, but also to study letters seriously, to teach and to learn, each man according to his ability and by the help of God, so that the religious rule of life, which brings with it honourable conduct and zeal for teaching and learning, may give regularity and beauty to language." He complains that he has noticed in a greater part of the addresses presented to him from the monasteries that the excellence of the sentiments was not matched by the elegance of the diction, a fault which could not be cured save by the diligent study of other men's writings.[1]

[1] For further information on the literary efforts of Charles the Great, see Jaffe, *Monumenta Carolina.*

We have only to read Alcuin's letters to see how real he believed the enthusiasm of Charles to be. He writes to his patron on one occasion: "I knew how strong was the attraction you felt towards knowledge, and how greatly you loved it. I knew that you were urging every one to become acquainted with it, and were offering rewards and honours to its friends, in order to induce them to come from all parts of the world to aid in your noble efforts." And after speaking of the king's invitation to himself, he adds, "Would I had been as useful in the service of God as I was eager to obey you." "I loved so much in you," he says again, "what I saw that you were seeking in me." Charles in his turn addressed Alcuin, in a letter written about 800, as his "beloved master, always to be named by us with love" ("dilectissimo magistro nobisque cum amore nominando Albino abbati"); thanking him in the same letter for his "welcome blessing on us and our family," and proceeding to dilate upon a point of ecclesiastical nomenclature on which Alcuin had written to him. He concludes with this sentence: "Since you have borrowed the words of the Queen of Sheba to Solomon about the happiness of those servants who wait upon him, and listen to the words of wisdom, if you know this to be true, come, be with me, listen, and let us be happy together in the Lord, rejoicing in the many flowers that bloom in the luxuriant meadows of Holy Writ" ("et pariter in Domino in pratis vernantibus varietate florum Scripturarum jucundantes delectemur").

It is unnecessary to say that we do not look to

Charles, or to Alcuin, or to any writer of their day, for anything striking in the way of literature, and still less for any wealth of new ideas. The zeal of the emperor and the abbot was for the preservation or revival of Roman letters, and in this they were imitators, but in no sense creators. If they wrote vaguely in a language not their own, it was from necessity rather than from choice. The German tongues were not yet literary. The "Heliand," a Saxon religious poem, produced a generation or two after the death of Charles, is almost the oldest known written work—not reckoning the ancient runes and lays which are said to have been collected by order of the emperor—in the newer continental tongues. Alcuin doubtless knew something of Bede, and, through him, of the English of Cædmon; and Charles himself would be able to understand Cædmon's verses. But for the monarch and for the ecclesiastic, Latin was the only tongue in which their ideas and purposes could find expression. The statecraft of Charles and the scholasticism of Alcuin employed as a matter of course the only form of speech which was common to the monarch and all his subjects, to the teacher and to the taught.

Nevertheless, it is to be observed—for it goes far to explain the darkness of the centuries which closed the first and began the second millennium of the Christian era—that Latin such as could have been comprehended by a Roman of the Augustan epoch had become by this time almost a sealed language to the generality of the inhabitants of Western Europe. "The revolution of language," Hallam says, writing of this period, "had now gone far enough to render Latin unintelligible without grammatical instruction. Alcuin and others who, like him, endeavoured to keep ignorance out of the Church were anxious, we are told, to restore orthography; or, in other words, to prevent the written Latin from following the corruptions of speech." The new tongues were but slowly assuming a literary shape; the old tongue was rapidly becoming unfamiliar. And as it was with words, so it was with ideas. The old philosophy, poetry, historic method and style were passing out of sight half-a-dozen centuries before Germans, Frenchmen, and Englishmen would be ready to evolve new systems of philosophy and a style of their own.

If it were just and sufficient to say that the occurrence of the six or seven darkest centuries which the world has seen—for darkness following the daylight of Greece and Rome must be considered relatively as well as absolutely—was due in the main to this break in the continuity of human speech, when dominion passed from nation to nation, but law and letters and religion could not flow without interruption from the old nationality to the new, this fact would surely be one of the most remarkable and significant in the history of the world. It would be a strong attestation of the absolute dependence of the literary spirit upon the written language, not alone for its existence—which is a truism—but also for its continuing effect and development. And though this fault in the linguistic strata is by no means the sole cause of intellectual relapse, still there is perhaps no other cause which accounts for it in an equal degree. If the education of Gauls and Teutons in Latin schools had continued steadily from the times of Ausonius, Ammianus, Cassiodorus, and Fulgentius, until the patronage of such monarchs as Charles and Alfred had encouraged scholars of the northern races to teach in their native tongue as well as in Latin, it is probable that the chasm of darkness between the Roman and the Teutonic brilliance would have been more rapidly and easily bridged. The devastating brutality of the Merovingians, which all but emptied Gaul of its Gallo-Roman schools, and against which the Gallic Church battled manfully but in vain, submerged the light of learning in Western Europe, even more completely than the Lombards submerged it in Italy, and the earlier Saxons and Danes in England.

It is when we bear these facts in mind that the literary work of Charles, his encouragement of schools and his patronage of learning, assume their true proportions. His own illumination, and the illumination of Alcuin, were feeble enough as compared with our own standards; but, if the spirit of Charles and Alcuin could have been diffused and maintained, the brightness would have steadily accumulated, and the millennium might have ended with an earlier renaissance. But the diffusion was confined within narrow limits, and the spirit of Charles, though it did not actually die with him, waned for several generations until it finally disappeared. It is true that the schools of Gaul, which had been founded or revived at the beginning of the ninth century, endured, and were even developed, under Louis the Pious and his immediate successors. In point of fact, poor as was the outcome of the Carolingian revival, it must be admitted that the schools of the later Franks made their mark in the history of education, and that the school of Paris in particular, which is known to have been in existence at the end of the ninth century, became the headquarters of scholasticism, and was expanded into a famous university.

XX.

THE LIFE AND WORK OF CHARLES.

CHARLES the Great reigned as emperor during the first fourteen years of the ninth century. Though, as we have seen, he concerned himself largely during the later portion of his life with the laws and internal government of the empire, yet these fourteen years were by no means years of peace. The submission of the Saxons was practically complete from 804; but almost immediately their place was taken by an enemy more formidable and more pertinacious, against whom Charles was too old to renew the determined policy of his youth. The northernmost Saxons, the Danes, and the Scandinavians, of whom we may speak collectively as Northmen, a hardy and persistent race, especially at home upon the sea, began to harry the Franks on the northern coast as early as 808. The Frisian shore was overrun in 810 and the succeeding years, and became a nearer point of vantage from whence a rapid succession of piratical attacks were made upon the exposed towns and villages on the western shores and estuaries. So long as the Franks remained strong and vigilant, even after the separation of Neustria from Austria, these attacks were held in check; but the time was at hand when the north-western section of the empire of Charles was unable to withstand the perpetual inroads of the teeming North.

These buccaneers of the olden time, some of whom were ancestors of the Normans who were soon to descend upon our own coasts, ruled the waves with almost complete immunity. Close on fifty separate expeditions, including Irish Kelts as well as Scandinavians, are mentioned by Frank chroniclers of the ninth and tenth centuries; and amongst them were some which ventured across the Biscay, and found their way as far as the southern shores of Gaul. The traders of the Armorican coast, and of the northern and southern ports, were no match for the fierce sea-dogs whose only trade was war and plunder. Charles himself, at the very beginning of the long epoch of Viking aggression, foresaw the danger which threatened his country, and wept, as one of his biographers tells us, when he thought of the evils which the Northmen were destined to bring upon his descendants and his people.

Meanwhile a dozen wars continued to rage along the whole extended frontier of the Empire; and, though Charles marched less frequently than of old at the head of his army, his three sons proved themselves worthy to continue his policy and to uphold his reputation. Pepin of Italy imposed peace upon the Duke of Beneventum without actually subduing him. Between 806 and 810 he fought several battles against the Saracens, and drove them out of Corsica;

and in 809-10 he struck a heavy blow at the Greeks in Dalmatia. The younger Charles, in addition to his constant, and on the whole successful struggle with the Saracens, contrived to keep the Gascons in subjection, and fought two campaigns against the Slavonians in Bohemia. Louis also distinguished himself in Spain, and led his troops against the still indomitable Bretons. Twice in the last four years of his life the emperor himself revisited the scenes of his earliest victories, in 810 driving back the Danes from the Weser, and in 812, in his seventieth year, advancing against the Wiltzes on the right bank of the Elbe.

Then, at length, not willingly but on compulsion, the hero of a hundred fights returned his sword to its scabbard. After the death of his two elder sons, in 810-11, he summoned Louis of Aquitaine to his side, and bade him prepare to assume the imperial dignity. Stimulated by Benedict and others, he had determined that the abuses which they had noticed in the practice and discipline of the Church should be reformed, and to this end he took it on himself to order the meeting of six national Councils at six of the principal metropolitan seats, Aachen, Reims, Châlon on Saone, Tours, Mainz, and Arles, which were accordingly held in the year 813, and took measures for the purification of ecclesiastical government within the empire. The Aachen Council was simultaneous with a General Assembly of the Franks, held in the summer, to which all the principal men of the country had been specially summoned, in order that they might promise allegiance to Louis. Charles took counsel with the most powerful amongst them, and, as Eginhard says, "invited" them to make his son their emperor conjointly with himself, to which they all agreed, saying that it was prudent and pleased them well. A little later, in the basilica of Aachen, the emperor, wearing his own crown, laid another upon the altar, and, having publicly addressed his son on the duties of the monarch towards God and man, the Church and the people, he asked Louis if he were solemnly determined to perform these duties. Louis swore it before the altar, and Charles then bade him take the crown and place it on his own head. All the congregation shouted, "Long live our Emperor Louis!" Thereupon Charles declared his son joint-emperor with himself, and cried aloud, "Blessed be Thou, O Lord God, who of Thy favour hast permitted me to see my son seated on my throne!"

The last days of Charles are thus described by Eginhard. After sending his son back to Aquitaine, he proceeded, according to his usual custom, and in spite of the weakness caused by old age, on a hunting expedition in the neighbourhood of Aachen, and, after spending the remainder of the autumn in this pursuit, returned about the beginning of November. In the course of the winter, in the month of January, he took to bed, suffering from a severe attack of fever. At once, as was his custom in cases of fever, he ordered himself a lowering diet, thinking that such abstinence would cure, or at least reduce, the illness; but pleurisy ("lateris dolore quem Græci pleuresin dicunt") followed, and, as he persisted in his starvation diet, chiefly consisting of infrequent draughts, he rapidly grew worse. On the seventh day after taking to bed he received the last offices of religion, and died in the seventy-second year of his age, and the forty-seventh of his reign.

Charles was buried on the same day in the basilica which he had built at Aachen. There is now in the nave of the church a marble slab bearing the inscription "Carlo Magno," but some of the relics buried with the body were removed by Otho III. in 997, and are now in Vienna. Frederic Barbarossa opened the vault for the second time in 1165, but caused the body to be enshrined again, the throne being now in the upper gallery of the nave.

The life and work of Charles the Great must be considered in relation to the times in which he lived. So far as his personal characteristics are concerned, the conclusion has already been drawn that Charles at Aachen, like Alfred in England, though in a higher degree than Alfred, represented a culture which was in advance of his generation, and which the Teutons over whom he ruled were not able to assimilate. A few there naturally would be who could live at his level of thought and art and refinement, and who, in the intervals of annual war, could return again and again to the life of mental activity and study. But such men would be very few amongst the Franks, whose bodily vigour was more conspicuous than the agility of their minds; and the few would have made little or no mark upon their generation if they had not been brought into prominence by the patronage of the monarch. A generation or two after the death of Charles the effect of his example began to disappear; the memory of his real service to learning gradually faded away, and gave place to more or less idle and exaggerated legends. The time for a renaissance of letters had not arrived; the intellect of the ancient world had but flickered up for a moment before its death, and the intellect of the modern world needed centuries of gestation before it could acquire the strength to be born. For Charles, though he was modern by race, drew little of his culture from the essentially modern ideas. The mould of his mind was Roman, and his models had been placed before him by Roman ecclesiastics. In so far as the Franks were mentally cultivated, it was because their minds had been partly Romanised, and the ambitions of Charles led him to imitate the empire which his ancestors had done so much to destroy. Beyond the Teutonic principles of law, and the traditions of popular meeting and election, not much that was political or intellectual in the ninth century can be traced as the special contribution of the Germans to the progress of mankind.

Their contribution, it is true, was both large and important, but it was practical rather than theoretical, domestic rather than political, and physical rather than mental. The Frank had beaten the Roman and the Gallo-Roman by his superior strength and energy; but civilisation and culture are not amongst the natural gifts of physical strength and energy. This is one of the main reasons why such culture as was to be found at the court of Charles the Great could not be expected to abide amongst the nation of the Franks, still less to survive the incursions of the Northmen. We cannot wonder that the imitative refinement of Aachen turned out to be little more than a transient phenomenon.

Nevertheless the legend of Charlemagne was more permanent, and produced a more potent result, than his eager encouragement of learning. Whilst the discussions at Aachen, the benefactions at Tours and elsewhere, and the high-minded appeals to the bishops, can scarcely be held to have led to any more effective advance than the slow evolution of scholasticism, there was something more widely striking and impressive in the imperial grandeur of Charles, his stately court, his energetic rule, his supremacy over Europe, his expeditions year after year, at the head of a magnificent array, surrounded by his paladins (knights of the palace), to beat back the infidel, to chastise his enemies, to succour the oppressed, and to impose Christianity on conquered nations. The eyes of those who saw him, and the imaginations of those who sang his famous deeds, preserved and embellished for future generations one of the most picturesque and romantic figures in the history of mankind, around which his glorious legend was developed and crystallised, until it became the inspiring model of chivalry and the germ-idea of the Crusades. This was a spectacle which could be appreciated and understood by all the Franks, and after them by all the Teutons. It supplied them with a literature in advance of learning, and with an ideal of life not hopelessly beyond their reach. There was a time, both before and after Clovis, when to be a Frank and not a brave and patriotic fighting man was almost impossible. Under the later Merovingians the energy and temper of the race began to show signs of relaxation, especially in and about the courts of the kings; and it was then that the election of Mayors of the Palace revived the older and stronger tradition. The vigour of the Carolingians was transfused through the nation, which regained its earlier force, and made its name once more a symbol of irresistible power. Eginhard mentions a proverb of Greek origin which shows how the more formidable qualities of the predominant race had re-asserted themselves in the time of Charles the Great:—"τὸν Φραγκὸν φίλε ἔχῃς, γείτονα οὐκ ἔχῃς"—"You may have a Frank as your friend, but beware of him as a neighbour." The Franks were aggressive and masterful, but in their best days they were simple in domestic life and loyal in war. It was chiefly under the Merovingians, and through the Merovingians, that they earned their worst repute for treachery and corruption.

Charles, as we have seen, the descendant of Austrian Mayors, was, by circumstances and by his own choice, a German emperor, and the distinction between the eastern and the western halves of the Frank dominions was emphasised after the extinction of the Carolingian house. But the dominant character of the Franks did not disappear with the Carolingians, even amongst the Franks who were gradually assimilated to the Gallo-Romans, and converted into Frenchmen; and it was through these later Franks that the old Frank energy passed into the veins of the Crusaders. "From what part of Europe the crusading impulse really came," says Freeman,[1] "we see by the name which all the nations of Western Europe have ever since born on Eastern lips. From those days till ours they have always been the Franks, Franks of course in the sense which the word *Franci* bore at Paris, not in that which it bore at Aachen. And among such Franks the Normans held a foremost place." So, indeed, it was throughout the long period of the settlement of the Easterns in the West, and of the Northerns in the South—the strongest strain of the settlers was always that which had been re-transfused with Eastern and Northern blood.

Something, again, has already been said of another permanent achievement of the first Frank emperor, the confirmation and enrichment of the Roman Church, concerning which it would be hard indeed to say whether the ultimate results of his intervention were more profitable or more disastrous for the Christian Church at large. The lust of empire affected both the popes of Rome and the Frank kings. The ambition of Charles was natural and honourable, and his exercise of imperial authority was undoubtedly benevolent. In order to secure his coronation he played, though reluctantly, into the hands of the pope, and strengthened the foundations of the temporal power, which he regarded as inconsistent with the religion of Christ, and an encroachment on the secular dominion. In succeeding centuries, the German emperors of the Holy Roman Empire took steps to check the growth of the papal states by force of arms, but they did not go so far as to secularise

[1] "The Norman Conquest," v. 356.

CHRIST AND HIS MOTHER.
(Ninth century fresco.)

what had come to be known as the patrimony of Saint Peter. Thus it fell out that the wealth of the Church corrupted the purity of the faith; and, in respect both of discipline and of dogma, all but the most undiscriminating apologists of Rome have admitted the truth of what Wyclif was one of the earliest to affirm, that there is a distinct contrast between the tenets of the first millennium and the tenets of the second, between the attitude and decisions of the Church before its temporal aggrandisement and the claims of the Vatican at a later period.

The influence of the Franks, and of Charles the Great in particular, upon the Angles and Saxons in England was indirect, but none the less important. It is the more difficult to measure its extent because both nations inherited many customs and characteristics from their common ancestors in Germany; but there can be no question that Englishmen were indebted to the Franks of Gaul for large and durable contributions, before as well as after the Norman conquest. The Anglo-Norman law has been spoken of by jurisprudents as a daughter of the Frank law. "The Frankish monarchy,[1] the nearest approach to a civilised power that existed in Western Europe since the barbarian invasions, was in many things a pattern for its neighbours and for the states and principalities that rose out of its ruins. That we received from the Normans a contribution of Frankish ideas and customs is indubitable. From the time of Charles the Great onward, the rulers of both Mercia and Wessex were

---

[1] "The History of English Law before the Time of Edward I.," by Sir F. Pollock and F. W. Maitland (Cambridge University Press).

in intimate relations with the Frankish kings." They were relations of marriage, of trade, of social intercourse and borrowed ideas; and, amongst these borrowed ideas, the maxims and methods of law are not the least significant.

The friendship between Charles and Offa, king of the Mercians (d. 796), was somewhat intimate, and the two kings took practical steps to encourage trade amongst their subjects. Charles proposed a marriage between his eldest son and the daughter of Offa, but was offended when the Mercian king claimed a reciprocal alliance for his own son. The quarrel was ultimately adjusted; the kings became good friends again, and renewed their correspondence. A letter from Charles to Offa asks for the recall of a Scottish priest who was residing at Cologne; others promise that English merchants and pilgrims shall be protected, and others again speak of gifts which had been sent to Offa, and to various Mercian and Northumbrian bishops. Like all the best Teutonic kings, Offa wrote or re-wrote the laws of his people, which Alfred incorporated with others in the following century.

XXI.

THE PARTITION OF THE EMPIRE.

AFTER the death of Charles, the power of the Franks in Gaul rapidly declined. The government of the empire, so far as it had been systematic and effectual, depended on the spirit and energy of one man. Without the strong personal authority of Charles, the wisdom of his ministers and commissioners would have been of little avail. To succeed him was a task demanding consummate skill and firmness, and these were qualities in which his son Louis was conspicuously deficient.

Louis the Pious, who is also called the Debonnair, presents the melancholy spectacle of a man essentially good by nature, full of lofty intentions, amiable and magnanimous in private life, quick to repent when he had done amiss, and quicker to forgive an injury, yet wanting in vigour and resolution, easily relying on the advice of others, and destitute of the worldly wisdom which would have enabled him to choose his advisers well. Men of his character are numerous in every age; they are doomed to suffer themselves and to bring suffering on others; and when they are born, as

Louis was born, to hold the reins of government, their life is apt to be a tragedy. So it was with the son of Charles the Great, who not only had to face the rebellion of half-subjected nations on the borders of the empire, with disaffection on the part of his *leudes*, and incessant ravages by the Northmen, but also experienced the fate of our own Henry II. at the hands of his turbulent and ambitious sons.

The Slavonians, Gascons, Bretons, and Burgundians were amongst the earlier foes who imposed on Louis the necessity of fighting for the preservation of his father's conquests. Expeditions against the two first-mentioned nations were followed by the revolt of the emperor's nephew Bernard, son of Pepin of Italy, who had not been confirmed in succession to his father, and whose animosity had been increased by the nomination of his cousins, the sons of Louis, to imperial and royal dignities. If Charles or Louis had recognised Bernard as king of Italy, he would virtually have established a hereditary dynasty in that country, whereas it was essential to maintain it as an integral part of what was looked upon as the rejuvenated Roman empire. The rebellion of Bernard was suppressed; he was condemned to lose his eyes, and died a few days after the infliction of this barbarous punishment. The cruelty is incongruous with most of what we are told about the character of Louis; but he took the responsibility upon himself, and performed a public act of penance for it at Attigny, in 822.

Louis, who had made enemies for himself at the beginning of his reign by suddenly substituting a decorous, if not an ascetic, court for the freedom and laxity permitted in the later days of Charles, weakened his authority in 817 by a premature bestowal of crowns upon his three sons. The eldest, Luther or Lothair, who was just nineteen, he associated with himself as emperor; Pepin, who was eleven, was made king of Aquitaine, and Louis, who was eight, became king of Bavaria.

They are shown, with their descendants, to the last of the Carolingians, in the table on the opposite page.

In connection with the sanguinary quarrels of the sons of Louis the Pious, Sir F. Palgrave makes the following very pertinent observation:—"Amongst other inherent germs of evil in the Carlovingian Empire was the absence of any definite law of succession or heritable representation: the children acknowledged the parent's power of appointing or partitioning his dominions, but never obeyed that power practically or honestly unless under compulsion, or when it suited their own interest. No certain principle could be discovered, whether an appropriation once made to this or that son or nephew was or was not revocable or irrevocable. Some portions of the empire had distinct constitutional rights, Aquitaine especially so: so also Armorica, so also Bavaria. Austrasia and Neustria were sometimes considered as united in one great national Assembly, and sometimes not. Popular assent was sometimes solicited and sometimes neglected."[1]

The successive subdivisions of the Frank empire

[1] "The History of Normandy and of England."

DESCENDANTS OF CHARLES.

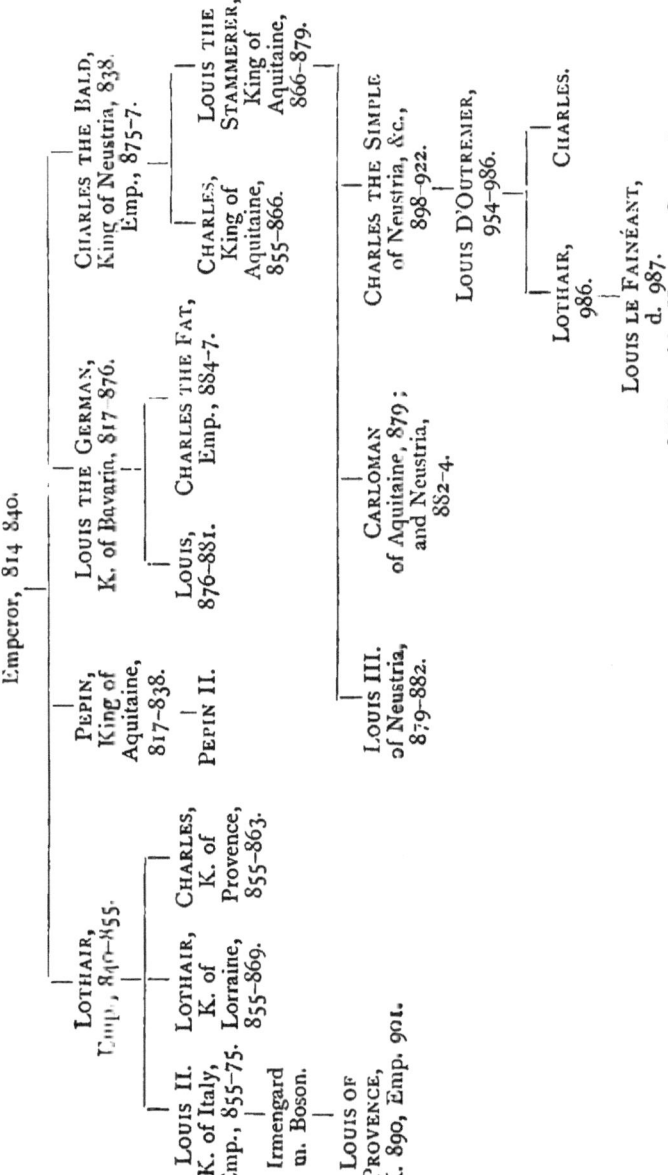

which will have to be mentioned in this chapter will be more clearly understood if we recall the partition of authority made by Charles the Great amongst his three sons. The empire, it will be remembered, was drawn together again before the death of Charles, and came entire into the hands of Louis. The States reserved by Charles under his direct government, or subsequently annexed by him, were as follows:—

1. *Neustria*, bounded by the English Channel, the Atlantic, the Loire, the Lower Meuse, and the Scheldt.

2. *Austria*, bounded by the Scheldt, the Upper Meuse, the left bank of the Upper Rhine (so as to include what was afterwards called Alsace), and the Alleman lands between the Upper Rhine and Danube.

3. *The Frisian Lands*, between the Rhine and the Weser.

4. *Saxony*, between the Weser and the Elbe, stretching southwards to Franconia and Thuringia.

5. *Thuringia*, between the Upper Weser and the Eastern Saale (tributary to the Elbe).

6. *Northern Allemannia*.

7. *Tributary States* to the empire were Moravia, partly corresponding to the present Hungary, right and left of the river Morava; Bohemia, right and left of the Upper Elbe; the Sorabian (Servian) land between the Saale and the Upper Oder; the land of the Wiltzes, north of the Sorabes, extending to the Baltic; the land of the Obotrites, between the

Wiltzes and the Nordalbingians; and the duchy of Beneventum, which was not under the direct sway of the Italian king.

The kingdom of *Italy* included the peninsula north of Beneventum, excepting the territories of the Church; the old Lombard lands eastward of Provence; Southern Allemannia, Bavaria and Carinthia, almost as far eastward as Vienna.

The kingdom of *Aquitaine* included the countries of Aquitaine and Burgundy, as already defined in this volume, bounded by Neustria, Austria, Allemannia, and Northern Italy, and touching the Pyrenees south of Toulouse; Provence, between the river Durance and the Mediterranean; Septimania; Gascony; the Marches of Spain, a little beyond Barcelona and Pampeluna; with Corsica, Sardinia, and the Balearic Isles.[1]

Louis the Pious, it will be seen, was more sparing in his devolution of authority. Outside of the Aquitanian kingdom he only assigned the duchy of Bavaria to the youngest of his three sons by his empress Hermengard, raising it to the status of a kingdom, bounded by the Lechs and the Ens, the Danube and the Eastern Alps. But even this subdivision, made so soon after the beginning of his reign, was taken as a sign of weakness, and, added to his elaborate prostration before Pope Stephen IV. on his coronation at Reims in 816, to his public penances, to the relaxation of his father's stringency of imperial rule, and to the too sudden and stringent

[1] See Lalanne, "Dictionnaire Historique de la France," under the word "France."

curbing of his court, had the effect of making his *leudes* restive, his sons presumptuous, his subjects unsettled, and his tributaries rebellious.

After the death of the Empress Hermengard, Louis married Judith, daughter of Count Welf of Bavaria, and by her, in 823, he had a son who is known to history as Charles the Bald. When this boy was six years old his father carved out for him a kingdom, including Allemannia, with Rhætia and a part of Burgundy. By this time the impatience of the Franks under the weak, yet autocratic rule of their emperor had come to a head. Judith—between whom and the Queen-Empress Victoria there is a titular tie, if not actually a tie of blood—appears to have been masterful and intriguing. She and her son were even more unpopular than Louis; and, as the result of a conspiracy in which the sons of Hermengard took part, she was suddenly removed from court, and imprisoned in a convent at Poitiers. The emperor submitted to his *leudes* at his palace of Compendium on the Oise (Compiègne), where he was deposed in favour of his son, Lothair, whilst Charles was deprived of his kingdom, and the Aachen arrangement of 817 was insisted on. There was, however, very little delay before a counter-plot reversed the decisions of Compiègne; and a General Assembly at Nimeguen restored Louis to his throne. Pepin of Aquitaine had taken part both in the plot and counter-plot, but he was still unwilling to lose the Burgundian provinces which had been conferred upon Charles. He revolted once more, and took up arms against his father, with the result that Louis deprived him of his kingdom, and gave it to Judith's son. The three sons of Hermengard again made common cause; Louis, deserted by many of his supporters, on what came to be called the Luegenfeld, or Champ des Mensonges, near Colmar, again submitted (833), and Lothair was once more recognised as sole emperor.

The English reader will find, perhaps, the best account of this period in the first volume of Sir F. Palgrave's "Normandy and England." He quotes the following passage from the Conquestio or Complaint of Louis, who was imprisoned in the Abbey of S. Médard at Soissons:—"They placed me here, striving to drive me to an abdication, being well aware how I honour the sanctuary, and how I venerate the memory of S. Médard and S. Sebastian." (Louis bestowed the neighbouring Abbey of Choisy on the Abbot and monks of S. Médard.) "They continually perplexed me by false intelligence. Sometimes they told me that my wife had become a nun, sometimes that she was dead; sometimes that my innocent Charles, whom they knew I loved above all things, was shorn as a monk." (Charles was at this time imprisoned at Pruym.) "And inasmuch as I, deprived of my kingdom, my wife, my child, could not bear these griefs, I passed my days and nights in tears and sorrow."

Then a new reaction took place; Pepin and Louis of Bavaria refused to acknowledge Lothair; Judith resolutely espoused the cause of her husband and her son; assemblies at S. Denis and Thionville played the same part as that at Nimeguen; and the twice-restored emperor confirmed Charles in his kingdom. The animosities and intriguing of the empress, the sons of Hermengard, the political clergy, the *leudes* and court officials, continued to be keen and warm for some years to come. Pepin regained a part of his old dominion, but did not acquiesce in the loss of the remainder; and a majority of his subjects appear to have remained loyal to him. There were Councils at Crémieu in 835, at Aachen in 836, and at Aachen again in 838. A raid of Northmen in 837 created a temporary suspension of this bitter and fatal

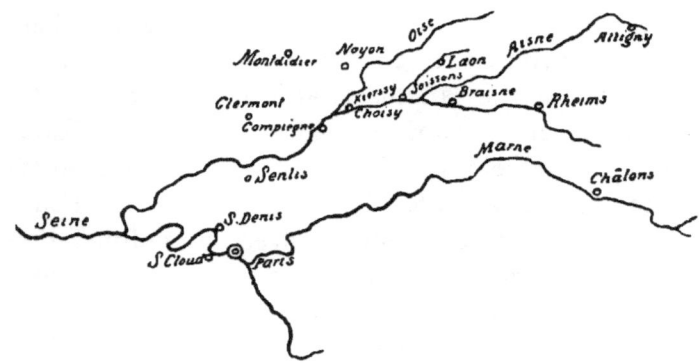

controversy. But in the following year there was another Council at Aachen, and a General Assembly at Kiersey on the Oise, the latter being held for the special purpose of crowning Charles, now a stripling in his sixteenth year, as king of (German) Francia, Burgundy, and Neustria. Aquitaine was left to Pepin, but in the same year, before he had had time to stir up fresh trouble, he died, at the age of thirty-two. His son Pepin was elected in his stead, though, like Bernard of Italy, he did not secure the confirmation of the emperor. The kingdom of Aquitaine was claimed by Judith for her son, and Louis summoned an Assembly at Worms, declaring his intention to make a new partition of the empire. Louis of Bavaria had again revolted, after the settlement made at Kiersey; but Lothair was now at his father's side, discharging the duties and forming the expectations of an eldest son. At Worms, then, in 839, Louis divided his empire into two parts, separated from each other by the Meuse and the Rhone, the sources of which are but a few miles distant from each other. Lothair, who had his choice in the inheritance, selected the eastern half, leaving the western to his half-brother Charles; whilst Louis, in spite of his rebellion, was allowed to retain the kingdom of Bavaria. It remained to quell the opposition of Louis and the younger Pepin; and the emperor had advanced as far as Mainz, on the way to Bavaria, when he was struck down by a fever, and died at Ingelheim, in June, 840.

This event had the effect of destroying the agreement which had been come to at Worms. In order to maintain the last dispositions of Louis the Pious, it would have been necessary for Lothair and Charles to combine against Louis the German and Pepin II.; but Louis was rapidly extending his sway over all the Frank lands east of the Rhine, and Lothair, at whose expense this aggression was being made, had neither sufficient honesty to keep the pledges which he had made to his father in the interests of Charles, nor sufficient wisdom to retain Charles as an ally against Louis. He had, in fact, broken his pledges on the morrow of his father's death by conspiring with his nephew Pepin against his younger brother, and this, apparently, before he recognised that Louis had made himself exceedingly formidable. It came to the knowledge of Charles that his mother, the Empress Judith, was threatened by her old enemies, and was practically a prisoner in Poitiers. He hastened to her relief, and by her advice entered into an alliance with Louis of Bavaria. The latter at once led a large army of Bavarians and Saxons across the Rhine, and joined forces with the army of Charles. Lothair and Pepin encountered them at Fontenai (Fontenailles), some eighteen miles from Auxerre, and a sanguinary battle, fought on June 25, 841, ended in the defeat of Lothair and his ally.

During the next few months the emperor was gradually recovering from this disaster, and preparing for a new effort, whilst Louis and Charles cemented their alliance, confirming it by a solemn exchange of oaths at the town of Argentaria, on the Rhine, some little distance to the south of Argentoratum, the modern Strassburg. The precise locality is doubtful. Some identify it with the Roman Argentovaria, now Arzenheim, nine or ten miles from Colmar; others with Colmar itself; and others again with the village of Arburg.

In order to give special weight to their pledges, the two kings exchanged them in the presence of their armies; and the circumstances are particularly interesting because a contemporary writer has preserved the exact words of the oaths taken by the monarchs and by their armies, in Gallo-Roman ("romana") and German ("teudisca lingua"), thus providing us with a convenient opportunity of illustrating side by side the forms which these two languages had assumed in the ninth century.

The oaths of Argentaria, taken in the spring of 842, were as follows :—

In the first place Louis, being the older of the two kings, pledged himself in these words :—" Pro Deo amur, et pro christian poblo et nostro commun salvament, dist di in avant, in quant Deus savir et podir me dunat, si salvaraeio cist meon fradre Karlo, et in adiudha et in cadhuna cosa, si cum om per dreit son fradra salvar dist, in o quid il mi altresi fazet ; et ab Ludher nul plaid numquam prindrai, qui meon vol cist meon fradre Karlo in damno sit."

That is to say—" For the love of God, and the Christian people, and our common salvation, from this day forward, in so far as God shall grant me knowledge and power, so will I succour this my brother Charles, both in aid and in everything, as a man by right ought to save his brother, in the (case) that he shall do even so to me ; and never will I take any plea (order) from Lothair, which by my will shall injure this my brother Charles."

We must remember that Louis (Ludwig) in Bavaria was surrounded by courtiers and officers who, with the exception of the clergy in the churches, rarely spoke any other language than that of Southern Germany, and that his army would speak Tudesque almost to a man. But the object of the oath-taking was that each of the two armies should hear the leader of the other army swearing in a language which they could understand ; and this is why Louis swore in Roman speech, for the men of Neustria and Aquitaine, whilst Charles swore in Tudesque for the men who lived in Germany.

It will be no waste of time to compare the oath of Louis, word by word, with the older Latin form of speech on the one hand, and with the modern French equivalent on the other. The reader will observe that every word is Latin in its origin; there is no trace whatever (beyond the proper names) of German or of Keltic contribution or influence.

Latin— Pro Dei amore et pro christiano populo et nostro
Romana—Pro Deo amur et pro christian poblo et nostro
French— Pour de Dieu amour et pour chrétien peuple et nôtre

L. communi salvamento de isto die in advenientem, in quanto
R. commun salvament dist di in avant, in quant
F. commun salut de ce[t] j[our] en avant, [en tant que]

L. Deus sapere et po[te]sse me donet, sic salvabo [ce]istum meum
R. Deus savir et podir me dunat, si salvaraeio cist meon
F. Dieu savoir et pouvoir me donne, ainsi sauverai ce [celui] mon

L. fratrem Carolum, et in adjumento et in quacunque causa, sic
R. fradre Karlo, et in adiudha et in cadhuna cosa, si
F. frère Charles, et en aide et en-chacune cause, ainsi

L. quam homo per directum suum fratrem salvare debet, in eo quod
R. cum om per dreit son fradre salvar dist, in o quid
F. que on par droit son frère sauver doit, en ce que

L. ille mihi alterno modo sic faciat; et a[b] Luthero nullum placitum
R. il mi altre -si fazet; et ab Ludher nul plaid
F. il me autrement ainsi fasse; et à Luther nul plaid

L. nunquam prehendam quod mea voluntate ce[isti] meo fratri
R. numquam prindrai qui meon vol cist meon fradre
F. [jamais] prendrai qui ma volonté ce[lui][à] mon frère

L. Carolo in damno sit.
R. Karlo in damno sit.
F. Charles en dommage soit.

The oath of Charles, repeated in German for the

better understanding of the army of Louis, was to the same effect—"In Godes minna ind in thes christianes folches, ind unser bedhero gealtnissi, fon thesemo dage frammordes, so fram so mir Got gewizci indi madh furgibit, so haldih tesan minan bruodher, soso man mit rehtu sinan bru[od]her scal, in thiu thaz er mig sosamo duo ; indi mit Ludheren in nohheinin thing ne geganga, the minan willon imo ce scadhen werhen."

As the Roman has been compared with the more ancient Latin, so the Tudesque oath may be placed side by side with the modern German equivalents of the separate words :—"In Gottes Liebe, und in diesem Christlichen Volk und unser beider Erhaltung, von diesem Tag von nun an, so wie Gott Wissen und Macht vergibt, so [will] ich halten diesen meinen Bruder, wie Mann mit Recht seinen Bruder soll, in dem dasz er mir so [English, same] thut ; und mit Luther in keinem Ding nicht gehen [will] das [mit] meinem Willen ihm Schaden werke."

The oath taken by the army of Charles was in these words :—"Si Lodhuvigs sagrament quae son fradre Karlo iurat conservat, et Karlus meos sendra de suo part non lo stanit, si io returnar non int pois, ne io ne neuls cui eo returnar int pois, in nulla aiudha contra Lodhuwig nun li iner." And to the same effect was the oath taken by the army of Louis the Germanic in their own tongue :—"Oba Karl then eid then er sineno bruodher Ludhuwige gesuor geleistit, ind Ludhuwig min herro then er imo gesuor forbrichit, ob ih inan es irwenden ne mag, noh ih, noh thero, nohhein then ih es irwenden mag, uidhar Karle imo ce follusti ne wirdhic." That is to say—"If Louis (or

Charles) keeps the oath which he has sworn to his brother Charles (or Louis), and Charles (or Louis), my lord, breaks that which he swore to him, if I cannot turn him aside, nor myself, nor any of those whom I might turn aside, I will not be with him in any aid against Louis (or Charles)."[1]

These oaths were in themselves very solemn, circumstantial, and stringent; they became still more so by the conditions under which they were taken, and by the events which followed during the next few years. The Thuringians, Bavarians, and South Saxons on the one part, the Gallo-Romans, Bretons, and Gascons on the other, distinct in history, customs, manners, and language, had been thrown together by their political necessities, and were to be linked in feeling for many a long day by the importance of their achievement and the permanence of its results. They were virtually, nay, actually, the founders of Germany and France as we have them to-day. Their kings were Carolingians, their leaders and their fighting men must have included a considerable number of Franks; and yet it is in the highest degree important to note that they were not Frank by great preponderance, nor characteristically Frank in spirit. All the nations which are mentioned above —and they are the nations expressly mentioned by the contemporary historian Nithard—had been fighting the Franks for centuries; and the moment had come when, at Fontenai and at Verdun, a great combination of anti-Franks, yet under Frank leader-

---

[1] Pertz, "Monumenta Germaniæ Historica": *Nithard*, bk. iii., ann. 842, "De Dissensionibus Filiorum Ludovici Pii."

ship, was able to throw off as much as was detachable of the Frank yoke.

The significance of the crisis from this point of view has been somewhat overlooked, and it is worth while to dwell upon it on that account. The battle of Fontenai, the oaths of Argentaria, and the subsequent compact at Verdun created two of the mighty States which were to play a leading part in the second Christian millennium—so much so that, as Sir F. Palgrave has said, "The history of modern Europe is an exposition of the treaty of Verdun." It is true that they definitely broke up the Frank empire as established by Charles the Great, which the ecclesiastics in particular had loved to picture as the Roman Empire restored, and which the Roman people and Church had helped to build on the old foundations. But that empire could not by any possibility have endured in its entirety as a political dominion including the whole of Italy, Germany, and Gaul. It was heterogeneous, incohesive, and certain to break to pieces, leaving the three chief component nations to stand apart in their original distinctness, though with a common civilisation and a common religion. The title of emperor remained, to be inherited, or fought for, or bestowed by election. The more descriptive title of Holy Roman Empire was to descend through the pages of German history, now as a substantial fact with practical and important consequences, now as a brilliant memory. The French monarchy was to vaunt itself as the eldest son of the Church, and to claim a special hereditary right to defend the integrity of Rome. But meanwhile the political empire of Charles the Great had fallen asunder, and the principal work of the Carolingians, and of the Franks, may be held to have been completed.

The army of Lothair, on the other hand, must have been far more characteristically Frank than that of his brothers. He was the Frank emperor, in possession of Aachen, with all the symbols and machinery of the imperial power. Though his authority east of the Rhine was diminished by the rapidly increasing influence of Bavaria, it is said that, in his anxiety to recruit his forces after the battle of Fontenai, he gained the adhesion of a certain number of Saxons by permitting the restoration of the pagan worship which his grandfather had so sternly suppressed—a cynical apostasy not out of keeping with the violation of the pledges which he had made to his father on his deathbed.

The emperor, however, in spite of his efforts and those of Pepin of Aquitaine to renew the strength of their army, and to take revenge for their defeat at Fontenai, did not muster courage for a fresh attack; and in the summer of 842 he approached his brothers with proposals of peace. They were now close to Châlon on Saone, having advanced so far from Argentaria; and the three brothers met to discuss the terms of peace and partition. But it was not until August, 843, that an agreement was come to at Verdun. Pepin was allowed to keep Aquitaine, and the remainder of the empire was divided, after much consultation and negotiation, into three parts, which were regarded as precisely equivalent. Charles the

Bald took everything to the west of the Rhone, the Saone, the Meuse, and the Scheldt, except a few districts on the left bank of the last-named river. Next to him came the Emperor Lothair, whose territory extended from the North Sea to the borders of Calabria in Italy, his eastward boundary being the Rhine and the Carnic Alps. The kingdom of Louis comprised the whole of Germany from the Rhine to the Elbe, and from the North Sea and Baltic down to the Alps.

This, as we have said, was virtually a definitive partition of the conquests of the Franks, which is a very different thing from saying that it was acquiesced in by all who were concerned in it, or that its details remained without change for any considerable length of time. As a matter of fact, Charles the Bald attacked Pepin in the year following the conclusion of the treaty of Verdun, and gained a victory over him in the neighbourhood of Angoulême, though it took him ten years to make himself master of Aquitaine, and he failed to overcome the resistance of the Bretons. Lothair also had trouble with Provence, but, most of all, the three brothers began to trouble each other again, each two in turn combining against the third. All this did not prevent Central and Western Gaul from developing steadily into France, or the kingdom founded by Louis of Bavaria from developing into Germany.

Lothair died in 855, and was succeeded in the kingdom of Italy and the imperial title by Louis II., whilst his second son, Lothair, became king of Lorraine (Lothringen, "Lotharii regnum"), and his youngest son, Charles, king of Provence. Charles the Bald, after setting his son on the throne of Aquitaine, and repelling an invasion by Louis the German, presently attacked his nephew in Provence, and, the young king dying in 863, his uncles divided the kingdom between them. They did the same thing in 869 with the Lothringian kingdom; and, six years later, Charles invaded Italy. The Emperor Louis died in this year (875), and the son of Judith seized the opportunity of having himself crowned as emperor at Rome. The king of Germany died eight months later, before he could contest with his brother the possession of the imperial crown; but in the following year his son and namesake defeated Charles at Andernach.

Exactly one year later, the last son of Louis the Pious came to the end of his strenuous and adventurous life, and Louis the Stammerer, who was already king of Aquitaine, succeeded him as king of Neustria, but not as emperor. Some writers have concluded that the imperial dignity would pass, on the death of Charles the Bald, as naturally as the kingship—as easily as it passed from the Emperor Lothair to his eldest son in 855. But the son of Charles was never emperor, and there was no succession between 877 and 884. There may have been, and probably would be, a claim, and more claims than one; but that was not sufficient. In 877 the line of Lothair was represented solely by his granddaughter Irmengard, who was married to Boson of Provence, and her blind son. The line of Pepin was extinct. The reigns of the three Kings of

Aquitaine and Neustria, in succession to Charles the
Bald, endured a little less or more than two years.
It is possible that they claimed the imperial crown,
but had not time to secure their coronation by
the Pope. Moreover, the son and grandsons of
Charles had to reckon with the rivalry of the sons
of Louis the German, and thus there was quite
enough to account for the inter-imperium of seven
years. Louis the Stammerer died in 879; his son,
Louis III., king of Neustria, died in 882; and his
second son, Carloman, king of Aquitaine, died in 884.
Charles the Fat, second son of Louis the German,
being for the moment, after the many casualties of
the past ten years, sole remaining king of the Frank
dynasties, was recognised and crowned as emperor
in 884. More than that, the empire of Charles the
Great was for the next three years reunited, but it
fell to pieces again on the deposition of Charles
in 887.

One of the chief crimes of Charles the Fat,
for which, amongst others, he had been deposed by
his subjects, was the conclusion of a disgraceful
treaty with the Northmen, by which he ceded to
them a part of Friesland. Ever since the latter
years of Charles the Great, the storm from the north
had been beating disastrously upon the shores of
Neustria and Aquitaine. Scarcely a year passed by
that was not marked by audacious inroads of Scandinavians, Danes, and Saxons. In 837 they plundered
Menapian and Frank cities on the Lower Rhine. In
841 Rouen was sacked and burned. A year later
they ascended the Loire, and sacked Blois and

Amboise. Next year the Gironde was visited. Within the two following years Nantes was sacked and Rouen occupied. In 846 the city of Paris, from which the defenders had fled at their approach, was seized and plundered, and Charles the Bald, who had taken refuge in the abbey of S. Denis, was compelled to purchase the withdrawal of his foe by a payment of seven thousand pounds' weight of silver. Saintes, Bordeaux, Tours, Orléans, Périgueux, Bourges, Arles, Nîmes, Chartres, Paris twice again, Noyon, Amiens, Meaux, Angers, Arras, fell in turn before the ruthless marauders, whilst the king of the devastated land was attacking or defending himself against his brothers. In 859 and 866 he renewed his purchase of a temporary peace. Picardy was ravaged in 883, and, two years later, siege was laid to Paris, which had now been strongly fortified by the valiant Counts of Paris. The assault was prolonged for eleven months.

Burgundy was overrun in 886, and it was now that Charles the Fat, at the moment when Eudes, Count of Paris, was making himself famous as a champion of the distressed and goaded land, submitted to terms dictated by the invaders. Verily the proud supremacy of the Western Franks had come to an end, when the last of their emperors, only four generations after the founding of the new Roman Empire, submitted on his own territory to a pagan foe. Count Eudes fought heroically at Paris, in Brittany, and elsewhere; but he could not, even after he had been elected to the Neustrian crown, expel the Northmen from the coasts on which they had begun to settle down. From 886 onwards the Norwegian Rollo, after establishing himself at Rouen, gradually mastered the whole country of the Lower Seine, with much of that of the Eure ; and at length, in 911, he obtained from Charles the Simple the recognition of his claim to the Duchy of Normandy. It was held by his descendants as a hereditary fief of France ; and a century and a half later the sixth of these descendants, Gallicised as the Frank warrior had never been, crossed the sea and became King of England.

XXII.

FRANCE AND GERMANY.

The deposition of Charles the Fat, the last Carolingian emperor, led to the formation of seven kingdoms west of the German frontier, whilst Germany was governed by Arnulf, who, in 896, was crowned emperor at Rome. Of the western kingdoms, that which was presently to take and keep the name of France passed into the hands of Eudes, Count of Paris. A kingdom of Navarre, including most of the marches of Spain, between the Pyrenees and the Ebro, asserted its independence. Rainulf, Count of Poitiers, enjoyed for a few months his assumed title of king of Aquitaine. Boson, Count of Autun, had already ruled over a kingdom of Provence, extending northwards to the Jura, and his son Louis the Blind succeeded him in 890. Burgundy beyond the Jura acknowledged Rodolf, or Raoul, formerly duke of that country. The Duke of Spoleto ruled at Langres with the title of king; and Berengar was king of Italy.

The Carolingians, however, were not quite extinct. Louis the Stammerer had left a posthumous son, Charles the Simple, who at the age of fourteen.

amidst the general anarchy which then distracted the land of the Franks, was brought forward by Zwintibold, duke of Lorraine, and crowned at Reims as king of Neustria. He had a son, Louis d'Outremer (whose mother Ogive was the sister of the English king Athelstan), two grandsons, Lothair and Charles, and a great-grandson, known as Louis V., or, more appropriately, Louis le Fainéant, who had a nominal reign in Neustria of less than one year, and who died by poison in 987. With him the line of Charles the Great finally passes away.

The line, but perhaps not the blood, of Charles was exhausted on the death of this unfortunate youth. For Louis the Pious is said to have had a daughter Adelaide, married to Robert the Strong, who may have been the descendant of a Gaul or Gallo-Roman, and who fought his way to greatness. He was amongst the earlier opponents of Charles the Bald, who gained him over by making him Count of Anjou, and giving him his sister Adelaide in marriage. Robert fought valiantly for his king against the Bretons and the Normans, and met his death in a victorious combat against the Northern invaders in 866. On the deposition of Charles the Fat in 887, Robert's elder son Eudes, Count of Paris, was made king of Neustria, and proved himself in every way worthy to wear the crown. After him his brother Robert was elected king. Robert's son, Hugues the Great, would have been king of Neustria by heirship, but he resigned his claim to the crown to his brother-in-law, Raoul, Duke of Burgundy. Hugues, successively Count of Paris and Duke of France, died in 986, in the same year as the Carolingian Lothair; and, on the death of the *roi fainéant* already mentioned, Hugues Capet, the young son of Hugues the Great, was elected by the nobles as king of France.

The following table should be compared with that of the descendants of Louis the Pious on p. 301. The claims of the family of Robert are now in constant conflict with those of the later Carolingians.

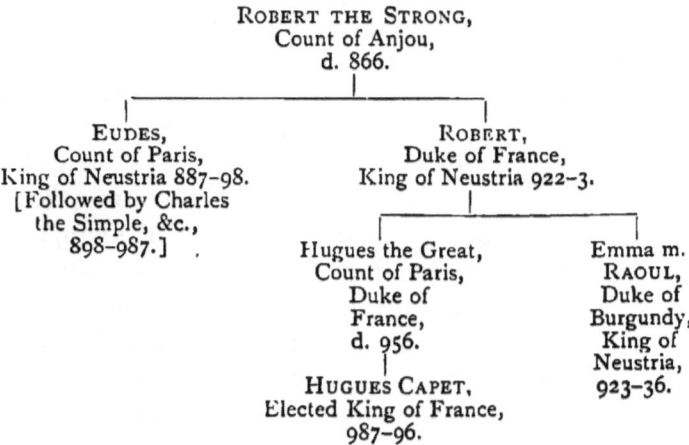

It is only now, in 987, that we can feel ourselves justified in speaking of a kingdom of France; and, even now, we must take the name rather as enlarged from the title of the Dukes of France, or Francia, than as a restricted use of the word applied by earlier Latin writers to the dominions of the Franks. There was a similarly localised use of the term, at a later period, in Central Germany, where Dukes of Francia ruled over a wide stretch of country extending between Lorraine and the borders of Bohemia and

Bavaria, with, of course, a better title to the name than could be possessed by Hugues the Great and his descendants.

In any case, the map of Europe from the tenth to the thirteenth century, roughly speaking, included a kingdom of France, with an eastern frontier which varied slightly from time to time, but was approximately marked towards the south by the Rhone and the Saone, and which, in the north, excluded the duchies of Lorraine and Brabant.

One fact of the highest importance remains to be mentioned, which goes far to explain the chaotic state of government in Western Europe at the close of the ninth century, and which accounts both for the rapid decline of the power of the crown and for the ultimate reconstruction of society on the feudal basis. One of the last acts of Charles the Bald, in June, 877, before he set out on his fatal expedition to Italy, was to summon a general assembly at Kiersey, where he dictated a capitulary more or less imposed upon him by the dukes, counts, and other holders of land, who had in the aggregate become too strong for farther resistance. This capitulary amounted to an edict acknowledging and declaring the heredity of fiefs. The fiefs, as we have already seen, arose out of the original assignments of territory for the purpose of government, to *duces*, *comites*, and others, who were appointed by the king to render service in their administration ; or out of benefices allotted by way of reward or favour, in order that the holder might receive the revenues during his life, or during the royal pleasure. It has been abundantly manifest that such fiefs were transmitted from father to son before the time of Charles the Bald; but the custom had grown up by assumption of privilege, through the weakness or goodwill of the monarch, and always subject to revocation if the monarch saw fit to exercise his inherent power. It had not attained to legal sanction before 877; but the significance of the edict of Kiersey was that by it the king pledged himself and his successors to leave the holders of fiefs, in the absence of treason on their part, and on conditions of military or other service, in undisturbed possession, and with the right of transmission and disposition.

There were at this time thirty great fiefs, the lords of which were in a large measure independent of the royal authority, or at any rate so powerful that the kings did not lightly attempt to constrain them. These nominal vassals were the Dukes of France, Aquitaine, Burgundy, Gascony, and Normandy; the Marquis of Septimania; the Counts of Toulouse, Barcelona, Carcassonne, Roussillon, Urgel, Poitiers, Auvergne, Angoulême, Perigord, Laonnais, Châlon, Vexin, Vermandois, Valois, Ponthieu, Boulogne, Anjou, Maine, and Brittany; the Viscounts of Béarn, Narbonne, and Limoges; and the Seigneurs of Bourbon and Beaujolais. In course of time the great fiefs began to split up, until, at the end of a few centuries, the feudal lordships exceeded one hundred and twenty.

At the accession of Hugues Capet, Duke of France, to the chief throne of the West, with the title of king of France, the royal domain, the only territory over which he could exercise unimpeded sway—though nominally overlord and king of all the fiefs in addition—consisted of his own duchy and part of the Laonnais : in other words, the counties of Paris, Senlis, Orléans, the Gâtinais, and a certain extent of territory surrounding Beauvais and Amiens. Arles at this time was still a kingdom, with dominion over Provence and the duchy of Burgundy, the last king dying in 1125 ; whilst Lorraine had passed back from the state of a kingdom into that of a duchy.[1]

The development of the system of feudalism cannot be adequately treated in the space at our command, but we may observe that it arose gradually, by historic growth and necessity, and that it began to assume definite shape in the ninth century, under the reign of the Carolingian Franks. A capitulary dictated at Mersen in 847 (after the conclusion of peace amongst the three sons of Louis the Pious), ordered that every freeman should be the vassal of a lord, whether of the king or of one of his great vassals, to whom he should owe fealty, and from whom he should obtain protection of his life and property. This was, in fact, the true personal basis of the whole feudal organisation, just as the capitulary of Kiersey indicates the basis of feudal tenure by service to the overlord. In each case the edict merely sanctioned and legalised a pre-existing custom. Voluntary vassalage had existed from early times amongst the Germans—the word "vassal" itself belonging to them—and the institution of feudalism, though, as has been said, a natural and inevitable product of the political situa-

---

[1] Lalanne, under the words *fief* and *France*.

tion, was built out of German rather than out of Roman or Gallic ideas.

The appropriation of public lands, especially by means of *beneficia* or *precaria* conferred on individuals by royal favour, whether spontaneously or at the importunity of petitioners, had gone to such a length that weak kings and popes were stripped of a large part of their possessions. "The Roman Church," says Gregorovius, speaking of the time of Pope John VIII., "desired to farm out her property as before. She strove in vain, however, to exclude the principle of German feudalism, and its inevitable results, the complete alienation of the property with which she had been vested, and the appearance of a crowd of dangerous hereditary tyrants." The alienation of the royal (and therefore national) domains, particularly when the fiefs were made hereditary, was an evil which had crept in as a consequence of a public benefit. Feudalism, in its essential features and at the time of its institution, made for the organisation of society and the protection of the individual ; and it is one of the evils incidental to human progress that institutions which in their origin contribute largely to the general weal can rarely be dispensed with after they have served their purpose until their gradual abuse and decay have counteracted much of the advantage which they originally conferred.

Any full account of the system of feudalism will be found to be laden with terms which have grown out of the original root in the Chattan dialect which, in a casual moment, was applied, more or less in scorn, to a confederacy of German freebooters.

There is one meaning implied in all of them, that of personal freedom or privilege, and this meaning is derived, not immediately from the Chattan word, though it had a signification not far removed from that of freedom (as in the colloquial German phrase, "frank und frei"), but rather from the condition and privileges of the Frank people in a conquered land. It was from the Franks, again, not from the word "frank," that a score or two of geographical names in Central and Western Europe have had their origin —and these names, as we should expect, are more numerous in Germany than elsewhere. Thus we have Franken Wald, Frankenau, Frankenhausen, Frankenheim, Frankenstein, two Frankenbergs, two Frankenthals, Franconia, Frankfort, Frankfurt, Frankenhofen, Fränkische Crumbach, and the Frankische Rezat, as well as the race-names of the Unter, Mittel, and Ober Franken. In Austria there is a Frankenfels; in Denmark, Frankekleist and Frankenhausen; in Belgium, Francorchamps; in France, a Franche Comté, seven Villefranches, and Franconville. The list is not exhaustive, but it is enough to bear witness to the predominance of the race during a long series of generations. Of the national name of Francia something has already been said in an earlier chapter.

Localised names of a more generic character are to be found in "francland," or "terra Francorum," which was at first merely indicative of the occupation of particular districts; but at a later period "francland," "franca terra," and "franca villa," were used of estates and occupations held by men who were not subject to taxation, or who were free from the conditions of villenage. An inhabitant of such a locality would be a "franchilanus," or franklin. It was apparently an old English "Villefranche" which was described by Sir John Fortescue, writing in the fifteenth century, in which "none can be found who is not a miles, an armiger, or a paterfamilias such as is there commonly known by the name of Fraunclein."

The use of the term "francus" as the opposite of "servus" produced in course of time the abstract nouns "francitas" and "franquitas," and the verb "franchire," to express the manumission of a slave, and his reception into the ranks of freemen. Charles the Bald gave a charter to the inhabitants of Barcelona, "whether Spaniards or Goths," conferring upon them the full immunity and liberty enjoyed by the Franks, which were implied in the word "francitas," or "francdad." There we see the actual name of the nation passing into the language for common use, in the sense of liberty, immunity, and privilege. Later instances of the same word and signification are "franc taupin," "Franc archier," and, by association, "franc tireur."[1]

In a similar manner, on the other side of the Pyrenees, the words "franchisia" and "franchise" had their origin, first as signifying the law or rights estab-

---

[1] "Franck archers were these : King Charles the 7, in the yeere 1449, being destitute of footemen, appointed that every three score houses in his realme should arme a man, who in time of war received paie of the King, and were exempt from all subsidies and payments : for the which cause they were al called francke, that is free."—*Danett's note to his translation of Philippe de Commines.*

lished for the Frank people, then as common words in the sense above mentioned, and eventually as distinctive terms for the privileges of municipal government. "Tenir en franchileges" was a phrase applied to the fullest and freest method of holding property.

The late use of the Roman word "franchire," with the meaning of "enfranchise," is quoted by Dufresne from a charter dated 1185 :—"Franchio, manu et ore manumitto a consuetudine Legis Salicæ Joannem Pithion de Vico, hominem meum, et suos legitime natos, et ad sanum intellectum reduco, ita ut suæ filiæ possint sibi succedere : dictumque Joannem et suos natos constituo hómines meos francos, et liberos ab omni usagio bono et malo Legis Salicæ, et pro hac manumissione et franchesia habui et recepi 18 libras Viennensium bonorum." In this case we have the noteworthy fact of a man purchasing his "franchisia," and becoming "francus," as a consequence of being liberated from the fetters of the Salic law, in order that his daughters as well as his sons might succeed to his property. That is to say, a state of things had arisen in which the Salic law was no longer a symbol of the highest freedom and immunity—at any rate to a man who wished to give his daughters an advantage which the Salic law denied to them. Pithion de Vico elected to divest himself of his status under the Salic law, with all its customs good or bad, and was ready to pay a good price to his feudal superior, so that his daughters might have reason to appreciate the providence of their father.

The "Francum plegium," which our English ancestors knew as "frankpledge," or "ten-manne-tale," was a custom observed probably by all the Teutonic nations, but at any rate by the Franks and the northern nations; and its name is derived either directly from the Franks or from the earlier use of the word which they had contributed to the common speech of their country. The pledge given by every ten men, or tithing, in a community, which was required of them in case of an infraction of the law by any one of their number, or of their families, was earlier in its origin than the custom which required every man in a feudal community to be covered by the authority and responsibility of his superior. It was also different in kind, being founded on the notion of mutual and equal responsibility, not on that of the control of many by one—which, as shown in Pithion's case, led often enough to the exploiting of many by one. The tithings were a development upon the more ancient hundreds, of which Tacitus tells us that "what was once a number is now a name only." The court of the hundred was one of the main instruments of justice under the Frank monarchy.

If feudalism was, in the limited sense which has been indicated, a bequest of the Franks to succeeding generations, so also was the Teutonic imperialism which began with Charles the Great in the year 800, and which, with sundry gaps and modifications in the meantime, subsists to the present day. No doubt the popes of Rome used the name and symbols of the old Roman Empire to serve (as they conceived it) for a bauble wherewith to flatter the ambition of the northern barbarians, in order that a German warrior in the trappings of a Roman Augustus might confirm them in their worldly possessions, and protect them against their enemies. But this was only the Roman point of view. The popes crowned the emperors, and thought their solid advantages cheaply purchased by so doing. There remains the fact that the German kings had both the ambition to wear an imperial crown and the power to wield an imperial sceptre. So far as the papal object was concerned, the

TURRET BELL NOW AT SIENA (1159).

popes might have gone anywhere for a puppet emperor, to Italy, to Spain, to Asia or Africa, provided that an instrument could be found of sufficient strength for their purpose. But the important fact is that they could find no such instrument outside of the German race, though they tried to do so more than once; and amongst the Germans they could find none sufficiently strong except the Frank, and his successor the Saxon.

The imperial dignity was not in its nature hereditary. The Frank emperors needed at least a nominal election by the Romans, followed by coronation at the hands of the pope; but Charles the Great, and some of those who came after him, secured the succession to their sons by having them crowned in their own lifetime. The emperors of the ninth and tenth centuries were as follows :—

1. Charles the Great, Emperor 800-814.
2. Louis the Pious, his son, Emperor 814-840.
3. Lothair, eldest son of Louis, Emperor 840-855.
4. Louis II., eldest son of Lothair, Emperor 855-875.
5. Charles the Bald, fourth son of Louis the Pious, Emperor 875-877.
6. Charles the Fat, grandson of Louis the Pious, through his third son, Emperor 884-887.
7. Guy, Duke of Spoleto, of Austrian descent, Emperor 891-894.
8. Lambert, son of Guy, Emperor, 894-898.
9. Arnulf of Bavaria, Emperor 896 (repudiated).
10. Louis of Provence, fourth in descent (through Irmengard) from Louis the Pious, grandson of Louis II., Emperor 901-915.
11. Berengar, Margrave of Friuli, grandson of Louis the Pious (through Gisela), Emperor 915-924.
12. Otho the Great, son of Henry the Fowler, a Saxon duke, elected King of Germany, Emperor 962-973.
13. Otho the Red, son of Otho the Great, Emperor 973-983.

14. Otho III., son of Otho the Red, Emperor 996–1002.

Though the Saxon Otho, summoned to Rome by Pope John XII., carried on the tradition of the Roman Empire, it was no longer the Empire of the Franks over which Charles the Great had held sway. He was, indeed, the king of a wider Germany, to whom Slavonians, Danes, and Hungarians were subject; he was arbiter of the fate of Italy, and at any rate the protector of France; but, as Gregorovius says, it was no light task to struggle against the self-assertion of the growing nationalities, the feudal privileges, and the Papacy. Yet the Othos undertook their task in the spirit of Charles. Saxons as they were, they called their country the land of the Franks, and their language the tongue of the Franks. Otho the Great " brought the Roman imperial power to the German nation, and this energetic people," in the words of the German historian, " assumed the honourable but thankless task of becoming the Atlas of universal history. The influence of Germany soon brought about the reform of the Church and the restoration of learning, while in Italy itself it was the German element which fostered the civic republics."

If Germany was the heir of Roman imperialism, France was the heir of Roman speech, law, and letters. If the Frank spirit of domination had created and sustained the German Empire, the energy of the Franks and of the Northmen had blended itself with the milder characteristics of the Romanised Gauls, and helped to make a nation which fought crusades, organised feudalism, regularised the newer principles of national government, upheld the Church in the moments of its greatest danger, and marched in the van of chivalry, scholasticism, and the Renaissance.

THE END.

INDEX

A

Aachen, the seat of government under Charles the Great, 245-8, 249 ff., 272 ff.
Adelchis the Lombard, 228
Adrian, Pope, 224 ff., 240-1, 249, 268, 278
Ægidius, Roman *Comes* in Gaul, 94, 103
Aëtius, Roman *Comes*, 90-93
Agde, Council of, 141
Alaric I., king of Visigoths, 78, 139 ff., 171
Alaric II., 103, 139 ff., 149
Altofleda, sister of Clovis, 118
Alboin the Lombard, 209
Alcuin, Abbot, English ecclesiastic, at Aachen and Tours, 271 ff., 275, 281, 289
Alfred of England, 7, 213-14, 290
Allemans, 6, 48, 50, 62, 68 ff., 102, 175, 203, and *passim*; see "Charles the Great" and "Clovis"; 302
Amalaric the Visigoth, 171
Ambrose, Archbishop, imposes penance on Theodosius, 122
Ammianus, historian, 73-5, 284
Anastasius II., Pope, congratulates Clovis on his victories, 152
Anastasius, emperor of the East, 145-7
Angilbert, Bishop, 240
Angilbert, son-in-law of Charles the Great, 269
Angles, 7, 35, 214, 222, 257, 296

Aquitaine, 9, 17, 139 ff., 165, 182, 189, 191, 203, 218, 228, 231, 254, 288, 300, 303, 320
Arbogast, Franco-Roman *Comes*, 77
Aredius intervenes between Clovis and Gundobald, 134 ff.
Argentaria, the Oaths of, 308-12
Arianism, 69, 113; its character, 126-9, 132, 209, and *passim*
Arian States, 138-43
Aribert the Lombard, 209
Arichis, Lombard Duke of Beneventum, 228
Ariovistus in Gaul, 23
Armoricans, 94, 102-4, 114, 119, 132, 167, 300, and *passim*
Arnulf, Bp. of Metz, ancestor of Charles the Great, 201
Astolf the Lombard, 211-12
Athalaric, Ostrogoth, 171-2
Athanasius, Bishop, 126-9
Attila (Etzel), the Hun, 91-3, 122
Audovera, first wife of Chilperic, 181
Augofleda, sister of Clovis, wife of Theodoric the Goth, 119
Augustus (Emperor Octavian), 27, 44, 53, 247; "Augustus" as an imperial title, 69, 94, 120, 146, 165
Augustulus, last emperor of Rome, 97
Aurelian, Emperor, 62
Ausonius, a Gaul, 53, 56
Austria (Austrasia), realm of the Eastern Franks, 153, (and Neus-

tria), 191, 196 ff., 200, 254 ff., 293, 302
Avitus, Bishop of Vienne, 125

B

Bagats (Bagaudæ), 61, 67, 90, 103, 124
Bajulus, the office of, 199
Basina, mother of Clovis, 95-7
Basques, 189
Batavians, 17, 29, 31, 38, 156-7, 246
Bavaria, 153, 171, 203, 212, 221, 238; as a kingdom of the Franks, 300 ff., 323
Belgians, 13, 23-4, 31, 75, 79, 88, 117, 156, 167, and *passim*
Belgic Thuringia, imaginary, 84, 99-100
Belisarius in Italy, 172-3
Beneficia of land, 216, 326
Bertha, mother of Charles the Great, 211, 219, 224, 268
Bertha, sister of Charles the Great(?), 201
Bertha, daughter of Charles, 269
Bernard, grandson of Charles, 299
Boson, king of Provence, 316, 320
Brabant, 83, 154, 212
Breviarium of Anianus, 144
Britain, 2 ff., 97. See under "Angles," "Alfred," "Alcuin," "Offa"
Brittany, 103, 120, 184, 193, 197, 253, 321; *see* "Armoricans"
Brunhilda, 181 ff.
Burgundians, 90, 102-4, 119, 203; war with Clovis, 132 ff.; their code, 136; 169, 172, 189, 203, 254, 318
Byzantium, 193, 207, 245, 247, 252, 279, 323; *see* "Empire of the East"

C

Cæsar, Julius, 12 ff., 22 ff.; his frontier policy, 26 ff., 65; "Cæsar" as a sub-imperial title, 69
Caligula, Emperor, 30
Capitularies, 258, 263 ff., 323, 325

Caracalla, Emperor, his benefits to Gaul, 58-60, 68
Cararic, king of Térouanne, 101; his kingdom annexed by Clovis, 150
Carausius from Britain, seizes Boulogne, 67
Caribert, king of Paris, 179, 182
Carloman, brother of Pepin the Short, 201, 204
Carloman, brother of Charles the Great, 215-19
Carloman, king of Aquitaine, 301
Caroline script, 275
Carolingians, *see* "Franks"
Charles the Bald, 5th Frank emperor, 301, 304 ff., 316
Charles the Fat, 6th Frank emperor, 301, 317 ff.
Charles the Great, 1st Frank emperor, 9, 210-11, 213; king of the Franks, 215; his first campaign, 218; sole king, 219; marries Himiltrude, 219, and Desiderata, *ibid.*; begins the Saxon war, 222; the Lombard war in Italy, 224; marries Hildegard, 225; visits Rome, 225; confirms his father's grants to the Pope; renewed visits to Italy, 228; his sons, Carloman and Louis, consecrated as kings of Italy and Aquitaine, 228; expedition to Spain, 230; death of his nephew Roland, 231; subdues the Saxons and Witikind, 234; defeats the Slavonians, Wiltzes, Avars, Bavarians, Huns, 238; confirms Leo III. as Pope, 240; reinstates him, 242; is crowned emperor, as Carolus Augustus, 243; the character of his empire, 245; his government, 248 ff.; his court, 267 ff.; his later wives and children, 270; his meeting with Alcuin, 271; patronage of learning, 276; his life-work, 286 ff.; his death, 290; his descendants, 298; his legend, 235, 270

INDEX. 337

Charles, king of Provence, 301
Charles, king of Aquitaine, 301
Charles the Simple, king of Neustria, 301, 319-20
Charles le Fainéant, 301
Charles Martel, Mayor of the Palace, 201; his character, 202; conquests, *ibid.*; defeats the Saracens, 203; appealed to by Gregory III., 204; dies, *ibid.*
Chattan origin of the name "Frank," 19, 86; *see* "Frank"
Childebert, king of Paris, 166 ff., 177
Childebert II., king of Metz, 179, 185, 208
Childebert III., 179
Childeric I., king of Tournai, 82-3, 93 ff., 166
Childeric II., king of Neustria, 179, 263
Chilperic I., king of Soissons, 179 ff.
Chilperic II., 179
Chilperic the Burgundian, 111, 133
Chramnus, son of Clotair I., 177
Christian authors in Gaul, 55
Christianity, its growing power at Rome and in Gaul, 50 ff.; Orthodox and Arian, 113; policy of the bishops towards the barbarians, 120 ff.; supremacy in Europe of the Roman Church, 126 ff.; its appeals to Visigoths, 125; to the Franks, 185, 204-5, 210-12, 221, 225 ff., 240 ff.; the dispute between the temporal power, 240; the dispute between the Eastern and Western Churches, 278; effects of temporalities, 294; and *passim*; *see* Gallic Church
Civilis, his half-told story, 31
Claudius, Emperor, 30, 45, 62
Cloderic, his kingdom annexed by Clovis, 150, 166
Clodion invades Gaul, 82; his origin, 84 ff., 89
Clodomer, son of Clovis, 114, 166-9, 177

Clodovald (Saint Cloud), 166, 169
Clotair I., 166 ff., 177; his descendants, 179 ff.; the sons of Clotair, 180
Clotair II., 183, 190
Clotair III., king of Neustria, 179
Clotilda, 111; married to Clovis, 113, 152, 167 ff.
Clotilda, her daughter, 171
Clovis I., king of the Franks, 16; his mother, 97; comes to the throne of Tournai, 101; wins Soissons and Paris, 105; fights the Thuringians, 109; marries Clotilda, 111; converted to Orthodox Christianity by his wife, 113 ff.; baptised by Bishop Remy, 117; his sister married to Theodoric, 119; "rex Christianissimus," 125; makes terms with the Armoricans, 119, 132; the Burgundian war, 133 ff.; the Aquitanian war, 139 ff.; Clovis attacks the Allemans, 139; checked by Theodoric, 145; receives the title of Consul, 146; resides at Paris, 147; subjugates North-eastern Gaul and becomes sole king of the Franks, 149 ff.; dies, 152; his sons, 165 ff.
Clovis II., king of Neustria, 179
Clovis III., 179
Clovis, son of Chilperic, 181
Commodus, Emperor, 34, 55
Complaint of Louis the Pious, 305
Constantine, Emperor, 64, 68 ff.
Constantius, Emperor, 69 ff., 157
Council of Nice, 69, 126
Council summoned by Charles the Great at Frankfort, on the adoration of images, 278
Councils of the Church in Gaul, 136-8, 141, 184, 189, 288

D

Dagobert I., king of the Franks, 179, 191; a patron of learning and art, 197
Dagobert II., 179

Dagobert III., 202
Danes, 175, 233, 238, 284-6, 333
Decumates Agri, 35, 46, 72, 83, 102
Desiderata, second wife of Charles the Great, 219 ff.
Desiderius, king of the Lombards, 219 ff.
Didier, Bishop of Vienne, 189
Didier, Duke of Toulouse, 184
Dieburg, 84 ff.
Diocletian, Emperor, 50, 55, 68
Dispargum (Scheidungen-burg), 82 ff., 98, 109, 157, 168
Domitian, Emperor, 33
Duisburg, 84, 150

E

Ebroin, Mayor, 199
Eginard, biographer of Charles the Great, 224, 231, 240, 245, 267, 271; account of his life, 276-7, 289, 293
Eloy (Eligius), S., 197-9
Emperors, Frank and Saxon, the first fourteen, 332
Empire (ancient) of Rome, *passim;* its collapse, 97. *See* under names of emperors.
Empire of the East, 50, 165, 185, 193, 207, 211, 245-7
Empire (Holy Roman), 243. *See* "Charles the Great," 294, 313, 330
Euaric, king of Visigoths, urged to champion Rome, 125
Eudes, Count of Paris, 320-1

F

Feudalism, origins of amongst the Teutons, 215, 246, 323
Fiefs, hereditary, 323-4
Fontenai, the battle of, 308
Franc (various meanings of the word), 18, 327
France, the kingdom of, 256, 322, 333
Francia, the land of the Franks, 57, 147, 153, 185, 191, 200, 255
Francia, the French duchy, 321-2
Francia, the German duchy, 322
Franconia, 327
Frank Reich, 191, 256
Franken (German geographical name), 45, 81, 85, 327
Frank (various meanings of the word), 18, 79, 293, 326
Franks, their relations to other nations, 1-10; their origin as a confederacy of Sicambrians, Chattans, Tencterians, &c., 11 ff., 21 ff., 31, and *passim ;* the evidence of Vopiscus, 15-20, 59; of Gregory of Tours, 16-17, 82, 98; of Sigebert, 19; of Lydus, 20; of Sulpitius, 59; fabled Pannonian (Trojan) origin, 17; their German home, 37 ff.; they break the Roman frontier, 50, 59, 60, 62, 72; their first settlements in Gaul, 64, 75, 86, 89, (Læti), 91, 154 ff.; a Frank sea-raid, 65-7; Frank usurping emperors of ancient Rome, 70; a Frank consul, 77; a Frank *comes*, 77; qualities of the Franks, 67, 74, 111 (*see* "characteristics" below); Salian Franks, 16, 74-5, 79, 83 ff., 107, 155 ff.; the Merovingians, 80 ff., 212, 263, 284 (*see* also under "Clovis," &c., and *passim*); Franks of the Thuringian border, 81 ff., 95, 110, 170; Clodion of Dispargum, 82 ff.; Merowig, fights with Romans, Gauls, and Goths against the Huns, 93; Childeric of Tournai, *ibid*. ff.; Clovis of Tournai, 101 ff. (follow up under "Clovis"); the typical Frank warrior, 105; conversion of the Franks, 117; Rome aids the Franks, 123 ff., and appeals to them, 125 ff.; the Franks, as Orthodox Christians, become champions of the Papacy, 211 ff., 240 ff.; characteristics and institutions of the Franks, 153 ff., 166, 180, 191, 212, 215, 248, 253 ff., 293; their laws,

INDEX.

155 ff., 257 ff.; their ranks, 108, 160 ff., 186-8, 193, 216, 262; complete masters of Gaul, 168 ff. (follow up under "The Sons of Clovis" and "The Sons of Clotair"); they elect Mayors of the Palace, 194 ff.; the Carolingians, 200; Pepin the Short usurps the kingdom, 204 (follow up under "Charles the Great"); the summit of their glory, 245; their arts and culture, 197, 249 ff., 271 ff.; incompatibility with the Gauls, 253 ff.; their influence on other Teutons, 296; decline of their power in the West, 298; Carolingians after Charles the Great, 300; their royal and imperial seats, 306; their language, 254, 282, (examples) 309; anarchy in the Gallic Franklands, 320; ultimate preference of the Franks for Germany, 8
Fredegonda, third wife of Chilperic, 181-8
Fredum, 160
Frisians, 28, 39, 41, 94, 199, 204, 271, 286, 302, 317

G

Galba, Emperor, 31
Galeswintha, second wife of Chilperic, 181
Gallic Church, 124, 137-8, 184, 139, 217, and *passim*
Gallienus, Emperor, 59-60, 62
Gascons, 154, 189, 203, 232, 255, 238, 299
Gaul, 3, 8, 13, 24, 41; Romanised, 52; the Frank kingdom of, 101; and *passim*
Gelasius, Pope, 152
General Assemblies, 223, 248, 257 ff., 288
Germanicus, 29
Germans, 4, 8, 21, 37, 71, 129; their tribes, 34 (Note); and *passim*
Germany, *passim*; 333

Godegisil the Burgundian, 133
Gontran, king of Burgundy, 179, 180, 184-5
Goths, 48 ff., 90, 102, 129 ff., 154, 172 ff., 328
Gratian, Emperor, 77, 147
Gregory I. (the Great), Pope, 125, 209
Gregory II., 209
Gregory III., 204-5
Gregory of Tours, 17, 82, 85, 108, 136, 149, 176, 206
Grimoald, Mayor of the Palace, 197, 199
Grippo, son of Charles Martel, 204, 212
Gundachar the Burgundian, 90
Gundobald the Burgundian, 133, 145, 168

H

Hadrian, Emperor, 43, 246
Haroun-al-Raschid, his present to Charles the Great, 252
Hermann, 29, 40, 74, 223
Hincmar, Archbishop, on the General Assemblies, 258
Honorius, emperor of the East, 78
Hugues Capet, king of France, 10, 324
Hugues the Great, 321
Hunald, Duke of Aquitaine, 205, 218-19, 255
Huns, 91-3, 122, 180, and *passim*

I

Italy, 80, 124, 139, 185, 208, 225 ff., 246, 251, 287, 299, and *passim*

J

John II., Pope, 209
John VIII., Pope, 326
Judith, Empress, 304 ff.
Julian, emperor of the East, 69 ff.; in Paris, 73, 76
Justinian, emperor of the East, 172, 177

K

Kelts, 3 ff., 23, 102, 120, 154, 191, 254-6, and *passim*

Kiersey, Treaty of, 211
Kynesioi, the westernmost race in Europe known to Herodotus, 3

L

Læti, (Lěti), 73, 75, 88-9, 161
Leo I., Pope, 123
Leo III., crowns Charles the Great, 240 ff.
Libri Carolini, 278
Limes Germanicus (or Imperii), 12, 43-7, 64, 81-7
Limes Rhenanus, 64, 84
Liutprand the Lombard, 210
Lombards, 4, 182, 185, 207 ff., 241, and *passim*
Lorraine, 315
Lothair, 3rd Frank emperor, 330 ff., 314-16
Lothair, king of Lorraine, 301
Louis the German, son of Louis the Pious, king of Bavaria, 300 ff.
Louis II., 4th Frank emperor, 301
Louis le Fainéant, 301, 321
Louis III., king of Neustria, 301
Louis d'Outremer, 301, 321
Louis the Pious, 2nd Frank emperor, 221, 269, 288, 298 ff., 305, 316
Louis of Provence, 10th Frank emperor, 301
Louis the Stammerer, king of Aquitaine, 301, 316-17
Luegenfeld, the Field of Lies, near Colmar, 305

M

Magnentius, a Frank usurping emperor, 70
Major Domus, *see* Mayors
Majorian, Emperor, 94
Marbod, 30, 33, 40
Marcomanni, 34
Marculfus, Frank monk and historian, 163
Marcus Aurelius, Emperor, 33-4, 37, 246
Martin, Bishop, 143, 275
Maurice, emperor of the East, 185

Mayors of the Palace, 178, 194 ff.; Sismondi on, 205-6
Mellobaudes, Franco-Roman consul, 77
Merovingians, 80 ff.; *see* under "Franks"
Merowig, founder of the Merovingian dynasty, 93 ff.
Merowig, son of Chilperic, 181, 183
Missi Dominici, 247, 252, 257 ff.
Mummolus, 182, 184

N

Narses in Italy, 175-7, 207
Neustria, 178, 191, 200, 302, 321; and *passim*
Nicephorus, usurping emperor of the East, 247
Northmen, 26, 175, 238, 286, 292-4, 299, 317 ff.
Novempopulania, 189

O

Odoacer the Herulian in Rome, 97
Offa of Mercia, his friendship with Charles, 297
Ordeal, the laws of, 161-3
Orthodox bishops, 130, 138
Oster Ric (Austria), 191
Ostrogoths, 145, 172; *see* Theodoric

P

Paris, 73, 105, 147, 166, 318, 320
Pepin of Héristal(?), Mayor of the Palace, 200
Pepin of Landen(?), Mayor of the Palace, 197, 200; his descendants, 201
Pepin the Hunchback, son of Charles the Great, 219
Pepin the Short, son of Charles Martel, 204, 212, 268
Pepin I., king of Aquitaine, 300
Pepin II., king of Aquitaine, 301, 317 ff.
Plague, 175, 184
Postumus, 60, 75
Probus, Emperor, 62; his policy in the Rhenish provinces, 64, 67, 75

INDEX. 341

Provence, 6, 172, 191, 193, 203, 303, 320

Q
Quintian, Bishop, 141

R
Radbod the Frisian, 204
Ragnacar, king of Cambrai, 101, 105, 151
Ravenna, exarchate of the Eastern Empire, 139, 172, 208, 211, 240, 249
Reccared, king of Visigoths, 184
Remy, Bishop, 16, 86, 117 ff., 127
Rhine frontier, 12, 27-8, 40
Riparian Franks, 14, 16-17, 39, 86; the Riparian kingdom, 101; its absorption, 149
Robert, Count of Anjou, 321
Rois Fainéants, 199 ff.
Roland, reputed nephew of Charles the Great, 201, 231
Roman frontier after Trajan, 43
"Roman Republic," 208, 212, 221, 226, 241 ff.
Roncesvalles, 231

S
Sala, the two rivers, 45, 87, 111
Salians, *see* under "Franks"
Salic law, 79, 155 ff., 162, 195, 263, 329
Saracens, 203, 215, 221, 230, 270, 288
Saxons, 94, 176, 182, 190, 203, 221 ff., 228 ff., 271, 282, 296, 302, 312-14
Scheidungen-burg, 85, 109, 157
Seneschal, 199
Septimania, 203, 303
Sicambrian League, 12-15, 87, 239
Siegbert, king of Riparian Franks, 101, 114, 149, 166
Siegbert, king of Metz, 179 ff.
Sigebert of Gembloux, 19
Silvanus, a Frank usurping emperor, 70
Slavery among the Franks, 163, 217
Slavonians, 215, 299, 333
Spain, 60, 66, 80, 102, 145, 175, 230-2, 288, 328
Stephen II., Pope, 205, 211
Stilicho the Vandal, 78-9
Suevans, 13, 23
Syagrius, king of Suessiones, 105

T
Tacitus, 11, 12, 31 ff., 49; "Germania" quoted, 34 (Note), 155 (Note)
Tencteri, 13, 25, 32
Tetricus, 62
Teutoburg forest, 29
Teutonic law, 154 ff.
Teutons, 4, 38, 42; and Romans, 38, 149, 282 ff.; and *passim*
Theodebald, king of Metz, 166, 176
Theodebert, king of Metz, 166, 172; his daughter, 173
Theodebert II., 179, 188-9
Theodoric, king of Ostrogoths, 133, 139, 145, 165, 249-51
Theodoric, king of Visigoths, 90, 93
Theodoric, son of Clovis, 145, 166, 170
Theodoric II., king of Orléans, 179, 188-9
Theodosius, emperor of the East, 77, 121-2; his code, 144
Thirty Tyrants, 60, 62
Thuringia, 81 ff., 98 ff.; 302, 312; and *passim*
Tiberius, Emperor, 30, 34
Totila the Goth, 172
Trajan, Emperor, 33, 44
Tribe names of the Teutons, 28 (Note)
Trojan origin of the Franks, legendary, 17
Tungri, 41, 65, 86, 88, 101

U
Urtheil (ordeal), 161; various ordeals, 162-3
Usipii (Usipites), 12, 13

V

Valentinian I., emperor of the East, 19, 77
Valentinian II., emperor with Gratian, 77
Vandals, 35, 60, 62, 78
Varus defeated by Hermann, 29
Veleda, Bructerian wise woman, 32-3
Verdun, the treaty of, 313
Vespasian, Emperor, 31-2, 42
Virgil, the Trojan legend, 17
Visigoths, 93, 102, 104, 144, 171, 190. *See* "Alaric"
Vitellius, Emperor, 31-2
Vitiges, the Ostrogoth, 172
Vocladensian Plain, 143, 203
Vopiscus, historian, 15, 19, 59

W

Warnaher, Mayor, 196
Wehrgeld, 160
Witikind, 229; in fable, 235; 238
Wintrion, Duke, 188, 196, 206

Z

Zacharias, Pope, 211

ROMAN PLACE NAMES, &c., MENTIONED IN THE TEXT, WITH THEIR MODERN EQUIVALENTS.

Agedincum Senŏnum, Sens
Agri Decumātes
Albis, Elbe R.
Alcimŏna, Altmühl R.
Amisia, Ems R.
Angli, Angles
Aquæ Mattiăcæ, Wiesbaden
Aquæ Sextiæ, Aix
Aquis (Aquisgrānum), Aix-la-Chapelle, Aachen
Aquitania (præ-Augustan), Gascony
Arausio, Orange
Arduenna Silva, Ardennes
Arelāte, Arles
Argentaria (?), *see* p. 308
Argentorātum, Strassburg
Argentovaria (p. 308), Artzenheim
Aremorĭca (Armorica)
Asciburgum, Asburg
Atuatuca, Tongres
Augusta Suessiōnum, Soissons
Augusta Trevĕrorum, Trier, Trèves
Augusta Vindelicorum, Augsburg
Augustodūnum (Bibracte), Autun
Augustodūrum Baiucassium, Bayeux
Augustonemētum, Clermont-Ferrand

Aulerci Cenomāni (Diablintes), Maine R.
Aureliāni Cenăbum, Orléans
Avenio, Avignon
Axŏna, Aisne R.
Bæterræ, Béziers
Batăvi, Batavians, Betuwe
Belgica, Belgian land
Beneventum, Benevento
Boihrĕmi, Bohemia, Böhmen
Bonna, Bonn
Bononia, Boulogne
Braina, Braisne
Bructĕri (mediæv. Borahtra-gau)
Burdigăla, Bordeaux
Burginatium, Schenkenschanz
Burgundi (Burgundiŏnes), Burgundians
Byzantium, Constantinople, Istamboul
Camarācum, Cambrai, Kamerijk
Campania, Champagne
Caninefates, Kennemerland
Carcaso, Carcassonne
Carisiācum, Kiersey, Quierzy
Catalauni (Durocutalauni), Châlons-sur-Marne
Cebenna, Cévennes
Chamavi (mediæv. Hamaland)
Chatti (Hessen)

INDEX.

Chattuarii (mediæv. Hattera-gau)
Colonia Agrippīna, Cologne, Köln
Confluentes, Coblenz
Dispargum (Divisio-burgum), Dieburg
Diutia, Diutz, Deutz
Divisio, Scheidungen-burg
Divodūrum Mediomatricorum, Metz
Durnomăgus, Dormagen
Durocortōrum Remōrum, Reims
Forum Julii, Fréjus
Fossa Drusiāna, the dyke of Drusus
Garumna, Garonne R.
Geldŭba, Gellep
Germania Inferior, Superior (Gallic provinces created by Claudius—the latter extended by Domitian across the Rhine, to the Limes Germanicus)
Gottŏnes, the Goths
Hermiŏnes, Hermunduri (?); Thuringians
Issala (Navalia), Yssel R.
Itius Portus, Wissant
Julia Apta, Apt
Laugŏna, Lahn R.
Lemānus Lacus, Lake Leman
Locoritum, Lohr
Lugdūnum, Lyon
Luppia, Lippo R.
Lutetia Parisiorum, Paris
Matrŏna, Marne R.
Mogontiācum (Magunt-), Mayence, Mainz
Mœnus, Main R.
Mosa, Meuse R.
Mosella, Moselle R.

Nicer, Neckar R.
Noviodunum Diablintum, Jublains
Noviomăgus Batavorum, Nimegten
Regīna Castra, Regensburg
Rhenus, Rhine R.
Rhodănus, Rhône R.
Rigomăgus, Remagen
Rura, Ruhr R.
Sala, Saale (Frank) R.
Sala, Saale (Thuringian) R.
Sauconna (Arar), Saône R.
Scaldis, Scheldt, Escaut R.
Segodūnum Rutenorum, Rodez
Sequăna, Seine R.
Siga, Sieg R.
Suēvi ("Suabians")
Tenetēri
Tervenna, Térouanne
Teutoburgius Saltus, Wiehengebirge M.
Teutŏnes, Teutons
Texuandri (Toxandri), Tessenderloo
Theodonis Villa, Diedenhofen, Thionville
Tolbiācum, Zülpich
Tullum, Toul
Tungri, Tongres
Turnācum, Tournai
Vacălus (Vahālis), Waal R.
Vandăli, Vandals
Vasconia, Gascony
Vetĕra Castra, Birten
Vincobōna, Vienna
Virodūnum, Verden (Germ.)
Virodūnum, Verdun (Gaul)
Visontio, Besançon
Visurgis, Weser R.
Vosĕgus, Vosges M.

www.ingramcontent.com/pod-product-compliance
Lightning Source LLC
Chambersburg PA
CBHW020239240426
43672CB00006B/582